MW01125720

THE
LET
THEM
THEORY

Also by Mel Robbins

BOOKS

The High 5 Habit: Take Control of Your Life with One Simple Habit *

*The 5 Second Rule: Transform Your Life, Work,
and Confidence with Everyday Courage*

The High 5 Daily Journal *

AUDIOBOOK ORIGINALS

*Take Control of Your Life: How to Silence Fear
and Win the Mental Game*

Reinvent Your Life

Here's Exactly What to Do: Simple Tools for a Happier You

Start Here: Pep Talks for Life

*Kick Ass: Life-Changing Advice from
the author of The 5 Second Rule*

Work It Out: The New Rules for Women to Get Ahead at Work

*Available from Hay House

Please visit:

Hay House USA: www.hayhouse.com®
Hay House Australia: www.hayhouse.com.au
Hay House UK: www.hayhouse.co.uk
Hay House India: www.hayhouse.co.in

THE
LET
THEM
THEORY

**A Life-Changing Tool That Millions
of People Can't Stop Talking About**

Mel Robbins

HAY HOUSE LLC
Carlsbad, California • New York City
London • Sydney • New Delhi

Published in the United States by: Hay House LLC: www.hayhouse.com®
Published in Australia by: Hay House Australia Publishing Pty Ltd: www.hayhouse.com.au
Published in the United Kingdom by: Hay House UK Ltd: www.hayhouse.co.uk
Published in India by: Hay House Publishers (India) Pvt Ltd: www.hayhouse.co.in

Lines from "The Summer Day" by Mary Oliver reprinted by the permission of The Charlotte Sheedy Literary Agency as agent for the author. Copyright © 1990, 2006, 2008, 2017 by Mary Oliver with permission of Bill Reichblum.

Project editor: Melody Guy
Cover design: Pete Garceau
Interior design and illustrations: Julie Davison

Library of Congress Cataloging-in-Publication Data

Hardcover ISBN: 978-1-4019-7136-6
Autographed ISBN: 978-1-4019-9706-9
E-book ISBN: 978-1-4019-7137-3

11 10 9 8 7 6 5 4 3
1st edition, December 2024

Printed in the United States of America

This product uses responsibly sourced papers and/or recycled materials. For more information, see www.hayhouse.com.

For my daughter Sawyer,
who co-wrote this book with me.

I have loved sharing this experience with you,
even though there were times you wanted to kill me.

As they say, *Let Them*.

Table of Contents

Your Relationships and the Let Them Theory

Choosing the Love You Deserve

Appendix

My Story

A t the age of 41, I found myself $800,000 in debt, unemployed, and watching my husband's restaurant business crumble. It felt like we had failed at life with no hope of ever escaping the debt.

I enviously watched as my friends found success after success in their careers while we struggled to get groceries on the table. I had just been laid off and had no idea what to do with my life: I'd already tried being a public defender for the Legal Aid Society in New York City, being a lawyer in a large firm in Boston, working for a few start-ups, doing business development at an advertising agency, becoming a life coach, hosting a call-in radio show, and even opening a small paint-your-own-pottery-studio. I felt completely lost, like nothing I did would ever be enough to dig us out of the hole we were in.

To deal with the anxiety and self-doubt, my main strategy became avoidance. Avoid getting up by hitting the snooze button. Avoid the pain with alcohol. Avoid responsibility by blaming my husband. Avoid looking for a job by procrastinating however I could.

If you've ever been in this situation, you understand how monumental even the simplest tasks seem: getting out of bed, opening your bills, being fully present with your family, cooking a nice meal, applying for a job, going for a walk, canceling that subscription, or even just being honest about the extent to which you're struggling. . . Everything feels impossible. Every morning when I woke up, the anxiety was coursing through my veins, and I thought, *Is this really what it's going to look like for the rest of my life?*

But you want to know the funny thing about being stuck? I knew exactly what I needed to do: get up, tackle the dreaded pile of bills, get the kids ready for school, make myself go on walks, reach out to my friends for support, make a budget, find a job. And yet, I couldn't seem to do any of it.

How I Changed My Life

I'll never forget the morning when everything changed for me. The alarm went off, and there I was, lying in bed, completely overwhelmed by our problems. Like so many of us, I was paralyzed by my own thoughts, and the last thing I wanted to do was get up and face another day.

But then, something strange happened. A thought popped into my head that would ultimately change my life. It was so simple, almost silly. I remembered watching a rocket launch and the way NASA counted down to blast off: *5-4-3-2-1*. I thought, *What if I just counted backward like that and launched myself out of bed?*

It seemed ridiculous, but I was desperate, so I gave it a shot. I counted backward: *5-4-3-2-1*—and I got out of bed. Just like that. I didn't think about how tired I was or how much I didn't want to face my problems. I simply moved before my brain had the chance to talk me out of it. It's like launching a rocket: Once you start the countdown, *5-4-3-2-1*, there's no turning back.

At that point in my life, I was so used to letting my thoughts paralyze me and fear and stress consume me that the concept felt completely foreign. I remember what a revelation it was when I thought to myself, *Wait a minute, I can feel horrible and still do what I need to do? Yes, Mel, you can.* And it worked.

In those five seconds, I had interrupted the cycle of overthinking. It felt like a small victory, but it was also a revelation. If I could push through those five seconds of fear, maybe I could push through anything.

So, I started using this countdown everywhere in my life.

5-4-3-2-1 Get up when the alarm rings.

5-4-3-2-1 Pick up the phone and start networking to find a job.

5-4-3-2-1 Open the bills that had been piling up on the counter for months.

I started calling this the "5 Second Rule." One 5-second move at a time, I forced myself to put one foot in front of the other and slowly step back into my life. I won't lie to you. It wasn't easy. The next couple of years were among the hardest of my life.

It's not easy to claw your way out of debt or face the painful issues in your marriage. It's not easy to quiet the anxiety or push through the self-doubt. It's hard to update your résumé and look for a job when you question the value you bring. It's a grind to force yourself to get back in shape and create healthier habits after you've let yourself go.

And it's definitely not glamorous to work all day, then come home, take care of three kids, spend a few minutes with my husband, and then stay up late every night, trying to figure out ways I can make more money.

But that's what I did.

The 5 Second Rule taught me that action is the answer. Thinking about your problems will never solve them. Waiting around to feel like doing something means you'll never do it. It taught me that no one is coming to save you. You must save yourself from yourself. You have to force yourself to make little moves forward, all day, every day, especially when you don't feel like it.

Using 5-4-3-2-1, I pushed through the excuses, the anxiety, the overwhelm, and the fear. And step by step, day by day, week by week, I slowly took the actions that put my life and career back on track. My husband started using it to push himself to face the issues in his business head-on, and it worked for him too. But it would be another three years before I told anyone else about the 5 Second Rule. I had been reluctant to share it with anyone because, first, I didn't know why it worked. And second, I didn't feel like I was in a position to give anybody advice.

But that all changed one fateful day when an old roommate recommended me as the "perfect person" to give advice on career change at a small event. I suppose she thought of me because I had changed my career so many times, even I had lost count. The event offered to fly me and my husband to San Francisco and put us up in a hotel. When you're struggling financially, that sounds like a free vacation, so I said yes. This was the first time I had ever given a speech on a stage at an event. The only public-speaking class I had ever taken was in high school, and as soon as I boarded the plane, that's when the panic started to sink in: *What on earth have I gotten myself into?*

When I walked on stage and saw 700 people in the audience staring back at me, my mind went blank, and I could feel my chest and neck turning red.

I then proceeded to have a 21-minute-long anxiety attack onstage. About 19 minutes in, I forgot how to end my talk on career change, so I blurted out the 5 Second Rule and how I use it, because I couldn't think of anything else to say. I must have blacked out, because I also don't remember the part where I gave everyone in the audience my email address. And as I walked off that stage, I thought that was the worst experience of my life. Thank God it's over.

It turns out that small event was one of the first TEDx conferences ever held. They filmed it, and a year later, posted the video online. Not only did it go viral—it's become one of the most watched TEDx talks of all time. The 5 Second Rule and its 5-4-3-2-1 countdown spread by word of mouth around the world. As it spread, people started to write to me at that email address, sharing stories about how the Rule was changing their lives. I was so moved by people's stories that I would sit up late at night, after I had put our three kids to bed, answering their emails one by one.

When I had been drowning in my problems, I felt like I was the only one who had trouble doing the things I needed to do. It's not true. We all struggle with motivation. It's a universal problem, and the 5 Second Rule seems to be a solution that not only works for me but also works for people all over the world.

The stories were amazing: People had used 5-4-3-2-1 to push through fear, procrastination, and excuses to change jobs; lose 100 pounds; get sober; launch and sell businesses; improve their health and marriages. The medical and clinical uses blew me away. Doctors and psychologists were using it to treat PTSD, OCD, and depression. Even as I'm writing this Introduction, we have heard from over a thousand people who have used the 5 Second Rule to stop themselves from attempting suicide and to ask for help.

As that TEDx talk became more and more popular online, I started getting invited to speak at other small events. I remember being asked to talk to a group of Realtors at a bar. It was embarrassing standing there with a beer in my hand, trying to talk over the music and people gabbing in the next room. But I survived. I spoke in church basements, a high school classroom, then a friend's brown-bag lunch at work, and it just grew from there.

I would break out in hives as I held the microphone, and I wasn't getting paid. But the more I talked about the Rule and saw how powerful it was for everyone who tried it, the more I became obsessed with understanding why such a simple hack could lead to such profound results.

So, I put my lawyer hat on and started researching habits, human behavior, and the science of motivation. I needed to make a case: Why does counting 5-4-3-2-1 work? I gathered evidence from the experiences of ordinary people who had been using it. I found compelling precedent from the accounts of therapists, addiction specialists, and medical doctors who had begun recommending it to their patients, and all the evidence pointed to a simple explanation:

Small, Consistent Action Changes Everything

Meanwhile, my friends and extended family had no idea what I was doing because I was too scared to tell them. Mel? Giving advice? Give me a break. She nearly destroyed her own life.

At this point in my story, my husband had left the restaurant business and was struggling with depression. We were still drowning in debt, so I was working a full-time job trying to keep our family of five afloat while dedicating nights and weekends to speaking at small events and basically writing a dissertation on the science of motivation on the side.

I knew I wanted to teach the 5 Second Rule full-time and somehow make this my career, but I didn't know how. Looking back, I can see how paralyzed I was with imposter syndrome. What right did I have to call myself an expert in anything? I suppose I was just waiting for some kind of permission to put myself out there.

Maybe you're doing that right now. Waiting for the right time. Waiting to feel ready or a little less afraid. Waiting for someone to come along and tell you that today is the day to start. The problem with waiting is no one is coming. The only permission you need is your own.

Deciding to get serious about trying to make money as a motivational speaker was one of the best decisions I have made in my life. I'll share more with you about what led to this breakthrough in the pages of this book.

Once I started getting paid, I put every dollar toward chipping away at our debt. That first year I gave 17 paid speeches. The next year, it was 47, and I was able to quit my day job. I couldn't believe what was happening. By the third year, it was 99 speeches plus a 24-city tour with JPMorganChase. I had become the most-booked female speaker in the world. I was being hired by companies I admired.

How did this happen? By forcing myself out of bed on those mornings I didn't feel like it. Learning how to push yourself to take action when you are afraid or full of self-doubt or overwhelmed with excuses is a life skill you can learn. Once you master it, you'll understand that you can achieve anything through small, consistent moves forward.

I found myself on the road 150 days a year, standing on stages teaching the 5 Second Rule and the science of motivation while my husband stayed home and took care of our three kids. Word about the Rule and my skill onstage grew and grew. One event had 27,000 people in the audience. CEOs from the world's top brands, professional athletes, medical doctors, neuroscientists, and bestselling authors had begun recommending my work to others. I started a newsletter because I no longer had time to respond to people's emails personally. I eventually wrote to the team at TEDx and asked if they could remove my email from the video online.

When people would ask if I had a Ph.D. or if I was a therapist, I would say, "No, I learned everything the hard way—by screwing up my own life and then having to fix it."

Armed with years of experience, evidence, testimony, and research, I was finally ready to make my case in the form of a book. In 2017, I self-published *The 5 Second Rule*.

The 5 Second Rule went on to become the most successful self-published audiobook in history, and the sixth most read book of the year on Amazon. That book has now been read by millions of people and translated into 41 languages.

Over the years of traveling across the country speaking on stages, I learned three important things: First, most of us are just trying to do our best to get ahead, pay our bills, raise a family, fall in love, have more fun, and reach the potential of our lives. We're just looking for simple ways to be a little happier and make our lives a little better. And we're not only looking for those resources for ourselves—we are looking for the people in our lives who need them too.

Second, I've been told over and over again that I have this amazing ability to distill complex ideas and scientific research into simple, actionable advice that anyone can use to improve their life.

And third, nothing brings me more joy than sharing what I am learning with people like you.

So I have made it my mission to find and share many simple tools to help anyone create a better life. And the "simple" part is key, because if you remember it, you'll use it. For example, did you know that high-fiving yourself in the mirror is one of the fastest ways to rewire your mindset for self-confidence? Me either, and once I learned about it, I dug into the research and it became the topic of my *New York Times* bestselling book *The High 5 Habit*.

The more results people achieved using the 5 Second Rule and the High 5 Habit, the more organizations, media companies, and corporate brands asked me to create programming for their teams and audiences.

So I launched 143 Studios, a Boston-based production company that produces award-winning content, events, audio series, online courses, journals, books, and professional development education for partners like Starbucks, Audible, Ulta Beauty, JPMorganChase, LinkedIn, and Headspace.

In 2022, we launched and started producing *The Mel Robbins Podcast*, which airs in 194 countries and is one of the top-ranked podcasts in the entire world. We've created free online courses that more than a million students have completed. And that little newsletter I created way back when is now read twice a week by a million and a half people. You can learn more about my media production company, the podcast, my newsletter, and our courses at www.melrobbins.com.

For everything I have accomplished, I had no prior experience or the "proper" credentials to pursue. I just made myself do it.

I was 41 when I had that anxiety attack on the TEDx stage. I was 46 when I got my first speaking paycheck. I was 49 when I self-published my first book. I was 50 when I started my production company. And I was 54 when I launched one of the fastest-growing podcasts in the world.

My life didn't change because of one thing that I did; it changed because of the thousands of mornings where I woke up and didn't feel like getting out of bed, but I *5-4-3-2-1* made myself do it.

Changing My Life Wasn't Glamorous; It Was Grueling.

I didn't achieve success or financial freedom because of some secret. I did it because I was willing to do what most people won't: I woke up every day, and regardless of how I felt, I kept slowly chipping away at my goals for over a decade, a painstakingly slow process.

Some days, all I focused on was just trying to be a little better than I was the day before. Often that's all you need to do. I am not special, or different, or gifted, or lucky; I just found the tools that worked for me and I used them. Today, my entire career and life's purpose is sharing those tools with you.

I don't say any of this to brag. I say this to tell you that you have no idea what you're capable of, and neither did I. Through action, I have achieved some extraordinary things, and so can you.

You'll never feel ready to change your life. One day, you just get tired of your own excuses and force yourself to do it. You're never going to feel like going to the gym. One day you just make yourself go. You're never going to feel like having that hard conversation. One day you just get sick of avoiding it, and you force yourself to start it. You'll never feel like looking for a better job. One day you just push yourself to start looking.

5-4-3-2-1 will help you push through your own internal obstacles and take action when you don't feel motivated to do so. And if you use it for long enough, you'll be shocked by what you can achieve.

The 5 Second Rule works because it helps you win the internal battle you have with yourself. But here's what it can't do: It can't remove the external battles you have to fight every day. No matter how many times you count *5-4-3-2-1*, it won't stop the traffic jams, or inconsiderate strangers, or a micromanaging boss, or your family's endless judgment, guilt trips, passive comments, and demands. And one thing I know for sure, the more you say *5-4-3-2-1* and push yourself to change, the more you'll wish other people would change too.

That brings us to this book.

For the past decade, I've been so focused on discovering, creating, teaching, and sharing simple ways you and I can improve ourselves. But in all this time, I have never tackled the number one factor (based on research) that determines whether you and I live a healthy and happy life: relationships. That's where the Let Them Theory comes into play. It's time we talk about how to effectively deal with other people and the surprising secret to creating better relationships with everyone in your life.

Two years ago, I stumbled upon these two words: *Let Them*, and it was like flipping a switch in my life.

The 5 Second Rule changed my relationship with myself.

The Let Them Theory changed my relationship with other people.

Let me explain.

The 5 Second Rule is about SELF-improvement. It will help you get YOURSELF out of bed on tough days, get to the gym, sit down and start writing, open your mountain of bills, take the risk, sign up for the class, finally look at your bank statement, do the last two weeks of laundry, or take the AI coding class you know you need to take.

Every time you count *5-4-3-2-1*, you will push YOURSELF through hesitation, procrastination, overthinking, and doubt. You'll teach YOURSELF how to take action no matter how you feel. That's why it works.

But over the years I have wondered, *Why do I need to constantly force myself to move forward? Why am I so afraid of failing? Why am I so nervous about taking a risk? Why do I have a hard time asking for what I need? What exactly is in my way?*

Have you ever truly stopped and considered these questions for yourself: Why do you hesitate? What is it that is causing you to procrastinate? Or feel so tired? Or overthink every decision? What's underneath all that doubt? What is stopping you from doing what you need to do or living your life the way you want to live it? What are you afraid of?

I was shocked when I discovered the answer for myself: It was other people. Or rather, how I was letting other people impact me. I was spending too much time and energy managing or worrying about other people. What they do, what they say, what they think, how they feel, and what they expect from me. The reality is, no matter how hard you try or what you do, you cannot control other people. And yet, you live your life as if you can.

You live as though, if you say the right things, people will like you. If you keep taking on more work, your boss will respect you. If you act in the right way, and cater to what your mom wants, and also keep your friends happy, somehow you'll find peace. You won't.

In this book, you'll learn how two words—*Let Them*—can set you free. Free from the opinions, drama, and judgment of others. Free from the exhausting cycle of trying to manage everything and everyone around you.

There is a better way to live.

The Let Them Theory is a proven method that teaches you how to protect your time and energy, and focus on what matters to you. You've spent too long chasing approval, managing other people's happiness, and letting their opinions hold you back. Learn how to stop giving your power away and start creating a life where you come first—your dreams, your goals, your happiness. But the best part? The Let Them Theory doesn't just change your life for the better—it transforms the lives of everyone around you too.

How This Book Will Benefit You

This book covers the Let Them Theory, what it is, why it works, and how to use it in eight key areas of your life where you've been trying to control things that you simply cannot control. It is packed with research, evidence, and stories of how you can apply the Let Them Theory—and you'll learn that this approach is supported by ancient philosophies, therapeutic modalities, and the core teachings of the world's major religions, Stoicism, and spiritual practices.

While much of what you're about to learn is supported by scientific research, this is not a textbook or an academic paper. This book is meant to be a guide to applying the Let Them Theory and these principles in the most important areas of your life. That's why it is written in a way that's easy to understand, fun to read, and filled with relatable stories and specific takeaways. Plus, you'll find summaries at the end of each section so the key takeaways are at your fingertips, and you can immediately put to use what you're learning.

I cannot wait for you to read this book and apply everything you learn. You'll quickly see how you've tied your happiness to other people's behavior, opinions, and feelings. The result? You've unknowingly sabotaged your ability to be happier, healthier, and get what you want.

That ends with this book.

If you can promise yourself that you'll stick with me through this book, read, absorb, and immediately start implementing what you learn, I guarantee you: Your life will get a little easier and your relationships will get so much better.

This will be one of the most liberating and empowering things you will ever experience. And it all begins with two simple words: *Let Them*.

The Let Them Theory

Let Them + Let Me

CHAPTER 1

Stop Wasting Your Life on Things You Can't Control

If you're struggling to change your life, achieve your goals, or feel happier, I want you to hear this: *The problem isn't you. The problem is the power you unknowingly give to other people.*

We all do it, often without realizing it. You make the mistake of thinking that if you say the right thing, everyone will be satisfied. If you bend over backward, maybe your partner won't be disappointed. If you're friendly enough, maybe your co-workers will like you more. If you keep the peace, maybe your family will stop judging your choices.

I know this because I've lived it. I spent years trying to be everything for everyone else, thinking that if I could just do enough, say the right things, and keep everyone happy, I'd finally feel good about myself.

But what happens instead? You work harder, bend further, and shrink yourself smaller, and still, someone is disappointed. Still, someone criticizes. Still, you're left feeling like no matter how hard you try, it's never enough.

It doesn't have to be this way. This book is here to help you take your power back. To stop wasting your time, energy, and happiness trying to control things you can't control—like other people's opinions, moods, or actions—and, instead, focus on the one thing you can control: you.

And here's the remarkable thing: When you stop managing everyone else, you'll realize you have a lot more power than you thought—you've just unknowingly been giving it away.

Let me introduce you to the simplest, most life-changing idea I've ever discovered: the Let Them Theory.

What Is the Let Them Theory?

The Let Them Theory is about freedom. Two simple words—*Let Them*—will free you from the burden of trying to manage other people. When you stop obsessing over what other people think, say, or do, you finally have the energy to focus on your own life. You stop reacting and start living.

Instead of driving yourself crazy trying to manage or please other people, you'll learn to *Let Them*.

So, what does this look like? Imagine you're at work, and your colleague is in a bad mood. Instead of letting their negativity affect you, just say *Let Them*. Let them be grumpy. It's not your problem. Focus on your work and how you feel.

Or maybe your dad makes another comment about your life choices, and it hits you like a brick. Instead of letting it ruin your day, just say *Let Him*. Let him have his opinions. They don't change who you are or what you've accomplished or your right to make decisions that make you happy.

The truth is, other people hold no real power over you unless you give it to them.

Here's why this works: When you stop trying to control things that aren't yours to control, you stop wasting your energy. You reclaim your time, your peace of mind, and your focus. You realize that your happiness is tied to your actions, not someone else's behavior, opinions, or mood.

It sounds simple—and it is. But I'm telling you, this shift will change everything. And, even though it's called *Let Them*, this book is about YOU—your time and your energy—because these are the most precious resources you have.

The Let Them Theory will teach you that the more you let other people live their lives, the better your life gets. And, the more you let people be who they are, or feel what they feel, or think what they think, the better your relationships will be.

Learning how to let adults be adults has changed my life. And it will change yours too, because when you finally stop giving your power to other people, you'll see how much power you truly have.

But perhaps the most surprising thing about the Let Them Theory is how I discovered it in the first place.

I'm almost embarrassed to tell you the story.

I discovered something that changed my entire approach to life at. . . a high school prom. (Now there's a sentence I never thought I'd write).

The Prom That Changed My Life

I don't know what it is about proms, but boy are they stressful. I went through four of them with our two daughters, so I figured our son Oakley's would be a breeze. I was wrong.

Our daughters had obsessed about every detail for months: dresses, dates, promposals, hairstyles, spray tans, makeup, corsages, bus rentals, post-prom parties. It was never-ending, and I was so glad when their proms were finally over.

Our son, on the other hand, wasn't sure he and his friends were even going to go. Despite my prodding, he communicated zero details or plans with us. (I know everyone with a son, a brother, or a boyfriend is nodding along with me right now.)

And then, of course, the week of the prom, Oakley decided he wanted to go. Everything was a last-minute scramble—the tuxedo, the specific sneakers he wanted to wear, the logistics. Even finding his date, something our daughters agonized over for months, was left for 48 hours before the big event.

When prom finally arrived, miraculously, we had the tux, the tennis shoes, the date, and the location of the pre-prom photos figured out. Somehow we had also been talked into hosting the post-prom party. Whew!

Right before we were racing out the door, my husband, Chris, fixed Oak's bowtie one last time. Our daughter Kendall, who was home from college, looked at her brother and said, "You look SO good, Oakley."

I stood there and took in the moment. What a handsome young man he had grown into. I couldn't believe how fast 18 years had flown by. I also couldn't believe that Kendall was almost done with college, and our daughter Sawyer had already graduated and was now working at a large technology firm in Boston.

As I stood there in the kitchen, I allowed this fact to wash over me: Time was passing, and I wished it would slow down. That's the cruel fact about time. It's going to keep passing, whether you slow down or not. The time that you have with the people that you love is like a melting ice cube.

One minute, it's there. . . The next, it's gone.

And here's the sad truth: You and I, we can't stop the ice cube from melting. The only thing we can do is make the most of the time that we have with the people that we love while we have it. In moments like this, when I really stop and pause, I always feel a little sad.

I don't know about you, but I feel like I am racing through life and not allowing myself to truly enjoy it. And I get so worked up about things that don't matter that I ruin the brief moments I have with those I love.

Did I really have to get so stressed out about the last-minute scramble and take it out on Oakley? No.

I'm sure you can relate, even if you don't have a child going to the prom. Maybe you've let comments from your family ruin an entire holiday together, or been so consumed with work or school that you cancel yet another plan with your friends. You can waste years of your life being distracted by meaningless things or late nights at work. It's easy to get yourself so stressed out about life that you forget the entire point is to live it.

As I stood there in the kitchen watching Chris fix Oakley's bowtie, I just tried to take it all in. I took a deep breath, walked up to Oak, and gave him a hug. I looked at him and said, "You look so handsome."

"Thanks, Mom." And then he saw what time it was and said, "Dude, we gotta go!"

And just like that, the moment was gone, and time was moving again. Life is funny like that. One minute you are tearing up about the passing of time and how old the kids have gotten, the next minute you're racing around trying to find your keys and getting annoyed that someone left their dishes in the sink, AGAIN.

On the way out the door, I opened the fridge and grabbed the beautiful corsage I had made from the local flower shop for Oakley's date. He took one look at it and said, "Mom, she doesn't want a corsage. DON'T bring that."

I stared at him. "But it's so beautiful," I said. "Are you sure?"

"I already told you, she said she doesn't want one."

"Well, how about I just bring it with us, and if she wants to wear it she can. . . and if she doesn't, she doesn't have to?"

He snapped at me, "Mom, please. I don't want you to bring it."

I rolled my eyes at our daughter Kendall, looking for some backup. She shook her head at me and said, "Mom, drop it. He's nervous. He doesn't really know the girl he asked. Don't push it."

I'll admit that I was annoyed and maybe even a little hurt. I had spent time scrolling online researching flower trends for prom, and I had ordered his date something really killer AND taken the time to drive down, get it, and pay for it. Here I was trying to do something nice for him, and instead of being grateful, he's barking at me. Plus, it was his first prom—what did he know?

So I stuck the corsage in my purse, and we headed out the door to the place where everyone was taking pre-prom photos. Once we got there, Oakley introduced us to his date, who pulled out a boutonniere for his lapel and asked Chris if he could help her pin it in place. I, of course, couldn't help myself.

I reached into my purse, pulled out that corsage like it was a winning lottery ticket, and said to her: "Oakley said you didn't want something, but I had this made up for you just in case."

Oakley shot me a look, and I immediately wished I had kept my mouth shut. He turned to his date apologetically. "You don't have to wear it."

She looked back and said, "It's okay. . . I'll wear it."

And that's when I noticed she had made her own corsage, which she was already wearing on one of her wrists. Kendall rolled her eyes. Chris shifted. If I could have evaporated in that moment, I would have.

Oakley grabbed the plastic container from me and slid the corsage on the free wrist she had graciously extended. And then Chris pinned the boutonniere on Oakley's tux. We took a couple of photos, and then, out of nowhere, it started to rain. And by rain, I mean... downpour. Rain hadn't been in the forecast, so not one of the 20 kids dressed in black tie, or their parents, had a rain jacket OR an umbrella.

These kids are going to get SOAKED, I thought. But it didn't seem to faze the kids at all. They just kept talking in a group, and that's when I overheard them say, "So, what do you guys want to do for dinner?"

I leaned toward Oakley and whispered, "Oak, you guys don't have a reservation for dinner before the prom?"

"Nope."

I looked at my husband and said, "They don't have a reservation for dinner?!"

He shook his head. "I guess not."

This didn't seem to bother my husband or my son. Boy, did it bother me. How the hell do 20 kids have no reservation or plans to eat before the prom? Our daughters had this handled months in advance.

Oak and his friends kept discussing their options as a group. I looked at them and said, "So what are you guys going to do for dinner?"

Oakley turned toward me and said, in that way that only a teenage boy can, "I think we're going to head out and go to Amigos."

Now, the Amigos Taqueria is this great little taco place in the center of town. . . but it's got maybe four tables. The entire place is the size of a shed. All the moms froze, and even the dads were now questioning this plan. Twenty kids in black tie were planning to head out into this rainstorm with no umbrellas or rain jackets to a fast-food joint that maybe ten of them can squeeze inside of. . . before prom?! I couldn't help myself.

You know that feeling when your body is two steps ahead of you, and you just can't stop yourself from saying something or doing something irrational? In my defense, I wasn't the only parent who intervened. Dozens of parents were now swarming their kids trying to take control of the situation. I broke out my phone and started searching for restaurants that might have a sit-down reservation available for twenty.

Nothing... There was nothing. I could feel Kendall watching me. She just stood there as I yelled out to the other parents, "I can't find a reservation anywhere. I'll look for a pizza place that delivers here."

And that's when she reached out and grabbed my arm, pulled me toward her, and looked me in the eyes.

"Mom, if Oakley and his friends want to go to a taco bar for pre-prom, *LET THEM*."

"But it's too small for all of them to fit in; they're going to get soaked," I said.

"Mom, *LET THEM* get soaked."

"But his new sneakers are going to get ruined."

"*LET THEM* get ruined."

"Kendall, they're brand new!"

"MOM! You're being annoying. *LET THEM* show up to prom in wet tuxedos and dresses. *LET THEM* go eat where they want. It's their prom. Not yours. Just drop it."

LET. THEM.

The effect was immediate. Something inside of me softened. I could feel the tension disappearing, my mind stopped racing, and the stress of trying to control what was happening evaporated. Why did I need to get involved? Why did I have to manage this situation? Why not worry about what I was going to do for dinner tonight, rather than what they were? Why was I stressing about them at all?

Let. Them. It's *their* prom, not *yours*. Stop controlling it or judging it, or managing it, and *LET THEM.*

So that's what I did. As the other parents kept trying to microman-age their kids, I walked up to Oakley and smiled. "What now?" he said. "Here's forty dollars for Amigos," I told him. "Have an awesome prom."

He smiled wide, gave me a huge hug, and said, "Thanks, Mom. We will."

Then I watched as Oak and his date stepped out the door, into the pouring rain. I watched them run through the storm and splash mud up onto her gown and ruin his new sneakers. And I didn't care. In fact, it was kind of cute.

Little did I know, that one moment would fundamentally change my entire approach to life.

Let Them … What an Amazing Idea

Within a week, I could not believe how different I felt. I started saying *Let Them* anytime I felt stressed, tense, or frustrated. . . and funny, I realized it was almost always regarding other people.

Let them be sold out of bagels at the bakery.

Let Oakley be mad that I'm not letting him stay out late tonight.

Let Grandma read the news out loud: "Did you hear about this. . .?"

Let them do construction during the Monday-morning commute.

Let them leave dishes in the sink.

Let the neighbor's dog bark all day.

Let my family be late to absolutely everything we go to.

Let my relatives be judgmental of my career.

Let people hate the photo I just posted online.

Let my mother-in-law disagree with my parenting.

Two simple words: *Let Them*, changed everything. It was as if I didn't care and was weirdly above it all. The things that used to bother me just. . . didn't. The people who used to annoy me. . . just didn't. The tight grip that I had on life started to loosen up. Situations at work that would stress me out or cause me to go home and complain to my family just rolled off my back. Brain space that was once overflowing with dumb worries, annoyances, and drama was now available for more important things.

The more I said *Let Them* the more I realized that a lot of what I worried about wasn't worth my time, nor did it deserve my attention. And not everyone was worth my energy. It was liberating.

The more I said *Let Them*, the more time I had for myself. Time to think. Time to breathe. Time to have fun. Time to spend on what mattered to me. Time to take care of myself.

I felt at ease, happy, and centered. The impact was undeniable. Even Chris noticed: "You seem different." And the fact is, I felt different. I felt so good, I just had to share *Let Them* online. So I posted a 60-second video explaining the Let Them Theory on social media. Here is what I said:

> If your friends are not inviting you out to brunch this weekend, *Let Them*. If the person that you're really attracted to is not interested in a commitment, *Let Them*. If your kids do not want to get up and go to that thing with you this week, *Let Them*. So much time and energy is wasted on forcing other people to match our expectations. And the truth is, if somebody else—a person you're dating, a business partner, a family member—if they're not showing up how you need them to show up, do not try to force them to change. *Let Them* be themselves because they are revealing who they are to you. Just *Let Them* and then you get to choose what you do next.

Within 24 hours, more than 15 million people had seen it. Within a week, 60 million, and there were tens of thousands of comments on the video. News outlets started writing articles about the theory and how effective it is. People around the world started flooding my DMs and inbox with questions, stories, and examples of how they were using it. Psychologists and therapists were writing blog posts about it.

I was so blown away by the immediate response, I recorded a podcast episode about the theory and my experience using it. That episode took on a life of its own. It was shared so many times Apple named it the sixth most shared podcast episode of the year, globally.

That was just the beginning, because then the *Let Them* tattoos started rolling in!

A lot of *Let Them* tattoos. . .

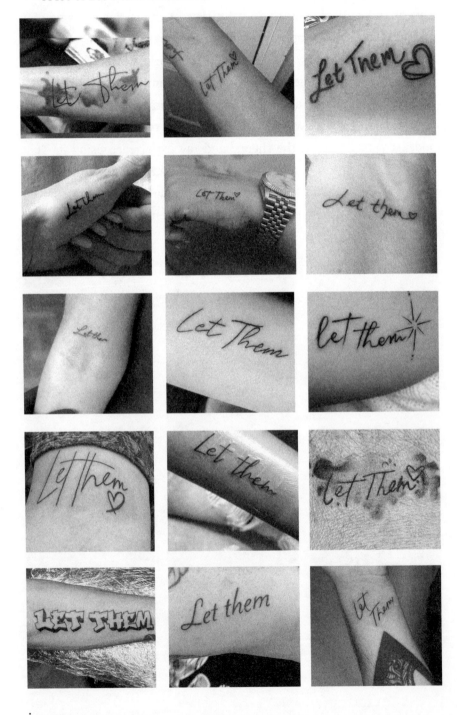

Let Them **is by far the most powerful thing I've ever discovered.** The fact that people around the world were getting *Let Them* permanently inked on their bodies is honestly what inspired me to write this book. I had to understand why these two words had such an immediate, profound, and universal impact on so many people.

Researching the Theory

I've spent the last two years researching the Let Them Theory: why it works, and how you can use it to transform your life and improve your relationships with other people.

In writing this book, I've spoken to many of the world's leading experts in psychology, neuroscience, behavioral science, relationships, stress, and happiness. You'll meet them as you read the book, and their research will help you apply the theory in countless situations in your life. As you'll soon see, the science is clear: This thing works. And it works really well.

But this book isn't just about introducing you to the Let Them Theory. It's about a fundamental law of human nature: *All human beings have a hardwired need for control.*

We all have an innate desire to control everything about our lives: our time, our thoughts, our actions, our environment, our plans, our future, our decisions, and our surroundings. Feeling in control makes you feel comfortable and safe, so naturally you try to control everyone and everything around you—oftentimes, without even realizing it.

But the fact is, there is one thing you will never be able to control. No matter how hard you try, you will never be able to control or change another person. The only person you are in control of is *you.* Your thoughts, your actions, your feelings.

For too long you've been working against this fundamental law of human nature. You've been fighting to change people, battling to control situations, worrying about what people say, think, or do; and in doing so, you've created unnecessary stress, tension, and friction for yourself and in your relationships. I did too.

The Let Them Theory has transformed my entire approach to life and how I deal with other people. Instead of resisting the natural flow of human nature, I learned to embrace it. Instead of wasting my energy on something I can't control—what others say, think, and do—I poured my energy into what I can control: me.

The result? I gained more control over my own life than I have ever had before. It was freeing. I stopped making other people the problem, and in doing so, my relationships improved in ways I never thought possible. It was like unlocking a door that had been sealed shut for years. And behind it? A life where I'm no longer weighed down by the need to manage other people.

In the coming pages, you'll learn all about the theory, the easiest way to start using it, and how awesome it feels when you do. You'll also learn about a surprising discovery I made early in our research. The Let Them Theory isn't just. . . *Let Them*. Yes, it begins with these two words, but that's not the whole story. *Let Them* is just the first half of the equation. There is a second, even more crucial step to this theory: *Let Me*.

In the next chapter, we'll unpack both *Let Them* and *Let Me* and explore the science and psychology behind each one of the two steps. Then, you'll learn about the eight core areas of your life where the theory will have the biggest positive impact. We'll talk about your relationships, career, emotions, opinions, stress, love life, struggles, chronic comparison, friendship, and most importantly, your relationship with yourself.

Over and over, you'll learn how you've been trying to control the wrong things and unknowingly made other people a problem. The truth is, other people should be one of the greatest sources of happiness, support, and love in your life. But they can't be if you keep trying to control what they feel, say, and do. That ends with this book.

Master the Let Them Theory, and you'll stop exhausting yourself trying to control the uncontrollable. This isn't just about feeling better. It's about redesigning how you live your entire life. I can't wait for you to discover the space and freedom to experience your life the way you've always wanted—on your terms.

Let's begin.

CHAPTER 2

Getting Started:
Let Them + Let Me

Not too long after I discovered the Let Them Theory, I was sitting on my couch, scrolling through social media, when I saw a photo of an old friend of mine. She looked fantastic. I glanced down to read the caption, where she was describing an amazing weekend she'd just had with her friends. And I could tell she meant it.

As I stared at the photo, I admired how tan, happy, relaxed, and refreshed she looked. And I found myself thinking, *Wow. I could really use a weekend like that.* Hell, I could just use a spray tan. I started swiping through the carousel of photos and realized I was seeing photo after photo that showed an epic girls' weekend away.

Brunch. Dancing. Shopping. Laughter. Swimming. Cocktails.

Then I took my thumb and my pointer finger and pinched so I could zoom in for a closer look at the group shot, only to realize that I knew every single one of the women smiling back at me on my screen. My heart sank. My friends had all gone away together.

You know that awful feeling in your stomach, the one that hits you when you realize you've been left out. It's like a punch. You try to brush it off, telling yourself it's not a big deal, but the hurt is real. I should have put my phone down, but I didn't.

I looked through those photos one by one—seeing a girls' trip through the eyes of the very same women who I had raised my kids with in our small suburban town—I tried not to let it bother me. But it did.

My mind started filling in all the details. I imagined how much fun they were having and how close they had become. I had known these women for years. We bonded over barbecues, carpools, soccer games, date nights with our spouses, and hard conversations about parenthood. So, naturally, I started to spiral.

I'm talking: Full. Stalker. Mode. I sat there, on that same spot on the couch, and felt it meld to my back as I poured over each and every one of their accounts. Five minutes before, I had been perfectly fine. But now? Well now, I found myself feeling the familiar swirl of emotions take over: rejection, insecurity, confusion. *When did they plan this? Why wasn't I included? Why am I never invited anywhere? When was the last time I went away with friends?*

As I kept on scrolling through their photos, turning those questions over and over in my head, Chris walked into the room, took one look at me, and asked, "What's wrong?"

I sighed, and told him the truth: "I just found out a bunch of my girlfriends went away for the weekend on a really fun trip. I obviously wasn't invited."

"That sucks," he said.

"Maybe I did something wrong," I said. "Maybe they're mad at me."

He crossed his arms and asked me, "Why do you care so much?"

I looked at him.

"It's not like you're close friends with them anymore, Mel."

He was right. I knew he was. But I still felt this urge to reach out and smooth things over. I'm sure you've experienced this before. You find out that you weren't included in something, and all you want is some kind of reassurance that there wasn't something you had done wrong.

Because honestly I didn't know. And if you are anything like me, when it happens you immediately assume that you have done something wrong. As I sat there on the couch wracking my brain for any evidence as to why I wasn't included, I couldn't think of anything. And that made me even more nervous.

I mean, sure, we had known each other for years. We had gone through early motherhood together, we had lived a lot of life together, and I really liked everyone who was on that trip. But, at the same time, I hadn't really spent time with them as a group in a long, long time. I had seen them around town at large gatherings, but I hadn't invested in those individual friendships; and I hadn't planned anything fun or reached out to them recently either. Intellectually, I knew this, but emotionally I was devastated. I felt like I was back in middle school again: the one left out of the sleepover, the one who didn't make the team, or who wasn't part of the inside joke.

Putting the Theory into Practice

I felt myself wanting to reach out to them and fix it. Call, text. Anything to make the anxiety go away. That's when those two words came in and saved me from myself. *Let Them.*

The old me would have obsessed over this for days. For weeks, really. My emotions would have gotten the best of me. I would have tried to pretend it didn't bother me. I would have tried to convince myself that I didn't care. I would have tried to rationalize it over and over in my mind. I would have turned my friends into villains to make me feel better. All of which would have made me feel worse and withdraw even more from these women who I genuinely liked.

But that didn't happen. It bothered me for about 10 minutes. As soon as I said *Let Them,* I felt a little better. The second time I said it, I felt a little better. The third, fourth, fifth, sixteenth time, thirtieth time I said it. . . I felt a little better.

I will be honest with you: In these types of painful situations, you're going to have to keep saying *Let Them* over and over, because when something hurts, the hurt doesn't just disappear. It rises up again and again. So don't be surprised when you find yourself having to repeat *Let Them* again and again.

Let Them go on the trip. *Let Them* take the weekend together. *Let Them* have their fun without you.

At first, those words felt like a rejection. Like I was giving in. But then I realized something important: *Let Them* wasn't about giving in. It was about releasing myself from the control I never had in the first place. Because here's the truth—no matter how much I tried to analyze the situation or how many ways I could try to control or fix it, nothing I did would change what had happened. Their choice to go away didn't have to make me feel bad, but my attempts to control the situation were making me feel horrible.

Let Them.

And just like that, the knot in my chest began to loosen. The pressure to "fix" the situation faded, and I realized something that changed everything: Their weekend away had nothing to do with me.

It wasn't personal. They weren't plotting against me. They weren't making a statement about my worth. And even if they were? *Let Them.*

What We're Really Trying to Control

We all have moments where we try to control the world around us—especially when we feel hurt, left out, annoyed, or afraid. Maybe you've found yourself trying to manage every detail of a group plan to make sure everyone is included; or maybe you've stressed about whether people are upset with you when they don't respond to your messages right away. It's exhausting, isn't it?

I'm a fixer by nature. I've spent most of my life believing that if I didn't step in, if I didn't manage the situation, things would fall apart. I had to be the one who kept everything together—relationships, work, friendships, even the emotions of the people I love. And when something didn't go the way I expected, it felt like a reflection on me. If someone was upset, if something didn't work out, if I wasn't included, I automatically thought I had to fix it, change it, control it.

In talking to so many psychologists while researching this book, I learned that the urge to control things comes from a very primal place: fear. Fear of being excluded, of not being liked, of things falling apart if we're not steering the ship. And it shows up in all kinds of ways. We hover over our kids, making sure they make the "right" decisions. We try to influence our partner's habits, worrying that if we don't step in, they'll somehow get it wrong. We even impose our opinions on friends, believing we know better than they do about how their lives should unfold.

I've felt that fear a lot in my life. Fear that if I didn't make things happen, I'd be forgotten. Fear that I wouldn't be liked or accepted. Fear that without me at the helm, things would unravel. And let's be real—control gives us the illusion of safety. When we're in control, we believe we can protect ourselves from pain, disappointment, rejection.

But it's just that—an illusion of safety. Because no matter how much we try to control people or situations, the truth is, we can't. People will do what they want to do. They'll make their own choices, live their own lives.

The fact is, none of that "control" actually makes you feel better. In fact, it has the opposite effect. Trying to control people and situations doesn't calm your fears. It amplifies them. Any psychologist will tell you, the more you try to control something you can't, the more anxious and stressed out you become.

Sitting on that couch, staring at my phone, I realized I wasn't just trying to control what my friends might think of me—I was trying to control my own discomfort. I hated feeling rejected, so my immediate reaction was to fix the situation before I had to feel anything at all.

That's when the Let Them Theory started to click at a much deeper level for me.

Let Them: A Tool to Implement Wisdom

The Let Them Theory isn't just a mindset hack—it's rooted in ancient philosophies and psychological concepts that have guided people for centuries. If you're familiar with Stoicism, Buddhism, Detachment Theory, or Radical Acceptance, you'll recognize that *Let Them* and *Let Me* applies these teachings and turns them into a practical, everyday tool for improving your relationships and reclaiming your personal power.

In Stoicism, the focus is on controlling your own thoughts and actions—not the thoughts or actions of others. This philosophy aligns perfectly with *Let Them*, which is about consciously allowing others to make their own choices and live their lives, without feeling the need to manage or influence their behavior. By practicing *Let Them* and *Let*

Me, you're applying the core principle of Stoicism: Focus on yourself, because that's where your true power lies.

Buddhism and Radical Acceptance teach that suffering comes from resisting reality. The pain we feel often stems from wishing things were different than they are. The Let Them Theory helps you not only accept reality but also separate yourself from the need to change it. You acknowledge that others' actions and choices are not yours to control, and in doing so, you reclaim your emotional freedom. This is Radical Acceptance in its most empowering form.

Detachment Theory teaches us how to emotionally distance ourselves from situations that trigger us. When you say *Let Them*, you're practicing emotional detachment. You create a mental gap between your emotions and the situation at hand, allowing yourself to observe what's happening without being consumed by it. The result? You remain calm, clearheaded, and in control of your actions.

To me, this theory is not the same as "letting it go." Personally, I've never been able to let anything go—because it never feels resolved. It feels like you've walked away from something that's bothering you, and just swallowed your feelings and moved on. *Let Them* is different. When you say *Let Them*, you're not giving up or walking away. You're freeing yourself. You're releasing that grip you have on how things should go and allowing them to unfold the way they will go.

When you let others be who they are, you're making an active, empowered choice to release control you never truly had. You're freeing yourself from the endless cycle of stress, frustration, and emotional upheaval that comes with trying to manage everything and everyone. The beauty of *Let Them* and *Let Me* is that it helps you master these practices, so you can stop being ruled by emotions and start living a more peaceful, intentional life.

How This Works in Real Life

Think about how this applies to different areas of your life. Let's say you're in a meeting at work and you've come up with an idea you're excited about. You've put thought into it, you know it has potential— but when you pitch it, the room goes quiet. People nod politely, but they move on, and before you know it, someone else's idea is getting all the attention. You feel invisible. You start second-guessing yourself, wondering if maybe you should've said it differently or tried harder to be heard.

In that moment, you can either let this dismissal crush you, or you can pause and say *Let Them*. Let them dismiss it. Let them go with a different idea. Their response doesn't change the value of your idea. It doesn't change your worth as a contributor. They might have gone with a different strategy, but that doesn't mean yours wasn't a great idea. You're still the same person with the same talents and ability to succeed, and the fact that you had an idea to pitch proves it!

The same goes for dating. Maybe you've been texting someone and things felt like they were going somewhere. But then, out of nowhere, they ghost you. No response, no explanation. It stings, doesn't it? You wonder what you did wrong, replaying every conversation, trying to figure out where it went off the rails. The temptation to text them again, to find some way to get closure, is almost overwhelming. Been there.

But here's where *Let Them* comes in. *Let Them* show you who they are. Their disrespect doesn't say anything about you. How you respond does. Stop asking why they are doing this. The question is, why do you want to be with someone who does this to you? You don't. Don't waste your energy chasing someone who's already left. Focus on what you can control: Processing your emotions and reminding yourself that you deserve someone who treats you with respect.

In both of these situations—whether it's work, dating, or anything else—when you say *Let Them*, you are recognizing what's in your control and what isn't. Instead of spiraling, you're choosing to steady yourself and detach. As I said earlier, other people hold no real power over you, unless you give them that power. And every time you say *Let Them*, you choose to take it back.

Or take me and the situation on my couch. I wasn't even aware that my friends had gone away together. The second I saw the photos from their trip, though, I reacted. My emotions took over. I felt insecure. I felt left out. I felt less than. And then I took it a step further and told myself that I had done something wrong. Which only made me feel worse.

The truth is, I did this to MYSELF. My friends didn't do anything TO me. They were just living their lives. They are allowed to go away. They are allowed to plan a weekend with whomever they want. The way I reacted to their trip is what hurt me.

This is so important to understand that I want to truly unpack this with you in detail. Let's use the visual of a seesaw on a playground to explain how the power dynamic between you and other people goes up and down, and how to use the Let Them Theory when it happens.

When someone does something (like planning something and not including you) you will react in an either positive or negative way. If you react negatively—and have self-destructive thoughts or heavy emotions—it will weigh you down. Your reaction is what tips the scales and changes the dynamic between you and someone else.

This graphic illustrates exactly how I felt when I saw that photo online.

A) WITHOUT LET THEM

INFERIOR
JEALOUS
INSECURE
LEFT OUT
LESS THAN

What caused me to go down? I did.

Anytime you internalize other people's thoughts, actions, and feelings as evidence that somehow you're a bad person or you've done something wrong, you just gave other people power. And it shifts the dynamic and balance in the relationship. You feel beneath them.

That's exactly what happened when I told myself I had done something wrong. I felt inferior, jealous, insecure, left out, and less than. Those thoughts and emotions are really heavy thoughts.

When you say *Let Them* you free yourself from the weight of all the negativity that just made you sink. It's like pushing off the ground on a seesaw. You go up and your friends on the other side go down. The power dynamic shifts.

B) SAYING LET THEM

SUPERIORITY
DETACHMENT
FALSE CONTROL
JUDGMENT

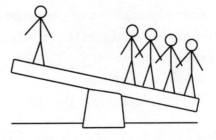

It feels so good to rise above other people and the situations that bother you. That's why people love saying *Let Them*, because when you're up, you now feel this false sense of superiority and confidence. You push through those heavy emotions and rise up. This will automatically make you feel better than someone else. You will feel wiser and weirdly above it all, which is why it is easy to detach from the situation.

And a little superiority can go a long way when you're in an emotional spiral. That temporary feeling of power over other people can help you move through the situation, accept what's happening, and process the frustrating or painful experiences in life.

It helps to feel better than the friend who doesn't call you back, or the lazy roommate who doesn't do their dishes, or the rude customer you have to deal with at work.

But then, that moment of Let Them is over.

Then you will think. . . now what? You'll be sitting up there looking down on other people, and you'll start to feel a little stranded in your superiority. And, after I initially started saying *Let Them*, I didn't really know what to do either. Saying it and getting that jolt of superiority felt good, and detaching from the emotion felt great. That was the easy part. But I didn't know what to do next.

And here is the danger of only saying *Let Them:* If all you ever do is say *Let Them, Let Them, Let Them,* it will lead you to feel more isolated. It will make you want to withdraw or shut down.

And that is exactly what the old me would have done with the situation on the couch. If I had just stopped at the *Let Them* part—I can imagine it now—I would have sat there in my superiority. I wouldn't have reached out. I would have gossiped about them behind their backs, sought out reassurance from other friends, and felt very awkward every time I saw them. And these are women that I actually like and want to be friends with!

I want you to stop and really think about a situation where you see friends of yours going out and doing things without you. When it happens, it hurts. It always hurts to be excluded. You want to be included on that golf trip. You want to be invited over to watch the game. You want to go away for the weekend. You would love to go out for drinks with your cool co-workers. You want to have great, fun friendships.

And I want that for you too. So let me ask you a question: *How exactly is feeling morally superior going to help you create those great friendships?* It's not.

Saying *Let Them* simply relieves you of the hurt and pain you feel... but only momentarily. It feels so good to blame other people and feel better than others.

But as your friend, I feel obligated to warn you that if all you do is say *Let Them* you're going to find yourself without a lot of friends, without a lot of social plans, and confused as to why the theory "isn't working" in your favor.

And that brings me to the major discovery that I made when I first started researching the theory. *Let Them* is just the first half of the equation. You cannot stop there. There is a second, critical part to the theory—*Let Me*.

The source of your power is not in managing other people; it's in your response. When you say *Let Me*, you're tapping into that power by taking responsibility for what you do, think, or say next. *Let Me* makes you realize that you are in control of what happens next and that life is more fun and fulfilling when you're not sitting alone in your superiority.

Let Me Is the Power Move

That's why the theory only works if you say both parts. When you say *Let Them*, you make a conscious decision not to allow other people's behavior to bother you. When you say *Let Me,* you take responsibility for what YOU do next.

What I love about *Let Me* is that it immediately shows you what you can control. And there's so much you can control: Your attitude. . . your behavior. . . your values, your needs, your desires, and what YOU want to do in response to what just happened.

It's the opposite of judgment. *Let Me* is all about self-awareness, compassion, empowerment, and personal responsibility.

Your friends who went away aren't better than you. And you aren't better than them.

This is the crux of the Let Them Theory: *Let Them* and *Let Me.*

The more you allow people to live their lives, the better your life will get. The more control you give up, the more you gain.

The Let Them Theory is not about superiority at all. It's about balance. It's about making room for both you and someone else. It's about giving other people the space and the grace to live their lives—and then giving yourself the same.

C) SAYING LET ME

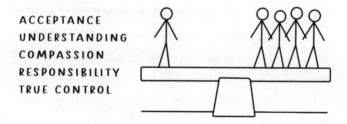

ACCEPTANCE
UNDERSTANDING
COMPASSION
RESPONSIBILITY
TRUE CONTROL

For example, with my girls' weekend spiral, first I said *Let Them,* which helped me rise above the situation and the hurt. It helped me separate myself from the emotions I was feeling. And that is the first step because getting emotional and blaming them or trashing myself, won't magically improve my friendships.

The superiority gave me the mental space to really look at the situation from above. The more I said *Let Them*, the more space I had to consider MY role in this situation, and what I wanted to do about it.

And when I stopped to look in the mirror, I saw a lot.

I had been so busy working the past few years, I had barely seen my friends. I hadn't invited anyone to do anything in a long time. Maybe I wasn't excluded. Maybe they didn't think of me at all. And if I'm not making an effort, reaching out, or bumping into them around the neighborhood, why would they think of me? Plus, if I'm being perfectly honest, I've been so busy with my own life, work, and kids, unless I saw my old friends post online, I didn't think about them much either.

No one owes me an invite. No one owes me a call. Yes, these things feel good; and yes, you deserve friends who reach out. But whose responsibility is it to create those friendships? And more importantly, *Let Me* be honest with myself: Have I been doing my part? When I stopped to ask myself that question, the answer was no.

When you are an adult, your social life is your responsibility. If you want more fun, you should get your butt off the couch and create a great social life (talking to myself here too).

Let Me stop expecting other people to always include me. *Let Me* take responsibility for what I want in life. *Let Me* figure out the deeper issue that I need to look at. *Let Me* be more proactive about reaching out to people. *Let Me* invite people to do something this weekend. *Let Me* throw a party for once. *Let Me* develop better boundaries with work so I have time for friendship. *Let Me* prioritize my social life, because clearly it matters to me, and it is my responsibility to create one.

Let Me reach out to a few of these women to reconnect. Not in a passive way. Not to smooth things over. And not to get an invite to their next getaway. But because once I said *Let Them* and *Let Me* and rise above my emotion, I connect with the deeper truth that I actually really miss a few of these women, and seeing that post online made me realize that I work way too much and I want to make an effort to rekindle my friendship with them. . . and a few other people now that I am thinking about it.

Before We Dive in: Two Warnings

As I researched this book, two important questions came up repeatedly from people who were applying the Let Them Theory, and I want to address them now before we dive deeper into the rest of the book.

First: Does the Let Them Theory apply to children?

Yes, you can absolutely use the Let Them Theory with kids, (with some very important caveats), but this book is specifically focused on how you apply the theory with adults. Throughout the book, I make clear distinctions between adults and children to avoid any confusion. And for those looking for guidance on how to use this approach with children, teens, and young adults, I've included a special guide in the Appendix at the end of the book that breaks this down in detail.

Second: What if using Let Them makes you feel lonely?

This is a critical point. Some people have shared that they feel lonely after using the Let Them Theory. If you're feeling this way, it's a sign you're applying the theory incorrectly. The Let Them Theory has two essential steps: **Let Them** and **Let Me**. These steps must go hand in hand. You cannot simply say *Let Them* and stop there. Many people forget the second step, *Let Me*—and this is a major mistake because *Let Me* is where your real power lies. It's in *Let Me* that you take responsibility for your next move, for creating the life, relationships, and connection you want. Without this step, you'll find yourself disconnected rather than empowered.

As your friend, I feel obligated to warn you that if all you do is say *Let Them* you're going to find yourself without a lot of friends, without a lot of social plans, and confused as to why the theory "isn't working" in your favor. It feels good to say *Let Them* because we like to blame other people. And as we've discussed, a jolt of superiority can help when you feel down. However, that's not the purpose of the theory.

Let Them is not an excuse to stop answering your phone, to shrug your shoulders, to refuse to talk it out with a friend or family member who is hurt, to stay in a situation that hurts you, or to ignore discrimination or dangerous behavior. It's not a license to give someone the silent treatment, ghost people, avoid hard conversations, or withdraw from your relationships.

It's not supposed to leave you feeling alone and invisible, but rather more connected and more fulfilled in every single one of your relationships. If you find that you're using the theory and it's making you lonelier please hear this: You are using it wrong. The theory is here to make your life better, not worse. So I am reminding you to ALWAYS remember to say *Let Me*. Because that is the part that will change your life.

Using the Let Them Theory, I saw how often I blamed someone else for the fact that I was alone sitting on my couch. Or not making the money I wanted to make. Or how often I said yes due to guilt. Or the decisions I made because I didn't want to disappoint someone else. Or how often I used the excuse of being too tired to make my health or fun a priority.

When you're an adult, your life, happiness, health, healing, social life, friendships, boundaries, needs, and success are all your responsibility. If you've been secretly hoping someone else would come and rescue you, fix your problems, pay your bills, create a social life, heal your wounds, change into your dream partner, and motivate you to be your best... it's not going to happen. No one is coming. And any time you spend blaming other people, or waiting for permission or an invitation, is wasted. Those days are over.

Your *Let Me* era is here.

You are capable of creating anything that you want if you are willing to put the time and energy into working for it. And that means you must stop wasting your time and energy on petty, shallow, and insignificant things. And it also means that you have to stop trying to control the one thing you can't: other people.

In the next section of the book, we're diving into four core areas of your life where the Let Them Theory will create the biggest and most immediate positive impact. You'll learn how to stop allowing other people's behaviors, opinions, reactions, and success to affect your happiness and stand in the way of what you want. And there's no faster way to get started and to feel the power of *Let Them* than using it to manage stress and protect your peace. So let's jump in.

You and the Let Them Theory

Managing Stress

Fearing Other People's Opinions

Dealing with Someone Else's Emotional Reactions

Overcoming Chronic Comparison

The more you let other
people live their lives,
the better your life gets.

— Mel Robbins

Managing Stress

CHAPTER 3

Shocker: Life Is Stressful

The fastest and most effective way to start using the Let Them Theory is to rise above the countless tiny stressors you face every day.

You know the ones I'm talking about: the never-ending notifications on your phone, the slow Internet connections, the unexpected changes in plans, the endless meetings at work, the inconsiderate behavior of other people, the long lines, the slow walkers. These small annoyances may seem insignificant, but they aren't.

I get that people can be annoying, and, yes, you have a lot on your plate. Modern life can feel like death by a thousand cuts—one thing after another that slowly drains your energy and stresses you out. It's not only easy to let it get to you, it's dumb.

You can't control how other adults behave, and stressing about it diminishes your power. You'll never reach the full potential of your life if you continue to allow stupid things or rude people to drain your life force.

Your time and energy are your most valuable resources, and in the next few chapters, you'll learn how to use the Let Them Theory to protect yourself from the unnecessary stress other people are currently causing in your life.

Just stop and ask yourself: Why do you have to let a long line at the coffee shop ruin your day? Why is traffic putting you in a bad mood? Why do you feel overwhelmed when someone interrupts you during an important task? Why does the person talking loudly on their phone in public irritate you? Why does a family member's unsolicited advice feel like a personal attack? Why does someone else's slow pace in a busy walkway make you feel rushed?

It happens to me too. Just the other day, I went to my favorite garden center to pick up some plants. There, the cashier was moving so slowly. There were only two lanes open and about five people waiting in each.

Beep. Beep. Beep.

I felt myself starting to get agitated. I had a meeting I had to get to back home. I wanted to turn to the person behind me, shake my head, and say, "Can you believe this?"

But I hesitated. I said *Let Them* to myself instead. The effect was immediate. I softened. Did it speed up the cashier? Nope.

It did something better. It protected me from this habit of letting little things become big stressors in my day-to-day life. The 10 extra minutes that this line was going to take wouldn't negatively impact the rest of my day, but allowing myself to get agitated and annoyed about something I couldn't control absolutely would. Why get stressed out about things beyond your control or that don't really matter? How does something so small have such a large impact on you?

When you let the world around you impact your emotional state and peace of mind, you become a prisoner to these external forces. You're letting trivial nonsense dictate your mood, drain your motivation, and steal your focus. There's this famous quote about life from Greek philosopher Epictetus, "It's not what happens to you, but how you react to it that matters." What does that mean? It means that your personal power is in how you react.

Learning how to respond differently to the annoying and stressful situations every day will change your life. Right now, you're giving away all your power because you're wasting your time and energy on things that don't matter; or you're burning up over things that are beyond your control. You have no idea how big of a problem this is. I didn't either.

The reason it's hard to manage your stress is that your reaction to what is happening around you is automatic and you feel your entire body go on edge. It's like you get swept up in the emotion, and the next thing you know, you send the text you regret. Or you say things in the heat of the moment that you don't really mean. Or you stand there in a really long line of people, and the anger and annoyance just build and build even though you wish they wouldn't.

These are all examples of how your reaction to stressful and irritating situations can become a big problem in your day-to-day life. You can't control what is happening around you, but you can control how you respond to it. Nowhere is this more evident than at an airport. In fact, if you want to feel stressed, just go to one.

The Airport Stress Test

From the check-in to security lines to people losing their minds over weather delays, missing baggage, people crowding the gates before they even start the boarding process, tight connections, getting rerouted, all the overhead space taken by the time you board, long lines at the rental car counter... the number of things that could stress you out are endless.

But let's use this fact as an example to help you understand what you can control and what you can't control. Remember the fundamental law of human nature: You can't control what other people say, think, or do. Anytime you try to, you lose your power. You must learn to focus on what you say, think, or do. That's how you remain in control.

Because no matter what is happening on the plane or at the airport, you still hold the power.

A few months ago, I was on a plane and the guy right behind me was coughing as if it were his last day on earth. You know that deep, chest hack that is bound to get everyone around them sick?

I didn't think anything of it for the first few minutes, but when it continued on and on, and then he started clearing his throat, and then he kept coughing, I started to get annoyed.

I was flying to an event where I had to give a speech, and over the next couple of weeks, I was speaking at a number of big events. I could not afford to get sick and lose my voice.

I turned around to look through the crack between the seats and saw him just open-mouth coughing into the air, as if no one else was on this plane. I thought: *Is this guy really going to get me sick? It's so selfish and rude of him. I can't get sick.* I considered my options.

Being passive-aggressive wasn't going to solve anything. As much as I kept huffing and puffing in my seat and glaring at him between the cracks trying to make evil-eye contact, he was either not picking up on my clues or he didn't care.

I considered flagging over the flight attendant and complaining, but he was sitting right there, so he'd hear me, which would feel really weird. So I decided to turn around like a mature adult and ask him politely, "Sir, could you please cover your mouth?"

There was an awkward pause.

He nodded and then he proceeded to cough openly for the rest of the plane ride. I know this, because I kept turning around and looking through the crack between the seats. Obviously, you feel bad for the guy. It's not like he wants to be sick. When you have to cough, you have to cough.

But in the heat of the moment, I was getting more and more annoyed. I was not only stressed out, but it was now ruining my mood and making it impossible to try to get some work done.

This is just one example of how something happening around you can easily stress you out and negatively impact your body and hijack your brain.

Your Brain on Stress

One of the experts that I interviewed while researching this book is Dr. Aditi Neurukar, a physician at Harvard Medical School and author of *The 5 Resets: Rewire Your Brain and Body for Less Stress and More Resilience*. Dr. Aditi was the medical director of Harvard's Beth Israel Deaconess Hospital's integrative medicine program, where she developed an enormous clinical practice in stress management using evidence-based, integrative approaches to help her patients feel better.

Dr. Aditi says, "Stress is a much bigger problem in your life than you realize."

According to Dr. Aditi, stress causes you to doubt yourself, procrastinate, burn out, doom scroll, and struggle with comparison. If you're having trouble focusing, feeling happy, or taking care of yourself, the reason is stress.

She also told me that if your inner critic is louder than ever, you're struggling with procrastination, you're constantly tired, you can't stop scrolling on your phone, or you have trouble disconnecting from work, it's all due to stress. Dr. Aditi explained to me that stress is way bigger than just the tension you feel in your body. Stress is a physiological state in your brain. This is important to understand because stress actively hijacks the functioning of your brain. As Dr. Aditi explained it, normally your prefrontal cortex is in control.

This part of your brain helps you run your day-to-day life. It helps you plan, organize, remember things, and guide your decision-making. To become the best version of yourself, you need to leverage this part of your brain.

The problem is that the second you "feel stressed" by the guy coughing on the plane, the line that is taking too long, or the test results you are waiting on, your brain goes into a stress response and that prefrontal cortex that is so important is no longer in control (and neither are you).

Your stress response is located in another part of your brain called the amygdala. Dr. Aditi described the amygdala as a "small, almond-shaped structure deep in your brain, located between your ears. It's one of the oldest structures of the human brain and many refer to it as our 'reptilian brain.' And it houses your stress response."

If you've ever heard someone refer to the "fight, flight, or freeze response," that's the exact same thing as your "stress response"—meaning that when you are stressed, your amygdala is in control. This can cause rash decision-making and more impulsive behaviors.

When life is normal and you're feeling good, your prefrontal cortex is the one driving most of your actions. This means that you can logically think through the pros and cons of situations and make well-thought-out decisions. In other words, you can choose how you are going to respond.

But, whenever something happens that makes you feel stressed, this is where you and I get in trouble because the response in our bodies and brains is automatic. Your amygdala takes over automatically. And, this part of your brain has one job: survival and self-preservation.

Your brain and body kick into fight or flight, and are only designed to work in this stressed-out state for short periods of time. You are supposed to reset back to normal functioning, where your prefrontal cortex is in control and you feel calm and confident again. But what happens when you don't reset?

The Real Reason You Are Exhausted All the Time

According to Dr. Aditi, 7 out of 10 people are currently living in a chronic state of stress. I used to be one of them. When you live in a state of chronic stress, you are locked in a constant state of fight or flight. Your amygdala is humming in the background, always on.

Dr. Aditi told me that when you're stressed, you not only *feel like* you're in survival mode, but from a neurological standpoint, your brain actually *is* in survival mode. Your goals. . . your dreams. . . your best self. . . your ability to be patient and nonreactive. . . it all goes right out the window.

Which is why you must solve this problem and stop allowing other people to create unnecessary stress in your life. There's too much at stake. You deserve to live a good life, but you'll never be able to if you are always in survival mode.

You'll never get that project done this weekend if you keep procrastinating because of stress.

You need to have more fun, but you won't allow yourself to have it if you can't disconnect from work.

You should be more present and connected to your spouse, but you never will be if you're constantly stressed.

The life you've always wanted is right in front of you, but you will never reach for it if your inner critic is constantly telling you not to. Stress is a major problem and it's time you deal with it.

Hacking Your Stress Response

So I asked Dr. Aditi how we reset our brain back to normal functioning.

She said the first step is to understand what stress actually is so that you know you have power in these situations.

For me, it was a revelation to learn that stress is your body and brain switching between two functions. It's empowering to know that I can switch back to normal functioning and that it's not hard to do, using the Let Them Theory.

How cool is it that you don't have to live your life feeling like everything happening around you has to stress you out? How amazing is it that other people's behavior doesn't have to be a huge problem in your life?

Next, you're going to use the Let Them Theory to reset your stress response. Think of it as an on-off switch—a little lever you can pull inside your brain whenever something happens that stresses you out.

The moment you say *Let Them*, you are signaling to your brain that it's okay: This isn't worth stressing about. You are telling your amygdala to turn off. You are resetting that stress response by detaching from the negative emotion you feel.

Here's how you do it: The moment anything happens that stresses you out, say *Let Them*. Put yourself in pause. Then say *Let Me* and take a breath.

Let Me take another breath. Slow your stress response. Calm your body and brain down. Take control and regain your power.

This seems so insignificant, but this one change will turn you into a different person. Catching your stress response using *Let Them* and *Let Me* empowers you to choose what you say, think, or do instead of allowing your emotions to hijack your response. No more rage texts, or snapping at your loved ones, or wasting hours crafting an email at work.

The fact is, not every email warrants a response and not every conversation needs your participation—and you do not always have to have the last word.

You'll start to see that a lot of what used to set you off isn't worth your time and energy; and the less you react to the things around you using *Let Me*, the more in control you feel.

Dr. Aditi said that taking deep breaths has been scientifically proven to help lower your stress response. Breathing in fully, feeling the air expand your belly, stimulates the vagus nerve, which sends a message directly to your brain that says, "We can calm down."

By saying *Let Me* and resetting your stress response—you are now back in control and can choose how to *intentionally* respond.

Own Your Reactions, Take Your Power Back

On that note: Let's go back to me on the plane, with the guy who is coughing behind me; I'm getting more and more stressed, and I can't focus on the work I need to get done, and I feel like a caged animal sitting there strapped to my seat.

So, how do you use the Let Them Theory to get someone to stop coughing?

You don't. You have to *Let Them* cough. *Let Them*.

I know… hear me out. Yes, it was stressing me out. Yes, I thought he was rude for not covering his mouth. And yes, I was worried about getting sick.

But let's come back to control: What could I control in this situation? I couldn't control whether or not another person was coughing. I could only control how I responded to the coughing.

Focusing on what you can't control makes you stressed. Focusing on what you can control makes you powerful. And that brings me to another important point: Who is responsible for me not getting sick?

Me, or this stranger on a plane?

Me. I'm responsible for my health. It's not this guy's responsibility to stop coughing because I want him to. It's my responsibility to respond in a way that takes care of my needs. I know what you are thinking.

Shouldn't everybody cover their mouth? Shouldn't everybody wash their hands? Shouldn't everybody follow basic guidelines of decency? Of course they should, but a lot of people don't.

My point is, trying to manage someone else, or a situation that is beyond your control, is only going to cause you more stress. I could get mad. I could keep turning around. I could yell at the flight attendant. I could get frustrated and yell at the guy, but to what end? Isn't there a more obvious and powerful solution right in front of my face?

I'm offering you a pragmatic and strategic approach to life.

Instead of getting enraged in my seat, I just *Let Him* cough, and then I *Let Me* focus on the simple actions I could take in order to protect myself.

I am going to cover my nose and mouth with my scarf, I thought. *And I am going to put my headphones on to drown out the coughing.* And that's what I did. And with my scarf over my nose and mouth, I turned up my music in my headphones.

Problem solved.

Every time you say *Let Them*, you acknowledge that you cannot control this situation that is stressing you out. When you say *Let Me*, you are following Dr. Aditi's advice and focusing on what you can control, which is your response to these stressful situations.

Dr. Aditi confirmed, "the Let Them Theory is like a sigh of relief for your stressed brain. It helps you reclaim control over your anxious thoughts so that your brain and body can finally get out of survival mode and back to thriving."

Let Me explain why this matters. If you allow yourself to get completely stressed out, you are giving all your power to other people.

In the past, I would have allowed this guy to stress me out. I would have gotten zero work done, been exhausted by the time the plane landed, and then called my husband to complain about this idiot who ruined my entire flight. I probably would have told the story over dinner that night with the clients who had hired me to speak at the event. I would have gone on and on about how "infuriating" this situation was for me. All of which would have left me feeling even more stressed out, more worked up, and more drained.

I am explaining this in detail because I want you to see what a problem this is. When you let other people stress you out, you surrender your power to things that either don't matter or are beyond your control. And it often spirals into other areas of your life for hours, weeks, and even years.

If you want to achieve your goals, be more present, feel more confident, and be happier, you must stop allowing other people to stress you out. In life, there will be things you can control, and things that you can't. There will be situations that are fair, and situations that are not. You get to decide what stresses you out and for how long.

What Dr. Aditi's research proves is that learning to protect your energy will improve your mood, mindset, health, focus, and ability to disconnect and unplug. I believe this is one of the reasons why so many people get the words *Let Them* tattooed on their body within days of learning about the theory.

It serves as a reminder that your peace is worth protecting. There is a certain kind of confidence that comes with knowing that other people can't disrupt your peace.

But let's take it up a notch.

A stranger coughing on a plane is a pretty straightforward situation. You will eventually get off the plane and move on with your life, so it is easy to use the Let Them Theory then.

But what about when it's not clear what you should do or what the right response is? How do you use the theory when your stress is coming from something much bigger. . . like your job?

CHAPTER 4

Let Them
Stress You Out

What about practicing *Let Them* and *Let Me* when it comes to something or someone that triggers your stress response every single day? According to research, work is the #1 cause of life stress for most people—and your manager has as much impact on your mental health as your spouse.

I'm sure I don't need to tell you that because, as rewarding as work can be, it is filled with stress. From 4 P.M. meetings on a Friday, to dealing with rude customers, passive-aggressive emails, a micromanaging boss, doing work that you don't enjoy, feeling unappreciated, seeing no opportunity for advancement, false promises, surprise layoffs, or being completely understaffed and having extra work on your plate—it's always something.

And if you're like me, and you've started your own business or are trying to be a good manager, just double that list.

So how do you use the Let Them Theory to not let work stress you out? For example, what if you've been doing a great job, hitting all your numbers, going above and beyond, and your boss just isn't promoting you?

When you ask for an update, you get the stereotypical response that "the company's profits are down this year" and "my hands are tied" but "you add so much value to this team" lip service. It sucks.

You feel frustrated, discouraged, powerless, hostile, or demoralized. Dr. Aditi says this is why she's seeing burnout in record numbers right now: People are stuck in a state of chronic stress at work. And she added, your stress at work isn't changing so you need to change your approach to dealing with it.

I know when I've been in that situation, that's exactly how I felt. And the fact that you need your paycheck to pay your bills only makes you feel more stressed-out and powerless.

But as overwhelming as work may be right now, you are not powerless. So, how do you use the Let Them Theory to get your boss to give you the promotion you deserve?

You don't. *Let Them* string you along.

I know it's tough to hear, because it's true. Yes, it's not fair. Yes, you've earned the promotion. And yes, you deserve to be angry about it.

But *Let Me* ask you this question: Who is responsible for YOUR career? That's right, you are.

Besides, you can't control if your boss is going to promote you, give you a raise, or even move you to the cubicle that's closer to the window. No matter how much hard work you've put in, or how many compliments you've received, the decision is up to them.

So if you're in a situation where you've put in the effort, you have had the conversation, you've asked for the salary increase, you've hit your numbers, and you still are waiting for that promotion or title change or new desk and it's just not coming, you have to stop being mad and choose what you're going to do about it.

Because, guess what? If you let your emotions get the best of you, it's going to make you crazy. If you let the stress of this situation take over, you will never be able to think strategically about your next move.

You cannot let the stress of this make you stupid. You've got to be smart about how you're going to respond. *Let Me.* That's where your power lies.

If something at work is out of your control and you've done everything you can to try to influence it, it is dumb to waste any more time trying to change the situation. And it is even dumber to constantly let it stress you out. You are way smarter than that. Your life and the possibilities in it are always way bigger than your current job.

You are never stuck. That's a lie you tell yourself. You can leave a job, a relationship, a living situation, a date, an interview, or a conversation any time you want to.

But instead, you're sitting there with your boss Steve, who you flip off every time the Zoom meeting ends.

You do not have to stay in any job that makes you feel frustrated, demoralized, or stressed. And you shouldn't. *Let Them* string you along.

It's time for the *Let Me* part. Stop fixating on your current situation, and start focusing on finding a better opportunity. Right now there's an amazing job with a kickass boss, a better salary, and a desk next to a window waiting for you to come find it. Your company is not the only company on this planet, and there's a million bosses out there who would be ecstatic to help advance your career.

Let Me go get it.

Is it hard to find a job? Yes. Can it take forever? Yes. Do you dread the idea of updating your resume? Yes. Is getting out there and networking intimidating? Yes. Your career is your responsibility and you have more power here than you think. It's time to start acting like it.

Let Me choose to spend my weekends differently. Instead of blowing off steam at the bars with your friends and complaining about work, how about you pour your time and energy into doing the work to find a job you deserve? Yes, it may take you six months to land something amazing, but those six months are going to go by whether you do nothing, or you go after what you want.

And consider this: If you stay in that job, who controls your future? That's right. Your boss Steve. But if you update your resume, start networking, and go on some interviews, who's in control now? That's right. YOU.

You can act like a toddler and call your boss every name in the book, but the harsh truth is that you're the one to blame—because you are choosing to stay in a job that makes you miserable.

That's on you. And you want to know what else is on you? Your dumb excuses for why you are not looking for another job. You have so much more power than you think. It's time to start acting like it.

You Control Your Next Move

One topic that I want to address in greater detail is how you can determine what the right response is for you when you say *Let Me*. The *Let Them* part is obvious.

When you say *Let Them*, you stop trying to control what someone else is doing. When you say *Let Me*, you take responsibility for how you respond to it, which is not always obvious.

Every situation is different and learning how to choose what type of response is worth your time and energy, and what isn't, will change your life. I have a story that will help you understand how to choose the right response for you.

The other day, I was taking our dogs for a walk at a popular spot at a local state park. As I pulled into the parking lot, a local park ranger stopped to pet my two dogs and say hello. And as we were chatting, he mentioned to make sure to keep the dogs on the leash and pick up their poop, because there had been a lot of complaints that dogs were running free, and that they were not being picked up after by their owners. And it was getting to the point where they may close the trails to dogs.

I thanked him for sharing that information, and assured him that I was not "one of those people" and would follow the rules. As I walked down the trail, there was a person walking 100 feet ahead of me, with their dog off the leash, running all over the place, and jumping up on people.

I started to get annoyed. I could feel the stress response rise up and my amygdala switch on. I was no longer enjoying my walk in the woods. I was focused like a laser on this dog and its owner, and I was getting more and more annoyed that this was exactly what the park ranger was talking about, and this one idiot was going to get us all banned from being here.

I kept saying *Let Them*, and it worked for the first five times I said it. But then her dog crouched right there on the middle of the trail and went number two, and I watched in horror as the owner kicks some leaves over it instead of picking it up in a doggy bag and removing it.

That was it. I went from feeling stressed to anointing myself as the dog police in five seconds flat. That brings me to an important aspect of using the theory. Your response to every situation is going to be unique and different every time.

There will be days when I just don't have the energy to chase this woman down, hand her a doggie bag, ask her to pick it up, explain the implications of what's going on, and request that she do her part.

And there will be days where I will run like an Olympic sprinter, chase her down, and do exactly that.

There will be moments when I just shrug my shoulders, say *Let Them*, and know it's not worth my time and energy. And, when I get to the point where the dog has made its mess, I'll *Let Me* be the bigger person, and I'll take a baggie and pick it up. And then I'll smear it all over her car in the parking lot (that last part was a joke).

While I don't want to have to pick up after other people, I like being the kind of person who cares about leaving public spaces in good shape for everyone to enjoy them. I love knowing that I leave places better than I found them. And I love acting like a leader, even when it's not my job to do so.

There will be other days where I feel that the best course of action is to turn around, walk back out to the parking lot, track down that park officer, wait with them until the woman comes back, and personally report her to the ranger so he can deal with her.

Every single one of these *Let Me* options are available to me and you. And as you were reading, you may even have thought of other options. The point here is, every situation is different, but one thing remains the same: You always get to choose how you respond.

I can't stop that lady from letting her dog poop in the middle of the trail, but I can choose what I do in response to it. I get to choose who I am going to be and how I am going to show up, and that is a very powerful feeling.

Every situation will be different based on how you feel, what's going on in your life right now, how much time you have, how important the issue is to you, what your values are, and what the most effective approach is.

Let Me is an opportunity for you to put your time, energy, and values at the center of your life. It's where you get to choose what's worth your attention and what isn't. How do you decide what's right for you? Particularly when it's a really stressful situation? Great question.

I find it helpful in these stressful moments to just say *Let Them*, take a pause, and consider: Is this going to bother me in an hour? Is this going to bother me in a week? Or is this something that just bothers me right now?

If I'm still thinking about it an hour from now, I should do something. If it's going to matter in a week or a year, then I definitely need to do something. In the situation with this lady and her dog, I knew it would bother me every single time I walked my dog at that state park.

In most cases, you will know what is right for you. And that leads me to the next example—which is the perfect topic to follow poop— and that's politics.

According to recent research, the majority of people report feeling very stressed about the current state of world politics. I feel it too. And how can you not?

We live in a moment where we are more polarized than ever, the stakes feel so high, and everyone seems so far apart and either angry or scared about where things are (or both).

It's impossible to have a civil conversation with most people who have a different point of view, because none of us really want to take the time to understand where the other person is coming from.

It would be easy, given how stressful politics can be at the local, state, national, and global level, to just throw your hands up in the air, disengage, and feel powerless to change the state of things.

So, how do you use the Let Them Theory to change the state of politics at a local, national, or global level?

You don't. The school board has already decided. The Senate has voted. These are the two candidates running. The election is over. It's tied up in the courts. *Let Them*. You can't change what just happened.

But I never said you couldn't change the future. Does it seem overwhelming? Yes. Does it feel like it won't make a difference? Yes.

Do it anyway. *Let Me* stay engaged and vocal on the issues I care about and do something that can change the future of my local, national, and global politics. Don't sit around and wait for someone else to clean up the mess that you see.

If it matters, be the one everyone else is waiting for. Create the change you want to see. That's the power of *Let Me*.

I like to remind myself of what Professor Margaret Mead said: "Never doubt that a small group of thoughtful, committed citizens can change the world; indeed, it's the only thing that ever has."

All it takes is one person to do the right thing. And if it bothers you enough, that person is you. Something can always be done. You can make a difference. And if it doesn't matter enough for you to get involved, then stop complaining about it. It just stresses you out. And as you are learning, that's dumb. Talk is cheap. If it really bothers you, dedicate some time and energy to changing it.

Over and over again, regardless of what situations and circumstances in which you find yourself using the Let Them Theory, you'll learn that no matter how big the problem is or how stressful something feels, there's always something you can do through your actions and your attitude to make it better.

That is the power of *Let Me*. You can't control everyone around you, or the world at large, or what people are doing at the park, but you can always control what you say, think, or do in response—and that's where true power comes.

And the more you tap into that power, the more you'll see all of the ways in which you've been sabotaging your own happiness and giving all your power away. And, like me, you didn't even know it. Your time and energy are paramount. The Let Them Theory really highlights this and empowers you to make better choices about what is worth your time and energy and what isn't. This doesn't mean avoiding difficult conversations or staying silent.

It doesn't mean being a doormat and letting people walk all over you; nor does it mean you have to pick up everybody's dog poop or run for political office.

What it does mean is that you get to choose what impacts you and to what extent. You get to choose what you participate in and what you don't. You get to choose when a job or relationship or issue is worth fighting for, and when it's time to leave. You get to choose, and that is why you are always in control of what happens next.

So let's summarize what you have learned about managing stress. Right now, you allow other people to create unnecessary stress in your life. The Let Them Theory teaches you to protect your energy by not allowing minor irritations to control your life, so you can focus on what truly matters.

1. **Problem:** Other people are going to do things all day that bother you, annoy you, or stress you out. It will happen. You can't control it. When you allow someone else's behavior to stress you out, you give other people power. That leaves you drained with no time and energy for yourself.

2. **Truth:** Your body's stress response is automatic. You will feel yourself getting annoyed. You will feel frustrated. You will feel the anger and agitation hit. You can't control the emotions that rise up inside of you. But you can learn how to reset your stress response so your emotions don't hijack you.

3. **Solution:** Using the Let Them Theory, you protect yourself from the stress other people have been causing you. Your power is in controlling your response to the

other person's behavior, to the annoying situation, and to the emotions that you feel.

When you say *Let Them*, you make a decision not to allow other people's behavior stress you out or bother you. When you say *Let Me*, you reset your stress response and take responsibility for how you respond.

It's time to reclaim all your time and energy for what matters most to you.

Fearing Other
People's Opinions

CHAPTER 5

Let Them Think Bad Thoughts about You

Poet Mary Oliver asked this question in her poem "The Summer Day": "Tell me, what is it you plan to do with your one wild and precious life?"

I don't know what your answer to Mary Oliver's question is, but I do know this: Whatever it is that you plan to do, other people are going to have an opinion about it.

In the next few chapters, you'll learn how to use the Let Them Theory to stop allowing other people's opinions to hold you back from pursuing what you want and limiting the potential of your one wild and precious life.

You have no idea how big of a problem this is. Neither did I. It's easy to put on a facade that you don't care what other people think, but the reality is, we all do.

The truth is, people will have negative opinions about you and there is absolutely nothing you can do to change this fact. When you allow your fear of what other people think to stop you from doing what you want to do, you become a prisoner to other people's opinions.

This fear impacts every aspect of your life. It makes you procrastinate. It makes you doubt yourself. It paralyzes you with perfectionism. It's the reason you overthink.

This is where that ends. It's time to give people the freedom to think what they want. *Let Them*. It's time to set yourself free and *Let Me* make the small moves boldly and unapologetically that over time will transform your entire life.

The Let Them Theory was a gigantic wake-up call for me. I knew that I was worried about other people's opinions, but I had no idea how big of a problem it was until I started saying *Let Them*. *Let Them* judge. *Let Them* disapprove. *Let Them* have their opinions. *Let Them* think bad thoughts. *Let Them* talk about me behind my back.

Right now, you move through life with other people's opinions as your road map. You take the left or right turn based on what you anticipate other people might think or say, rather than making the turn you want to make. When you navigate your life trying to predict what people are going to think and say about you, you give your power away.

Instead of overthinking every move you make, what if you just *Let Them* think whatever the heck they want to think? It's life-changing to free yourself of this burden. Remember the fundamental law of human nature: You can't control what another adult says, does, or thinks. Try to and you'll regret it. The more you *Let Them* think what they want, the better your life gets.

What if you gave yourself permission to live your life, and you gave other people permission to think whatever they want about it? What if you pour your time and energy into your hobbies, your habits, your happiness?

What change would you make if you weren't worried about being judged? What is something that you are afraid to admit that you want? What belief are you nervous to be more vocal about? What have you been too scared to try because you have never done it before? What challenge or race or adventure have you been secretly yearning to do? What do you wish would happen at work but you are too afraid to ask? What conversation have you been avoiding? What picture have you been waiting to post?

That last one really hits home for me.

Welcome to Your Biggest Roadblock in Life

Ten years ago, I was just getting started as a motivational speaker. I was brand-new to the speaking industry. And, like a lot of new businesses, in the beginning, there was no money. To get started and get my foot in the door, I would reach out to small women's conferences and pitch myself to speak for free.

If you're starting a business, or you've got a side hustle, or you've started trying to make money online through social media, you're probably nodding your head, because in the very beginning, you're putting in a lot of work with zero return.

I started getting frustrated that a year had gone by, and I was getting better onstage and the audiences were getting bigger, but my bank account was getting smaller. Why? Because I was working a full-time job during the week and doing these speaking gigs for free on the weekends.

And as I wrote about in the Introduction of this book, this was during the period of time when my husband and I were struggling with massive financial debt, so I was highly motivated to figure out how to make money doing this.

I asked some of the more experienced speakers for advice on how to start getting paid, which is what I recommend you do in whatever business, venture, or side hustle you dream of launching.

Every business has a formula. Follow it. I say that because one of the things I see people get hung up on all the time is this belief that "I need to be different." That is a fancy way to say that you're afraid other people will think that you copied them. This is an example of how your fear of what other people think holds you back from following the most obvious, easiest, and most proven path to success.

Let Them think you copied them. Because you did. And they copied the formula from someone else. Because they did. Formulas exist because they work time and time again. You will make it unique because you will be putting yourself into the formula. Do not reinvent the wheel. Follow the formula and use it to your advantage.

Which is exactly what the experienced speakers told me to do. Every successful speaker does the same three things. And, until you do these things, you're not really in the speaking game.

Here is what they told me to do:

1. Build a simple website with photos of you on a stage, plus a description of your keynote and the main takeaways.

2. Get testimonials from a few event planners at past events you have spoken at and put them on the website.

And then most important:

3. Start posting about speaking online. Turn your social media into your marketing. Post photos from events. Post content related to your speech. Post photos with the event planners that hire you. Social media is how people find you. Social media demonstrates that you are a player in this industry. And social media is what will lead people to that one-page website so they can book you.

That is the formula. Follow it, and you will start getting paid. So, armed with that advice, I knew exactly what I needed to do. Plus, the stakes were really high. I needed the money to get my family out of debt. I was very clear about what I needed to do.

But did I follow the formula? Not really. Yes, I created a website. Yes, I asked for testimonials and put them on the website. But did I post on social media? Nope.

At the time, my social media was personal. It was filled with photos of my kids, pictures from family trips, and selfies with friends. All of my followers were friends, former classmates, and family members. I had never posted anything about my desire to become a motivational speaker or the fact that I had been doing it for free for over a year.

And if you've ever wanted to use social media to launch a business, or promote some new aspect of your life, or to share your art, you know how hard it is to look at your account that has only photos of your personal life and make the decision that you're going to turn this into a marketing channel.

It took me TWO YEARS to start posting about my business on social media. Why?

Because I Was Afraid of What People Would Think

Who were you afraid of, Mel? My friends.

I worried that if I stopped posting photos of my kids and pictures from barbecues and get-togethers with extended family, and started posting photos of me speaking at conferences, that people would judge me.

Who does she think she is? Who the heck is hiring her to speak? What does she possibly have to say? What a phony.

I tried to post. But I'd thumb through my photos from the event and select one or two. Then the fear would kick in. As I drafted a caption,

I would start to feel worried about other people's negative opinions: *Does this sound too arrogant? Is this caption professional enough? If I post this, will people unfollow me? Will my friends think I'm full of myself? Should I start a separate account from scratch?*

I would then convince myself that it wasn't worth it to post. You want to know why? Because I burned through so much energy trying to craft the perfect, most compelling, and marketable image and caption—something that would both promote me and ensure that no one would think a negative thought—that I exhausted myself.

I created hundreds of draft posts. And they just sat there, in my drafts... for years. And when I did get the jolt of confidence to post, I would leave it up for five minutes and check it obsessively; and if there weren't as many likes as I wanted, or the comments weren't as positive as I had hoped, I would delete it.

This stupid fear kept me from marketing my business, something I wanted to make my full-time career, for years. I gave other people's opinions more weight and importance than my own ability to get ahead in life. Talk about giving your power away.

And when I look back at it now, it makes me sad.

I stopped myself from taking the actions that would have helped me achieve my goals, make more money, get out of debt, be able to buy nice things for my kids, and get a lot more clients a lot faster. Isn't that stupid? Of course it's stupid. And yet I'm sure you struggle with the same fear when it comes to "putting yourself out there."

Whether it's your business, your art, your music, your videos, or posting a photo of you in a bathing suit, if you're censoring yourself it's because you fear people's opinions. That's why you cover up your acne and insist on standing "on your good side" in every photo. And this is the same reason why you don't speak up at meetings. Online you are afraid to look bad and at work you are afraid to sound bad. You're afraid of what other people will think if they see the real you.

Every time you edit what you post, or stay silent in class or at work, or hide in the back of the group photo, you are engaging in self-rejection. You're the one telling yourself that you're not good enough. The constant questioning, editing, deleting, overthinking, and asking other people, "Does this look good?" only magnifies your self-doubt. And you want to know the crazy part? You're doing it to yourself. I did too.

Most advice on this topic sucks. Most people tell you to just "stop caring" about what other people think. But no one tells you how. It's time for a new approach. Using the Let Them Theory, you'll adopt a revolutionary approach to squashing this fear once and for all: Give people the freedom to think negative thoughts about you.

It is a radically beautiful idea that will unlock your confidence, free your self-expression, and catapult you into a whole new chapter of your life. Give people the freedom to think something negative about you.

Let Them. It not only works. It's science.

You Have Zero Control over Someone Else's Opinion of You

The fact is, it is impossible to control someone else's thoughts. Therefore, fearing what other people think, or trying to control their thoughts, is a complete waste of your time.

You will never feel in control of your life, your feelings, your thoughts, or your actions until you stop being consumed with or trying to control what other people think about you.

I will say it again: Adults will have negative opinions about you—no matter what you do. Why? Because adults are allowed to think whatever they want.

It is physically and neurologically impossible for you to control what someone else thinks. The average human being has about 70,000 thoughts a day. Most of which are random and cannot be controlled. Which is why it's ludicrous to waste any of your energy worrying about what other people think or trying to change what they think.

You can't even control half the thoughts that pop into your own mind. Why the heck do you think you can control what pops up in someone else's? You can't. It is scientifically impossible. That's why the Let Them Theory is so revolutionary.

Instead of fearing other people's opinions, you are just going to allow them to think what they want. In fact, I recommend that you assume people will think negative thoughts about you. Because people do have negative thoughts about you.

This is normal.

And by the way, people who love you think bad thoughts about you. . . every day! I have bad thoughts about the people I love every day! This is normal. To prove it, I'll go first.

When my husband wakes up, he usually lets out a huge fart. My first thought is, *You are disgusting.* I love Chris more than any human being on the planet. But I have bad thoughts and negative opinions about him all the time.

Same thing with my dog. At 5 P.M. my dog, Homie, is so annoying because he knows it's dinnertime. He follows me around, he pants like crazy, he jumps up on me, and you know what I think: He is a giant pain in the rear end, and he needs to chill. But I still love him.

My oldest daughter, Sawyer, who I wrote this book with, is a complete control freak; and when things aren't just right, she gets overbearing and too intense. She goes into an OCD cleaning spiral that just stresses everyone else out. But I still love her.

Every time our middle daughter, Kendall, FaceTimes me from Los Angeles, it feels like she is wearing a new outfit. I think she is irresponsible with her money and the last thing she needs is more clothes. But I still love her.

And our son, Oakley, is literally perfect. Just kidding. For the first hour he is awake, he refuses to make eye contact and speak to people. I think he is rude. But I still love him.

By the way, I asked my children to describe some adjectives they think about me. They said: messy, disorganized, loud, overfriendly, all-over-the-place, controlling, always late, know-it-all—and they have a lot of opinions about how much I share online about our life. And yet, they still love me. (Sawyer also wanted you to know that writing this book with me nearly drove her to sever parental rights because of the number of times I completely blew up the manuscript—for context this is version 11.0.)

Why am I telling you this? Because everybody has critical opinions about people they love as well as total strangers. It is a fact of life.

Embrace it and accept it. Instead of trying to change reality, start using it to your advantage. *Let Them.*

Here's another truth: Just because someone has a negative opinion doesn't mean they feel negatively about you as a whole.

I can think a bad thought about my husband and still love him and treat him with so much respect and kindness, because two things can be true at once. You can be annoyed by the way someone is acting and still love them to death.

This is how you feel about the people you love! You think their friends are bad influences. You think they are overreacting. You think their boyfriend treats them poorly. You think their business idea is going to fail. You think they are self-centered. But you still love them.

My point is simple: Adults will have negative opinions about you and everything you do. *Let Them* judge. *Let Them* react. *Let Them* doubt you. *Let Them* question the decisions you are making. *Let Them* be wrong about you. *Let Them* roll their eyes when you start posting videos online or you want to rewrite the manuscript for the 12th time.

Instead of wasting your time worrying about them, start living your life in a way that makes you proud of yourself. *Let Me* do what I want to do with my one wild and precious life.

This approach is liberating because right now you are living your life and making decisions trying to anticipate what everyone is going to think. When you let the fear of what people might think dictate your choices, you limit your potential and hold yourself back from pursuing what you truly want.

It's the reason you procrastinate, doubt yourself, get paralyzed by perfectionism, and, most importantly, it's why you wake up every day and avoid the work that would actually help you get ahead.

You are so afraid of judgment, you don't take any risks at all. Isn't that what you are afraid of? That you'll be judged?

That, if you get divorced, or quit the real estate business, or go back to school, or cut your hair, or try out for the soccer team and get cut, everyone will have an opinion about it? Of course they are going to have an opinion about it. So what?

This stupid fear is stopping you from trying new things, taking risks, being yourself, and making the small moves that, over time, will change your life. How sad.

The Let Them Theory will help you be more courageous. Doesn't it seem smarter to accept reality and give people the freedom to judge?

You can't control what someone thinks, so there's no reason why you should be afraid of it—or allow it to stop you anymore. Your time is way more valuable than that, because you've got important things to do with this one wild and precious life.

Starting today, you are going to grant people the freedom to think negative thoughts about you. *Let Them.*

"But I Don't Want People to Think Negative Thoughts About Me."

I know what you are thinking: *But I don't want people to think negative thoughts about me, Mel.* I know you don't. Neither did I. But the fear of what other people *may* think is a major source of your self-doubt.

I'm not good enough. (For whom?)

I'm not smart enough. (For whom?)

They are going to be mad at me. (Who is going to be mad?)

My parents won't approve. (So?)

If I do this, no one is going to like me. (Who is no one?)

What will my friends think? (Whatever they want.)

Does this make me look bad? (To whom?)

Every one of these common fears is all tied to other people. That's why I'm repeating this fact over and over again: Adults will have negative opinions about you, and your outfit, and what you just said, and what you did last week, and what you want to do.

Let Them.

Adults are allowed to think whatever they want to think. So are you. This is why the Let Them Theory will set you free. Instead of living your life on the defense, you're going to get on the offense. You're going to play the game of life the way you want.

Here's another truth: You are so much stronger than anyone's opinions about you. Stop giving your power to other people and step into your potential.

Let Me live my life in a way that makes me proud. *Let Me* make decisions that align with my values. *Let Me* take risks because I want to. *Let Me* follow the path my soul is turning me toward.

Doing what makes you happy, being brave, taking risks, and following your own path will always be more important than other people's opinions about it. This is YOUR life. Stop letting other people's opinions ruin it.

Write the book. Ask them out. Wear what you want to wear. Go surf all day. Go back to school. Drop out of school. Move. Get a dog. Book the trip. Stop drinking. Embrace your sexuality. Take the path that you've been scared to follow.

The more you use the Let Them Theory, the more you'll realize that, underneath this fear, your soul has been nudging you all along in the direction that is meant for you.

Every time you say *Let Them*, you clear all of the noise and distraction on the surface and create space for something deeper: your voice, your intuition, your truth, and your unique path in life.

It's always been there. It's just been buried beneath all this fear.

As you use the Let Them Theory to free yourself of the burden of other people's opinions, you'll begin moving through life with your values, your needs, and your goals as your road map. Instead of anticipating what other people might think, you'll navigate your life in a way that makes you proud of yourself.

And that right there is the secret. When YOU are proud of yourself, you hold all the power.

Make Decisions That Make YOU Proud

This brings me to a very important point about prioritizing your needs while also maintaining supportive and loving relationships. The point here is not to move through life as a selfish or narcissistic person who doesn't care about other people.

The point is learning how to put your needs first as you're balancing what works for you with the expectations and feelings of other people. In life, you don't want to be a doormat, but you also don't want to be an inconsiderate bulldozer. It's a balance.

Let's say you have a crazy-busy weekend coming up. On one hand, you have a close friend celebrating a big milestone birthday—and it's one of those really fun weekends where friends are all getting together to celebrate.

For you it means making a four-hour drive to get to where the party is going to be held. And you know that the right decision for you is to be there. On the other hand, you promised your parents months ago that you would come home this same weekend because your grandparents are visiting.

You want to do both.

You want to be a good friend, you want to be a good child, and you want to be a good grandkid, so you move heaven and earth to drive four hours north of the city to be present for the Friday night festivities for your friend.

And you are glad you did.

You stay up late, laughing with friends, and down a bottle of wine. You have an absolute blast. Then, the next morning you wake up at 7 A.M. You roll out of bed, pull on your sweats, leave a note saying you're sorry to miss out on the rest of the weekend, and get back in the car to drive another four hours to your parents' house to spend the rest of the weekend with your grandparents.

As you are driving on the road, you are proud of yourself for making the effort.

Little do you know (you'll find out later), the birthday girl was upset that you left and apparently said: "I don't know why she even bothered coming if she could only stay one night."

Let Her.

Four hours later, you're at your parents'—a little hungover and a lot tired. You step out of the car in your sweats and hug your grandma who is so excited, she is teary-eyed.

Then you hug your mom, and she whispers in your ear, *"Your grandmother was so disappointed you weren't here when she arrived last night."* And then she adds, *"We need to leave for lunch in ten minutes. You need to change."*

Let Her.

I am telling you this story to prove two points: First, even when you bend over backward and try to please everyone, and make it work, even THAT won't guarantee that other people will think a positive thought. *Let Them.*

Second—and this is the most important point—don't be the person who bends over backward to make everyone happy. I used to be that person. It left me depleted and feeling like nothing I could do was ever good enough.

Now that I know the Let Them Theory, I bend over backward to make *myself* happy. *Let me* explain.

The reason to make a herculean effort, or to show up both at your friend's birthday party and to see your grandparents, is that it makes YOU proud of yourself. Don't go to your friend's birthday so they think you are a good friend. Go to your friend's birthday because it makes YOU feel like a good friend.

Don't go home to see your grandparents because it makes your mother happy. Go home to see your grandparents because it makes YOU happy to prioritize your grandparents and family.

When you operate in a way that makes you proud of yourself, it doesn't matter what other people think. They're going to be mad that you left early. They're going to be mad that you arrived late. Someone is always going to be disappointed by the decisions that you make. Don't ever let it be you that's disappointed. And don't let guilt drive your decisions.

When you go to your parents because you feel "guilty," you've turned your parents into the villain. When you choose to go because you'd be mad at yourself if you didn't, you're in control of your decisions.

This is a very straightforward example of how to stop worrying about what other people think, and let your values drive your decisions.

But what about those moments when your opinion and someone else's really do clash? Like what if your mom doesn't like the person you are going to marry? What do you do then?

I've been there.

CHAPTER 6

How to Love Difficult People

In my opinion, it's easier to use the Let Them Theory with strangers, co-workers, and even friends, because you will likely have a little distance from them to recharge after using it. You can walk into your bedroom and shut the door. You can go home after work. You can walk off the plane.

And most of the time, you won't even know about it when someone is thinking something negative about you. Family, though? Family hits different. Family is with you for life.

Your family tends to be a lot more blunt and in your face with their opinions: They are mad that you aren't coming home for the holidays. They constantly question why you are still single. They think you've ruined your life by dropping out of school. They hate your friend group. They disagree with how you are living your life. They make it clear they don't like who you're dating. They don't want you to quit your job to start that business. They wish you would take better care of yourself and they are very vocal about it.

Family tends to be a lot harsher to your face because they have a stake in your happiness and your success. A lot of the time when your family cares, they show it by pushing you. When they don't like your friends, or they think you're headed down the wrong path, or they wish that you would take better care of yourself, they let you know it.

Most of the time, it's how your family shows you that they care. They want more for you, they want you to be happy and they see all your potential when it's going to waste. However, it can very easily cross the line from caring to control.

Family has had opinions about you since you were born. They have known you the longest. They feel entitled to their opinions because they think they know what's best for you. (Which is typically also what feels best for them.)

Plus, everyone in your family has expectations about each other and the way the family should operate. These familial relationships cut deeper than the rest because you have known them for a long time—and these relationships form an interconnected system. Which also explains why your family tends to react more dramatically to any change you make—because you are part of that family system. Any change you make will send either positive or negative waves through the entire system.

Knowing that people will have a reaction because you're part of an interlocked web of relationships that has been in place for generations can help you navigate this better.

I'm not saying that those expectations or that system is right. I'm just saying that it's the reality. And I find understanding the larger context of any situation helps me stay in control of how I show up in my family.

For example, if you decide to get a divorce from your spouse, or you no longer want to follow the same traditions, or you marry some-one outside your religion, or you pursue a unique career path, or you have different political beliefs, this will send shock waves through the entire family system because it disrupts everybody's expectations and beliefs about who you are and how you should live your life.

Nowhere is this more apparent than when the dynamics of step-children and stepparents get added to the interlocked web. This is a major shock to the family system and can either make or break it, for better or for worse. All expectations for how the household runs when new individuals are introduced are thrown out the window. Change can be really hard to accept. Especially for the kids who are being forced to just accept this change and operate as one big happy blended family.

The Let Them Theory will be a game-changer in helping you navigate your role as a stepparent. As the adult, it's your responsibility to *Let Them* grieve. *Let Them* see you (and your kids) as a threat, because no matter how good your intentions are, you are a threat. They have to compete with you for time with the parent. It's true. They are seeking control, just like you are. *Let Them* feel their emotions. *Let Them* have time alone with their parent. If they don't have to like you. *Let Them*.

Don't ever forget that stepchildren, in particular, need under-standing, grace, and compassion from you. They aren't just learning to accept a new adult in their life; they are also grieving the loss of the family they wanted. This is NORMAL.

Understanding the larger context, will help you focus on the *Let Me* part and operate with more grace and be the wise and compassion-ate adult. The more grace and kindness you display, the more space you create for a change in the dynamic to happen.

These dynamics between stepchildren and stepparents are hard. There is nothing seamless about them. But they also have the potential to be a lot more beautiful with the help of the Let Them Theory and a specific tool you're about to learn in this chapter.

I once heard a therapist say at a conference, "If it weren't for families, I wouldn't have a business." When it comes to family, your relatives are entitled to their opinions, but that's different from them rejecting your right to live your life, be your own person, and love who you choose to love. Whether their opinions are right or not is not the point. It's how you relate to their opinions that matters.

So, what happens when your loved ones don't agree with the way you are living your life or who you are as a person? I can relate. Here's what you are going to do about it. *Let Them.*

Don't try to change their opinion. Give them the freedom to have it. Whether it's your stepkids, your sister-in-law, your grandmother, or your brother, they are allowed to think whatever they want. And they are even allowed not to like you or the person you love. So, *Let Them.* And then, *Let Me* choose how to respond.

Frame of Reference

My friend Lisa Bilyeu, who is a bestselling author, host of *Women of Impact* podcast, and co-founder of the billion-dollar nutrition company Quest Nutrition, shared the concept of Frame of Reference with me.

It is a tool to help you deal with situations where someone disapproves of who you are, who you love, what you believe, or how you are living your life, and you want to navigate this at a deeper level.

I've been there and maybe you have too.

Our global podcast audience went crazy over Frame of Reference when Lisa described it as a mindset tool that's helped her relationships. *Frame of Reference* is a fancy way to say "understanding the lens through which somebody sees something" and it works beautifully with the Let Them Theory.

I'll give you an example from my life. When I met my husband, Chris, I was ecstatic and madly in love. And when he proposed I was absolutely over the moon. At the time, I remember my mom not seeming as excited as I expected her to be.

So I had this conversation with her where I told her I wanted her to be excited for me, and I asked her to act as though she was the one who chose him for me.

And she said, "But I didn't choose him for you, and if it were up to me, I wouldn't have, so I am not going to act like I did."

At the time, I was so angry I didn't know what to do. I didn't want to cut her out of my life, but I had no idea how to handle the situation. Here I am madly in love with someone I know is my soulmate, and my mom tells me to my face, "I would never have picked him for you," and then refuses to act excited for me.

I went on to marry Chris, but I felt this tension of disapproval underneath the dynamic between me and my mom for years. It was hard for me to forget what she said. And I didn't know how to let it go.

Over time, the tension dissipated, and 30 years later, my mother adores Chris. She likes to joke, "Chris, you're my favorite son-in-law" (he's also her only son-in-law).

So how did I navigate this? It's only recently using the Let Them Theory and this tool, Frame of Reference, that I have really understood why she felt the way she did. It has been a real game-changer in my relationship with my mom and my ability to hold space for her when I disagree with her opinion.

See, if I stand in my mother's shoes, knowing what I know about her life, I wouldn't want me to marry Chris either. Why? Because Chris is from the East Coast and marrying him meant that I would probably settle in the East and never move back home to the Midwest or live near my mom and dad ever again.

Because my mother's Frame of Reference is that once she left home and met my father, she never moved back home again either. My mom left the family farm she grew up on in upstate New York when she was 17 to attend college in Kansas. She met my dad there, and they fell in love. By the time she was 19, she was married and had me.

It's not what she or my dad had planned, but it's what happened. In fact, when my dad's parents found out that my mom was pregnant with me, my grandmother said to my 19-year-old mother, "I hope you didn't just ruin our son's life."

Can you imagine? When I think about how young my parents were and the fact that they were living in Kansas and had no family around them, it makes me so sad.

This was my mom's lived experience, and it formed her Frame of Reference about raising a family so far away from parents, and how hard it is to have no support from family around you.

My mom and dad ultimately settled in Michigan after my dad finished his residency and medical school, and growing up I rarely saw my grandparents or extended family because they lived so far away. It was just me, my mom, my dad, and my brother. Our own little family of four against the world.

So when I left home to go to college on the East Coast, it must have triggered this whole fear that I might never come back home. And when I met Chris in New York, who was also from the East Coast, it solidified my mom's biggest fear that I too would start my life far away and never move back home to my small Midwestern town.

And that's exactly what happened. My mom's biggest fear came true. When you look at it from my mother's Frame of Reference, she saw her story playing out in front of her, all over again. I was going to move away and meet somebody and never come home.

And she was right. I'm sure she wanted me to marry someone from Michigan so I would settle down close to them. Thirty years ago when

I met Chris, I didn't think about my mom's Frame of Reference. I was just offended and angry and concluded that she "didn't support me."

I can now see that she supported me—she was just scared of losing her daughter. She loves me and didn't want me to live so far away. Using the Let Them Theory, I can give her the freedom to wish my life took a different path, and I can also really deeply understand where she is coming from.

I can also empathize with how hard it must be to see your daughter marry someone who will take her away from you. I wouldn't choose somebody like that for my daughters and son either.

I wouldn't want my daughter Sawyer marrying somebody from Europe and going to live in Paris. I mean if it makes her happy, she should. But would that be my choice? No. This may seem unsupportive or controlling, but I'm sure every parent can relate. And I'm not saying that to be controlling. I'm saying that because that's how I feel. My opinion may be negative, but I am allowed to have it. Which I am sure my daughter would feel is very unsupportive.

And the same thing with my daughter Kendall. She currently lives in LA, and she could very well meet somebody that lives in California and proceed to settle down and raise her family out there. That would mean that I wouldn't see her or her kids as much as I would if they were living here on the East Coast.

And I'm allowed to have that opinion, just like Sawyer is allowed to move to Paris and Kendall is allowed to decide to raise a family in LA.

My mom is also allowed to have the opinion that she wouldn't have chosen someone from the East Coast for me. I'm glad it didn't stop me from marrying Chris, and living and raising a family where we wanted to be.

But now I am grateful for the Let Them Theory because I also deeply understand my mom, and why she felt reluctant 30 years ago.

It wasn't judgment; it was grief. She wasn't wrong. She was right. But I wasn't wrong either.

In fact, we were both right. Because we have different Frames of Reference.

Seeing it through her lens helps me put our relationship back in balance. There was no longer a power struggle; there was understanding.

One reason why it's so challenging to navigate these types of situations is because you both believe you are right. From their lived experience, or Frame of Reference, they believe their opinion is right. From your lived experience, or Frame of Reference, you know your opinion is right.

With the Let Them Theory, there is space, with acceptance and understanding, for both of our opinions to be true. There is space for a deeper connection, honesty, and love.

It takes an extraordinarily mature person to be able to detach from your emotions and want to step into someone else's shoes. It's hard to understand that someone can love you and have opinions that are deeply hurtful and at times bigoted.

When this happens in life, how you choose to respond is a deeply personal choice. I can't tell you what you should do if someone in your family is judging you. What I can do is give you the tools to determine how you want to respond to the situation.

Do you want this person in your life? If you do, the Let Them Theory will create the space for it. What I've found in my own experience and in researching this book and hearing about the experiences of so many other people, is that when you give people the space to come to their own conclusions—and you focus on showing up as your full self in a loving and compassionate way—over time, people often change their opinions on their own.

So, as hard as it may sound, *Let Them* have their opinions and focus on how you are going to respond. What I love about this idea of stepping into someone else's Frame of Reference is that understanding where someone is coming from may not change their opinion or yours, but it will deepen the connection that you have while you navigate your relationship.

It helps you create space for two things to be true at once, and that space is where love can exist. And trust me, I get it—it's easy to be irritated or offended by your parents. It's easy to blame them.

It's also easy to feel frustrated and annoyed with the dynamics with your siblings, or your divorced parents, or your in-laws, or your stepparents, or your adult children. It's easy to choose not to understand their perspectives.

You have to decide whether or not you're going to accept people as they are (your family or stepfamily especially) or create the distance that you need. All it takes is one person to change the way they show up in a family, and the entire system can change for the better. And that person is you.

One of the reasons why I love the Let Them Theory is that anytime you improve yourself, it improves all your relationships, and this is particularly true with family. I have felt the impact in my own family.

The stuff that used to bother me doesn't stress me out anymore. I don't allow myself to get sucked into the drama. And I stay laser focused on how I show up and live my life in a way that makes me proud.

One of the things that I have determined for myself is that it is important for me to have a close relationship with my family. And wasting my time and energy allowing them to stress me out or trying to control situations that are beyond my control is a waste of time.

Because the truth is: You have limited time with your loved ones. At some point, you're going to realize that your parents aren't going to be here forever, and that this was their first time as a human being too.

People can only meet you as deeply as they've met themselves. Most people haven't gone to therapy, haven't looked at their issues, and they don't want to.

Let Them. Let your parents be less than what you deserve. Let your family life be something that isn't a fairy tale. They are doing the best they can with the resources and life experiences they have. Now you get to choose what happens moving forward.

I'm not saying this to justify anything bad that happens. I'm not saying that you don't deserve better. Everyone deserves to feel seen, supported, and loved, particularly by their family.

But the fact is, most human beings have never done the work to understand themselves, heal their past, or manage their own emotions. If they haven't done that for themselves, they are incapable of doing that for you and showing up in a way that you deserve.

Let Them. When you recognize that, you have a choice in your life.

Let your family be who they are. Your dad is not changing. Your mom is not changing. Your siblings aren't changing. Your in-laws aren't changing. The only person you can change is you.

When you say *Let Them*, you are seeing your family exactly as they are for the first time in your life, perhaps. They are human. You have no control over what happened. You have no control over who they are. You can only control what you do from this point forward.

Accepting the reality of your situation doesn't mean you're surrendering to it. Instead, it's about reclaiming your power to shape your future. Learn how to let adults be adults and accept people as they are. Then decide how to make the best of it, and I promise you your family dynamics will get better.

This acceptance allows you to see your family with compassion, and more importantly, it allows you to see yourself as an individual who has their own unique Frame of Reference and path in life.

Then you move to the second part, which is *Let Me*. *Let Me* figure out what kind of relationship I want to create, based on the kind of person I want to be and the values that I have.

This could mean spending time with your family not out of guilt, but because it matters to you. That might mean defining your own traditions even though it upsets your family. That might mean being one that always makes the effort even when it is not returned. It might mean saying "I love you" or "I understand" or "I forgive you" for the first time.

That might mean having the hard conversations that you have been avoiding out of fear of their opinions or judgment. That might mean freeing yourself from guilt and making some changes. And it might mean separating yourself because you no longer are willing to accept less than you deserve. And it might mean going all in while you still have time.

So let's summarize what you have learned about fearing other people's opinions. You currently allow your fear of other people's opinions to control you. The Let Them Theory teaches you how to stop giving other people's opinions power over your life; and it empowers you to live your life in a way that makes you proud of yourself.

1. **Problem:** You are giving other people's opinions too much power. When you let the fear of what people might think dictate your choices, you limit your potential and hold yourself back from pursuing what you truly want. This fear causes you to procrastinate, doubt yourself, become paralyzed by perfectionism, and, most importantly, give up on your dreams.

2. **Truth:** People will have negative opinions about you no matter what you do. It will happen. *Let Them*. You can't control it. Allowing someone else's opinion to distract or consume you is a waste of your time and energy.

3. **Solution:** When you *Let Them* think what they want, it gives you the freedom to do what you want. When you align your thoughts and actions with your values, you will be proud of yourself. And when you are proud of yourself, you won't care what anyone else thinks.

When you say *Let Them*, you make a decision to let people think negative thoughts about you. When you say *Let Me*, you focus on the one person who's opinion truly matters—yours.

You get one wild and precious life, so go live it in a way that makes you proud.

Dealing with Someone Else's Emotional Reactions

CHAPTER 7

When Grown-Ups Throw Tantrums

N ow let's dive into how you have allowed other people's emotional reactions to influence your decisions.

The reality is adults are as emotional as children, and it is not your responsibility to manage someone else's reactions. As long as you let other people's emotional immaturity dictate your choices, you'll always come last in your own life.

I had no idea how big of a problem this was for me, and neither do you. From navigating guilt trips, to fearing disappointment, to worrying about someone's reaction or if "now is the right time," to tiptoeing around someone's mood, you're allowing other people's behaviors and reactions to drain your energy.

But it goes deeper than that. Their passive-aggressive behavior, guilt trips, and emotional outbursts are driving your decisions. This is why you say yes when you really want to say no. You cave when you should stand firm. This is why it's hard for you to set boundaries. This is why you walk on eggshells when certain people are in a bad mood.

Sure, it feels easier in the moment to give in to your sister's guilt trip, but, in the long run, you lose a crucial piece of yourself. When every interaction with your girlfriend or boyfriend leaves you emotionally exhausted, ask yourself this: Why are you always the one who has to adjust? Why do you take on the responsibility for someone else's happiness—at the expense of your own?

You will always come last if you let other people's emotional immaturity have power over you. Instead of taking on the weight of someone's disappointment, anger, or guilt, you'll learn a liberating new approach: Just *Let Them* react.

When you say *Let Them*, you give other people the space to feel their emotions without needing to fix them. When you say *Let Me*, you do what's right for you, even if it upsets someone, which is how you take responsibility for your own life.

It's time to stop being manipulated by someone else's guilt, anger, or disappointment. Other people's emotional reactions are not your responsibility to manage. I learned this from my therapist, Anne Davin, Ph.D., who is a depth psychologist, writer, and the smartest woman I've ever met. One day, I was talking with her about creating boundaries with a particularly difficult family member.

The thing is, I don't want this person to bother me. It's just that they have this way of constantly making it about them. I bet you have someone in your family like this. You know an evening with this person is going to be incredibly draining. If the attention is not on them, they have endless ways of bringing it back to them—positive or negative.

What If We Are All Just Eight Years Old?

So I was talking to Anne about this person and she said something that changed everything:

"Mel, most adults are just eight-year-old children inside of big bodies. The next time you're with this person and you feel yourself getting triggered by something they say or some way that they act, I want you to just imagine the fourth-grade version of them present in the room with you. Because what you're describing is someone who has the emotional maturity of an eight-year-old. And, like it or not, that's most adults."

Honestly, as I sat there and processed what she was saying, it made a lot of sense. It's true. Most people don't know how to process their emotions in a healthy way, much less communicate their needs in a direct and respectful fashion. I know I certainly didn't.

Just think about it: Why else does your mom pout instead of saying what's wrong? Why does your friend give you the silent treatment? Why does your boyfriend send you passive-aggressive texts when you're out with friends? Why does your sister blow up, then act like nothing happened an hour later?

It's because adults, at their core, are just as emotional as children. The difference is, they are better at hiding it. . . most of the time.

But here's what's beautiful about the Let Them Theory: It doesn't make you more judgmental—it makes you more compassionate. Instead of getting frustrated, you begin to understand that most people simply don't have the tools to handle their emotions maturely.

The truth is that no one has been taught how to do this. To handle your emotions, you have to understand them and know how to process them in a healthy way. And in my experience, most people have no idea how to do this. I know I certainly didn't.

Emotional maturity isn't something you're born with or that just happens. It's a skill that takes time, practice, and a desire to learn. My therapist is right. Most people you meet still act like an eight-year-old child when they don't get what they want or when they feel uncomfortable emotions.

But now, with the Let Them Theory, you'll learn to respond with compassion, set your boundaries, and stop letting other people's emotional immaturity run your life. And you're going to need this tool because the connection between adults and childlike behavior is irrefutable:

Child Behavior = Adult Behavior

Children run away from you	Adults avoid confrontation
Children sulk or pout in the corner	Adults give the silent treatment
Children shut down	Adults act stoic
Children throw tantrums	Adults erupt, rage text, and vent
Children slam doors	Adults slam doors too
Children lie	Adults lie too

If you read that list and someone immediately popped in your mind for each scenario, the same thing happened for me when I unpacked this with my therapist. The reason why children act like this is because they cannot regulate their own emotions.

I'll give you an example. Let's take a child in a toy aisle, who has selected a Lego set and wants it. The moment they are told they cannot have it, what happens?

Their little body floods with emotions: sadness, disappointment, surprise, anger. Which is why they have a dramatic emotional response and start crying, shut down, or flop down on the floor into a full-blown tantrum.

The solution is not to give the kid the toy or the Lego set. The solution is for the parent to help the child process the emotions that they're feeling in a calm, understanding, and compassionate way.

That might look like bending down and saying, "I know this is hard. I know you want the Lego set. It's okay to be upset. I get disappointed too. It's not fair. I get upset when I don't get the things that I want."

Let Them cry, beg, or do whatever they need, for as long as they need.

If kids are not allowed to experience the full wave of emotion (without an adult saying "calm down," or "this is silly," or "you're over-reacting"), they never learn how to process normal human emotions in a healthy way. Instead, they become an emotionally immature adult who takes it out on the rest of us.

So I just assume that most adults have never learned how to process their emotions in a healthy way, because no one's parents knew how to do this either, and if yours did, then you are one lucky person. A child cannot learn how to do this on their own. Like I said earlier, it's a skill that takes time, practice, and a desire to learn.

Of course, in researching this book, I realized that as a parent, I completely screwed this up. I would have bought my kid the Legos. Or, I would have erupted in frustration and yelled "Stop crying!" Or, I would have walked away from them, left them on the floor, and turned the aisle, hoping that they would notice I was gone, suddenly get scared, and stop crying. . . which explains why all three of my children now need therapy.

I wish I were kidding. I screwed this up because I didn't know how to regulate my own emotions. I was never taught how to do it as a child either. I grew up in a family where we didn't talk about our feelings. People tended to just erupt in anger when they got overwhelmed and then pretend nothing had happened.

And that brings me to a very important point about the Let Them Theory, and I need to make sure I am crystal clear: Adults are 100 percent responsible for the emotional and physical needs of children. Children cannot give themselves the emotional and physical support that they need.

It is your responsibility to help a child regulate their emotional responses in a healthy way. It is also your responsibility to teach a child that emotions are normal and how to process them.

In fact, in researching this book, Lisa Damour Ph.D., who is a clinical psychologist and *New York Times* bestselling author, told me that when a child (or adult) experiences disappointment because they can't have what they want, or sadness over a loss, that these are mentally healthy responses to life experiences. These emotions of sadness and disappointment are signs that you are mentally well.

Do the Feelings Fit the Circumstance?

When you are eight, being upset when you can't get the Legos that you want is a normal reaction. When your friend at school says something that hurts your feelings, being sad is a healthy reaction. When you want to watch TV and your parents say it's time for bed, getting upset is a normal reaction.

By the way, the same is true for adult experiences. When you are an adult, if you get fired, feeling frustrated and demoralized is a normal reaction. When you go through a breakup, it's normal to go through a depressive state. According to Dr. Damour, these are all appropriate, normal emotional reactions. They are evidence that your mind is working exactly as it should.

But growing up, you were probably taught to repeatedly repress what you feel. When you tell a child to "get over it" or "stop crying" or "calm down," you are training them to suppress how they feel. To distract, avoid, or numb these normal human emotions.

Dr. Damour told me that is why so many people live with anxiety, depression, addiction, or chronic pain—because they have avoided all the emotions over the years that then build up inside of them without any outlet.

I am going to say it again: It's your responsibility to help a child create space to process their own range of emotions. But it is not your responsibility to manage another adult's emotional reactions.

This is so important to understand. *Let me* unpack this further in detail.

~~Adult~~ Childlike Behavior

Let's take the very common experience of someone in your life giving you the silent treatment. The silent treatment is what an immature adult does when they're upset and they don't know how to process their emotions in a healthy and respectful manner.

So instead, they stop talking. They pretend nothing is wrong. And often, they ignore you. And if you've ever been on the receiving end of the silent treatment from a friend, a family member, or a co-worker, it's painful, and your immediate instinct is to try to figure out what you did wrong.

And that's exactly what the person giving you the silent treatment wants—they want your attention. Just like a child pouting off in a corner wants the parent to come over and soothe them, an adult that gives you the silent treatment wants you to ask, "Are you okay?" and "Can I do something?" and "What did I do wrong?"

They use the silent treatment because they don't know how to process their own emotions, and they are trying to get you to come over to them and ask what's wrong so they don't have to do it for themselves.

I had a friend who used to do this all the time in high school. One minute we were great and the next minute she was not talking to me. And I never knew what I did wrong. I would try to call her, say hello in the hallways, and sometimes beg for forgiveness for something I didn't even know that I had done.

She'd never address it, and then suddenly one day she'd decide she was over it—and then we were back to being best friends. I was always just so relieved when she started talking to me again that I'd just play along like nothing ever happened.

What I know now is that it was easier for her to give me the silent treatment and avoid having an honest conversation than to come to me and share how she was feeling. She didn't even know how to do that.

One more thing to understand is that it really has nothing to do with you. When someone gives you the silent treatment, it all stems from their inability to understand their emotions or past demons.

Let Them. Any time an adult acts like an eight-year-old child, *Let Them.*

This strategy is going to change your life. For you it might be a parent that gets angry, storms out of the room, and refuses to talk to anybody for several days or a weekend.

Or, in the case of one of my best friends, her mother suddenly stopped talking to her for a month. And then one day she would come down the stairs in the morning, and it was as if nothing had ever happened.

Using the Let Them Theory, you'll never again be the victim of someone else's emotional immaturity or emotional abuse—because you will know exactly what to do.

First, it's never your job to manage another adult's emotions. When someone pulls the silent treatment on you, or plays the victim, or erupts in frustration, *Let Them.* And then I want you to visualize an eight-year-old trapped inside their body. When you do that, something wild happens. You don't feel scared of this person. You actually pity them. You feel compassion instead of contempt.

You will also realize that their inability to process normal human emotions like sadness, insecurity, disappointment, anger, fear, and rejection is not your fault. And it's also not your problem to solve. This has been happening to this person since they were a child.

It is not your responsibility to manage their emotions or try to fix them. Your responsibility is to protect yourself from their emotional spiral, and to see it for what it is: A person who has no idea how to handle or express their emotions in a healthy way.

Let Them go silent. *Let Them* erupt. *Let Them* play the victim. *Let Them* sulk. *Let Them* deny that it happened. *Let Them* make it all about them.

Then, *Let Me*. *Let Me* be the mature, wise, and loving adult in this situation. *Let Me* decide if I want to address this directly or not at all. *Let Me* remind myself that managing another person's emotions is not my job. *Let Me* remove myself from any text chain, dinner table conversation, relationship, or friend group where this is happening.

Instead of expecting other people to change, demand the change of yourself. Hold yourself to a higher standard and stop allowing this type of emotionally immature behavior to be your responsibility to manage.

Stop staying in situations where someone's repeated emotional immaturity is starting to feel more like abuse. Stop feeling sorry for people who play the victim all the time. Stop explaining away someone's clearly narcissistic patterns.

The more time you pour into a relationship with someone who acts like an eight-year-old, the more you're going to feel like a parent to a child. When you recognize that you are dealing with someone who has a lot of internal work to do, you can draw healthier boundaries around the amount of time and energy you are willing to give to them.

Because until this person does the work to build the skills of emotional intelligence, they will always pull the silent treatment, play the victim, or be passive aggressive. This isn't a personality trait, it's a pattern.

But What If You're the Problem?

What do you do if you're realizing as you're reading this that there are times in your life when you're the one who's emotionally immature?

You get overwhelmed by your emotions. You sulk. You give the silent treatment. You rage text. You play the victim. You snap at other people. You make it about you.

If you are having this realization, here is what I want to say to you: You're not alone. I had that realization about myself too.

It's so easy to see this immature behavior in other people, but it takes a level of bravery and emotional intelligence to see it in yourself. For me, I wasn't even an eight-year-old. I used to be so emotionally immature, I probably clocked in at closer to five.

I got so easily overwhelmed by my emotions that I would throw tantrums, whether it was venting at my husband or erupting at my kids over something stupid. I had periods of my life where it was all about me, and it ruined a lot of friendships. Even to this day, when work gets incredibly stressful, I send long, angry texts to my business partner about how frustrated I am by things. And it's not okay.

Even as I am writing the Let Them Theory book and using *Let Them* in my life, I'm constantly learning how to create space to process my own range of emotions. This is the hardest part of the Let Them Theory to put into practice—learning to feel my raw emotions without immediately reacting. It's hard. I still catch myself wanting to snap back or immediately take control of the situation. . . all the time. And yes, I still get frustrated when I slip up. But that's the point: It's not about being perfect; it's about being kind to yourself and continuing to grow.

It's a lifelong process, and many days, it feels like I'm starting all over again. I know this is a skill I will be working on for the rest of my life, and so will you.

The Let Them Theory has been monumental in helping me be more compassionate toward myself. It has also helped me create a deeper understanding of how to handle my emotions.

Using the Let Them Theory is straightforward when someone else is throwing the tantrum. Learning how to use it to process your own emotions will put you at rockstar status. I can't even begin to tell you how much more money I make, how much smarter I am, and how I'm a better parent, a better spouse, and a better friend now that I have a better handle on my own emotions. I am finally starting to feel like a mature adult.

Here's how you use the Let Them Theory to process your own emotions in a healthy way: When you feel your emotions rising up, *Let Them*. Allow the anger, the frustration, the hurt, the disappointment, the sadness, the grief, the tears, and the feelings of failure to come up. *Let Them*.

And then, *Let Me* not react. Don't reach for your phone. Don't turn on the TV. Don't make a drink. Don't open the fridge. And for crying out loud, don't text anyone. Just notice the feelings and *Let Them* rise up.

The reason why you must learn how to *Let Them* rise is that once they do, they also fall.

Do You Know What an Emotion Really Is?

Emotions are just a burst of chemicals in your brain that ignite and are absorbed into your body within six seconds. Because your emotional reactions happen so fast, they can often be completely unconscious. You may first notice your emotions through the physical sensations that accompany the chemical burst, such as sweating, muscle tightness, or a racing heartbeat.

Research shows that most emotions will rise up, and then fall away, within 90 seconds, if you don't react to them.

You cannot control your emotions from rising up. Trying to is a waste of your time. The better strategy is learning to just *Let Them* rise up and then fall without reacting. There is also nothing you can do that will ever allow you to control the emotional reactions in another human being, no matter how hard you try.

Emotions are also contagious. Seeing someone else sad, afraid, disgusted, or angry can cause you to experience these same emotions in your own body. This explains why someone else's tone of voice, their shift in energy, their bad mood, and their body language can immediately trigger you to feel on edge.

And one more thing to understand is that whenever you or another person are hungry, or tired, or stressed-out, or under the influence, or lonely, or angry, or hurt, you'll be even more emotional. I say this because whenever I do or say something I later regret, there is usually stress, alcohol, or hunger involved. Knowing all this helps me to make the changes to better manage my emotions and helps me stay in control of what I say, do, and think.

That's one of my biggest takeaways from using the Let Them Theory: You will never be able to control what is happening around you. You will also never be able to control your emotional responses, because they are automatic—just like how your stress response turns on automatically.

But you can always choose what you think, say, or do in response to other people, the world around you, or the emotions that are rising up inside of you. That's the source of all your power.

Learning how to let other adults manage their own emotions will change your life. So will learning how to let your own emotions rise and fall while still communicating what you need to, even when it is very painful to do so. And there will be times when making the right decision for yourself is going to be one of the hardest things you have to do in life.

CHAPTER 8

The Right Decision Often Feels Wrong

Recently, a listener of the *The Mel Robbins Podcast* wrote to me with this question:

> Mel, I'm engaged and soon to be married. The wedding is a few weeks away and I know this should be one of the happiest moments of my life. But it's not. The closer we get to the wedding, the more my fiancée and I are fighting. I can't stop shaking this feeling of dread. Deep down, I am afraid I am making a huge mistake. I don't know what to do. The invitations are out, my parents and hers have already put down the deposits for everything. I don't want to disappoint my family. I don't want my parents to lose their money. I don't want to break my fiancée's heart. I don't want her parents and everyone else we know to be mad at me. How do I call this off?

Just reading the question, I could feel my heart seize. I bet yours did too. When the stakes feel this high, the right answer always feels wrong.

On the surface, the answer is simple, even though it doesn't feel like it. He should call it off. If you're dreading the wedding, you are making a mistake. If you can't stop thinking about calling it off, then you should.

Just because the right decision seems clear, doesn't always mean it's an easy decision to make. That's because the human experience is largely an emotional one.

What seems logical on the surface doesn't feel logical when you know it will cause other people a lot of pain.

Too often in life, when you're in that dilemma, you choose to inflict the pain on yourself instead of making a decision that you know is right for you but is going to be painful for other people to accept.

The groom who wrote to me knows, intellectually, what he needs to do. The problem is his emotions. He wrote to me because he is seeking reassurance. He has absolutely no idea how to handle what he's feeling, or how to deal with the emotional upset it will trigger in other people.

Agonizing over a difficult decision is a mentally healthy response to a very difficult situation. The fact that he is worried about other people is a sign that he's a good person.

There will be many times in your life when people are going to be mad, disappointed, or heartbroken by the things you say or do. There just will be. You have to be able to separate yourself from your emotions and the emotional reactions of others when you're determining the right decision to make.

You can't let your emotions drive your decisions, because they will often stop you from making the *right* decisions.

This is a hell of a lot more difficult than it seems. It can be devastating to make the right decisions. It can be absolutely heartbreaking to be honest with someone. It can feel like that decision might destroy you from the inside out, especially when it hurts someone you love.

Just take the situation with our groom who wants to call off his wedding and doesn't know how. You probably felt a wave of dread wash over you as you read through the message, and you and I don't even know this person.

That's how powerful emotions are.

You feel the weight in your chest as you picture him sitting his fiancée down and saying, "We have to talk." You can imagine him making the phone call and telling his parents. You can almost hear the sobbing as his fiancée buries her face into her hands. Your heart tightens as you picture the grief clogging her throat when she calls her parents. You can feel the anger swelling up in her dad's chest as he experiences the heartbreak of his baby girl. "Dad, he ended it," she might say. "He called off the wedding."

You're just reading and thinking about the situation, and it's creating an emotional reaction inside of you. And this is why letting people down and breaking their hearts is one of the hardest things you'll have to do in life.

Adults are allowed to feel how they're going to feel—and they're allowed to be angry. Broken. Devastated. Overwhelmed. Embarrassed. And extremely pissed off at you.

You can't control it.

But you *try* to control it by avoiding the truth. We've all done this. It's why you've found yourself staying in the wrong relationships or the wrong jobs or the wrong patterns of behavior for years.

It's why you still haven't called out your friend for talking behind your back, or confronted your mom, or taken a leave of absence, or confessed to your best friend that you are in love with them.

It feels easier to avoid it, because avoiding it means that you don't have to face it. But easier now makes it way harder later. Avoiding the hard conversations now won't make them any better next year.

In fact, from experience I can tell you that the longer you wait, the more painful it gets. Choosing not to do what's right for you will do nothing but cause you more pain.

So, did the groom call off the wedding? I don't know. Do I hope he did? Yes. I hope so for his sake, and I hope so for hers. Everyone deserves to be with someone who wants to be with them.

In life the most courageous, honorable, and kind thing to do is tell someone you don't want to be with them. It's hard to be honest, especially when other people are emotionally immature.

You don't want to deal with their guilt, venting, and bad moods, so you just avoid them. You're not avoiding confrontation—you're avoiding someone else's emotions. The only conflict is the conflict you're going to feel internally about how your decisions are going to impact other people emotionally and how they're going to react.

It's why people stay in marriages for a decade that they know have ended. It's why people stay in jobs for too long. It's why people pick majors and career paths and stay in them because they're afraid of making a decision that's going to cause someone else to feel something. And if you understand that emotions are a normal part of life, and that adults are allowed to feel the ups and downs and can survive it, you would be more courageous. It's not your job to protect everybody else from feeling emotions. Your job and responsibility is to live your life in a way that is aligned with your values, and in a way that gets you.

Sometimes that's going to hurt someone. It's going to disappoint them. It's going to cause pain or heartbreak knowing that your decision will hurt someone else—and it's going to be one of the hardest things you're going to do in life. When I know my actions may disappoint or upset someone, I find it helpful to remember Dr. Damour's framing that negative emotions are a mentally healthy response to life's upsets.

People are allowed to be upset when you change your mind, and disappointed or heartbroken when you break up. People are allowed to be depressed when they lose their job.

So how do you do this, and how do you manage the excruciating level of guilt and discomfort YOU are going to feel when you make a hard decision that you know is the right decision for you?

Learn to Ride the Emotional Wave

What's helped me is thinking about emotional discomfort like learning to ride a wave in the ocean. Because, at their core, emotions are like waves. They rise, they fall.

Some days, your life is going to be steady, still, and calm. Other days, like the day you call off the wedding, there's a hurricane that hits, and you're going to feel like you're drowning. But you will not drown.

Will it suck to call off the wedding? Yes. Will it be one of the most painful experiences of your life? Yes. Will her dad want to kill you? Definitely, for at least a few months. Will your parents lose their deposit and be angry with you? Yes. Will their hearts break because they love your fiancée too? Yes.

They're going to grieve the loss of what they thought would have been great.

And then slowly, as you *Let Them* feel whatever they need to feel, and you let yourself feel whatever you need to feel, and you don't try to control it or avoid it or change it, life has a way of going back to a new normal.

Eventually your parents will understand not only why you made the decision, but they will also be proud of you for having the bravery to do it. *Let Them.*

Let Me is the part where you remind yourself that this too shall pass. You are stronger than anyone else's emotional reaction. *Let Them* have their opinions. *Let Them* have their reactions. *Let Me* have mine. Let your emotions rise up and give yourself the space to process your emotions too.

Never let someone else's emotional reactions keep you from making the hard decision. *Let Me* be honest with myself and others. *Let Me* do the hard thing that is painful now, because it is the right thing to do and will save me from so much pain later. *Let Me* give myself the opportunity to have the life I deserve.

So let's summarize what you have learned about dealing with someone else's emotional reactions. Right now, you allow other people's emotional reactions to dictate your choices. The Let Them Theory empowers you to take a step back when another adult is acting like a child.

1. **Problem:** You're allowing other people's emotional immaturity to have power over your life. You're allowing somone else's outbursts, guilt trips, and reactions to dictate your actions, leading you to constantly manage their emotions rather than focusing on your own. This means you're always prioritizing the emotional needs of others at the expense of your own happiness.

2. **Truth:** Other people's emotional reactions are not your responsibility to manage. You cannot control how others feel or respond; nor can you fix their emotional immaturity. Most adults have the emotional capacity of an eight-year-old and you can't change that.

3. **Solution:** Using the Let Them Theory, you can stay in control even when an adult is acting like a child and having an emotional outburst. Make the right decisions for you, even if they make other people upset. You maintain your power when you stop taking on the burden of others' emotions and act in a way that aligns with your values.

When you say *Let Them*, you give others the space to experience their emotions without making it your responsibility to manage or fix them. When you say *Let Me*, you find the courage to make the right decisions for you, even if it will feel wrong to others.

It's time to grow up and act like a mature adult.

Overcoming Chronic Comparison

CHAPTER 9

Yes, Life Isn't Fair

The truth is: Life isn't fair. But at some point, you've got to wake up, accept that fact, and stop obsessing over what other people have, what they look like, and what they've achieved.

So let's talk about something that every single person on this planet struggles with: Allowing other people's success to paralyze you.

The reality is, you can't control another person's success, luck, or timing in life. The only thing you can control is what you do with the example other people set and the actions you take next.

When you see other people's lives as evidence that you're a failure, or you're unattractive, or not good enough, you become your biggest obstacle. Mindlessly scrolling on social media, or feeling inferior to someone else makes you feel stuck, hopeless, and perpetually behind. You are torturing yourself for no reason. You're letting other people paralyze you, which leads to procrastination and self-criticism.

When you focus on how unfair life seems and compare yourself to others, you're draining your motivation and keeping yourself from moving forward. It becomes a self-fulfilling prophecy. You are failing because of your chronic habit of comparing yourself.

You are the problem. And the first step is accepting the truth: Life isn't fair. It's just not.

It's not fair that you're drowning in student debt because you couldn't afford the tuition.

It's not fair that your sister looks like a supermodel and everyone flocks to her at the bars, while you're sitting there off to the side buying your own drinks.

It's not fair that your supervisor keeps giving you the crappy shift at work.

It's not fair that your country is torn apart by war.

It's not fair that you were born diabetic and have had to manage your insulin for your entire life.

It's not fair that your friend has a nice house or apartment because their parents paid for it.

It's not fair that your colleague got promoted and you didn't. It's not fair that you just got diagnosed with breast cancer. It's not fair that your friend seemingly has the perfect family life, while yours is so bad they wouldn't even put you guys on a reality show. It's not fair that your friend has a fast metabolism and can eat whatever she wants. It's not fair that you have asthma because you grew up in a polluted area. It's not fair that the cost of living and gas prices keep rising. It's not fair that your face is breaking out with acne.

You're right. It's not fair.

The fact is, every human being is dealt a different hand in life and you can't control the cards that someone else is holding. The more time you spend staring at someone else, the more you miss the entire point of the game.

In life, you're not playing against anyone. You're playing with them. Someone will always have better cards than yours. It's not about the hand you've been dealt; it's how you play it.

And while you've been busy comparing yourself to everyone else, you've missed one of the greatest secrets in life: Other people teach you how to be a better player, and that's how you win.

It's true, a lot of people have been dealt a "luckier" or "more successful" hand of cards. *Let Them.*

They are going to achieve things faster. They have a leg up. They have more resources. They have more support. There is nothing you can do to change it. It's a fact. *Let Them.*

Because worrying about it, or making yourself feel bad, is an insult to your intelligence. You can figure out how to win. You can learn how to work with what you've got and start where you are and create anything you want in life.

But you will never do that if you give all of your power to this stupid and toxic habit of comparing yourself to other people. Stop it.

Wishing everyone flocked to you instead of your sister at the bar, or that it was you on those European vacations, or that you were taller or had a healthier complexion, or a better job, or the wedding proposal, or more money isn't going to make it appear. It just makes your confidence disappear.

Any world-class card player will tell you, it's not about the hand you've been dealt. It's about how you play the hand. Winning the game of life requires you to focus on the cards you have and choosing what to do with them.

And look, I get it! It sucks to look at the hand you are holding and feel you have been dealt the unluckiest hand on the planet. It's easy to say "Why me?" It's easy to feel sorry for yourself. It's easy to look at someone else and make yourself feel bad because they have the body, the bank account, a loving relationship, perfect health, the car, the trust fund, the safety, the discipline, the friend group. . . because it is not fair. And you know what? Life is never going to be fair.

Some people are just really lucky. I have friends who seem to have had everything figured out from the day they were born. It feels like they have gotten everything they wanted. Positive things and experiences just pop up left and right. Everything always seems to just work out for them.

Why did these people get so lucky and I didn't? It's so easy to feel sorry for yourself and get angry at these people, right? They have the world's best family; they met the love of their life in college; they are superattractive and a gifted athlete. Nothing seems to go wrong for these people. And as far as you can tell, they don't struggle with depression, anxiety, or any kind of childhood trauma like the rest of us.

But comparing yourself to someone else's luck in life is a waste of your time.

When Comparison Is Torturing You

"But, Mel, I can't stop obsessing over how much more attractive other people are, or how I wish I were taller or didn't have asthma, or wishing that my parents didn't get divorced and my family life was better."

Comparing yourself to other people is unavoidable. It is human nature to look around and see what everyone else is doing and how you measure up.

The problem isn't the tendency to compare. The problem is what you're doing with the comparison that matters.

So ask yourself: What are you doing when you compare? Are you torturing yourself, or is it teaching you something important?

The fact is, there are two different types of comparison that people engage in: torture or teacher. In order to use comparison to your advantage, you must first identify which type of comparison you are doing, and it's very easy to tell the difference.

The first type of comparison is torture. This is when you find yourself obsessed over, caught up in, or beating yourself up over something that you will never be able to change. Comparison feels like torture when you're focused on fixed attributes of someone else's life.

For example, someone else's natural beauty, body type, family history, height, metabolism, parents, country of origin, past experiences, and any God-given talents like athleticism, perfect pitch, genius brain power, ability to learn languages at the blink of an eye, photographic memory, artistic talents. . . you get the gist.

You may be envious of these fixed characteristics of someone else's life, but these are the types of things people were usually born with and not something they worked hard to achieve. They were dealt these cards, and their cards are not going anywhere (and neither are yours).

And more importantly, no amount of effort on your part will make these cards magically appear in your life.

Here's how you know it's fixed. Is there anything you can do in the next 30 seconds to change this? If not, you're never going to be able to change these things.

It's critical that you understand the difference between things you can and cannot change, because comparing yourself to someone or some aspect of their life that you cannot change, no matter how much you try, is just torturing you.

Therefore, any time you spend obsessing over a fixed aspect of someone else's life versus your own is an act self-torture. It is useless for your growth and detrimental to your happiness. If you can't change it, you must learn to allow it. *Let Them.*

This is not easy to do.

I have watched our oldest daughter, Sawyer, engage in this first type of comparison and torture herself for years. She is hyper fixated on her younger sister, Kendall, who has a completely different body type, bone structure, metabolism, and athletic abilities. To top it off, Kendall was born with an amazing singing voice and perfect pitch.

Sawyer cannot change this. Kendall cannot change this. And I can't change this.

But over the years, I have watched Sawyer make herself miserable and give so much of her power away by engaging in torturous comparison. As a result, she hates her body. She beats herself up about her metabolism. She complains about how hard it is to lose weight and how easy it is to put it on. She's made it clear how unfair it is that Kendall can fit into her clothes, but she can't fit into Kendall's.

And you know what. . . she's right. It's not fair. And no amount of exercise, or supplements, or singing lessons will ever even the score that Sawyer is keeping in her mind: Kendall is winning and Sawyer is losing.

This is what psychologists call *upward comparison*. Upward comparison is this tendency to measure yourself against people and their attributes that you think are better than yours. Research shows it destroys your self-esteem.

You rarely engage in *downward comparison*, which is looking around and seeing how much better off are than the majority of people in the world. According to the U.N., one in four people do not have access to clean drinking water. The truth is, if you have running water, electricity, and the time to read this book, you're doing better than most people.

That brings me back to this type of torturous comparison and beating yourself up over aspects of your life that you cannot control or change.

I've watched with so much sadness in my heart at how miserable Sawyer makes herself. And I can't save her. I can't stop her from engaging in this kind of comparison. And no amount of complimenting or reassurance is going to change her behavior. She must choose to change this for herself.

Because until she stops torturing herself, she will never see the big, beautiful, amazing life that is right there waiting for her to embrace it. She will never embrace the beauty of her own body. And she will always see what she is not, instead of the magnificence of what she is. While she's focused on her sister, she is not seeing what the rest of us see, which is her unique talents, brains, and athleticism.

You must stop obsessing over the cards in someone else's hands. Life isn't fair. Someone will always seem to have better cards than you and comparing your hand to theirs will always make you lose. Stop focusing on the other players; that's not how you win the game of life. Learn to play with other players, not against them.

The sad fact is I have seen too many people develop an eating disorder or mental health problems or struggle with addiction or shame because of the torturous nature of this type of comparison. And I don't say this lightly because I know it can lead to very serious struggles and challenges that many people face, including people I love deeply.

Psychologists will tell you that the root cause of many disorders is an obsessive need for control. As you are learning in this book, any time you try to control something that you can't, it just makes you feel more out of control and powerless.

That's why it's imperative for you to recognize when you are engaging in this first type of comparison.

Stop. *Let Them* live their life. *Let Me* focus on mine.

You're too smart to waste your life torturing yourself. Hold on to your power, because you're going to need it to unlock the potential of your own unique life. What I've found is that being happier requires you to allow yourself to be happier.

It is impossible to enjoy your life or love yourself and beat yourself up at the same time.

So let's move on to the second type of comparison. This type of comparison is a gold mine for you.

CHAPTER 10

How to Make Comparison Your Teacher

You just learned about the first type of comparison, which feels like self-torture. Now let's talk about the second type: comparison that is teaching you something. And here's how you know that comparison is good: You're looking at aspects of someone else's life or success that you could create for yourself.

With time and consistent effort, these aspects of your life, career, or health could be changed.

The list of things you could change is endless: from your job, to creating a better friend group, to finding your purpose, to spending more time with your kids, to vacations, to creating financial freedom; getting up earlier, finding and creating the greatest love story of your life, being an amazing cook, or getting in the best shape of your life; buying a huge ring, a fancy watch, or a sports car; renovating your kitchen, building a second home, creating a better relationship with your stepparents, developing healthier habits, writing a book, healing your trauma, gaining more social media followers, having better boundaries and more time for yourself, launching a business, or developing a better reputation.

I wrote a long list on purpose. The fact is, 95 percent of the things that you want in life are things that you can create if you are willing to work hard, be consistent and disciplined and patient. Very little about your life is fixed in stone.

If someone has done something better, and bigger, and cooler than you could ever imagine, *Let Them*. *Let Them* have their success. *Let Them* beat you to it. *Let Them* do it in the smartest and the coolest way. Their success gives you the formula. Remember my story about not posting on social media? Whatever it is that you want, someone else can give you the formula. *Let Them* lead the way.

For most of my life, I didn't understand this. If someone achieved what I wanted, I told myself they had beat me to it. I looked at people around me and saw other people's wins as my losses. And when you see other people's wins as your losses, it will make you feel defeated before you even start.

If you're not careful, comparison can become the reason why you doubt yourself, procrastinate, and continue to stay stuck. You're capable of achieving the same success, but instead of working to create it, you're actively arguing against what you want. This is an example of how you've turned other people into a problem, and they don't need to be.

There is enough happiness, success, and money to go around for absolutely everyone including you. It is in limitless supply.

No one is taking anything from you. Happiness, success, and money are waiting for you to get serious about creating them. I will say this again: No one else's wins are your losses. That's why you have to change the way you look at other people's success.

The truth is, there are more than 8 billion people on this planet. If you are looking for evidence that someone else makes more money, has the coolest wardrobe, has the best friend group, went to a more prestigious school, is in the best shape, sold their company, is a *New York Times* bestselling author, has traveled the world, or quite literally has anything you could ever want. . . you'll find it.

The problem isn't the tendency to compare. The problem is not using comparison to your advantage. Using the Let Them Theory, you will learn how to flip comparison from a major problem in your life into your greatest teacher.

They've Always Been Your Teacher

Recently I was talking with a friend of mine named Molly. Molly is an extremely talented interior designer. She has built a successful business, has a number of employees, and does beautiful work for her clients.

The last few times that she and I have connected, she always asked me for advice about social media, asking questions like, "Mel, how can I get myself out there? I know I need to be doing more on social media, and doing a better job marketing my business and work online, but I don't know where to start."

For every business, there's a formula, so I gave her a simple list of things she could do: Start posting every day. Create videos explaining your projects. Post before-and-after photos. Hire an intern that creates a library of short videos for you. Take a free online course to learn more about the social media platforms, and pick one to focus on.

Just like in the example I gave you earlier, from when I wanted to build my speaking business years ago, the steps you need to take are always very simple. The problem is not doing them.

Molly called me the other day, and immediately I could tell something was off. "Molly, you don't sound like yourself. Is everything okay with the kids?"

She said, "Yeah, yeah, yeah. The kids are fine. I'm not."

And I said, "What happened?"

She said, "Well, I saw something the other night that sent me into a spiral. And I've been freaking out ever since."

And so I'm listening and I'm thinking, *What the heck could have happened? My gosh. This is really serious.*

It turns out that there is someone in Molly's neighborhood that she's known for a long time. She is not exactly Molly's favorite person—you know, the kind of person who is always drawing attention to themselves and just rubs you the wrong way. The energy between them has never clicked.

This person has no interior design experience or background. And now, they've gotten into the "design" business, started posting on social media, and suddenly their posts are blowing up. This person is getting thousands of likes on her posts, and what really burns Molly up is that everyone in the neighborhood is now talking about how "talented" this other woman is.

As Molly vented to me, "These are just photos of her own house, and she didn't even design it!"

The night before, after a long day of work dealing with her design clients, Molly had put the kids to bed, sat down on the couch, and started scrolling. Guess who was all over Molly's feed? This irritating woman.

She couldn't help herself. She read every single comment and she stalked the woman's website. The website looked modern and clean, whereas Molly's hasn't been updated in three years. The way in which the other woman was marketing herself was so impressive. It made her look very professional, like she'd been doing this for years. And that sent Molly into a downward spiral.

She is going to steal my clients! Everyone is going to think she is better than me. How does she know how to do all this? Why didn't I do this sooner? Argghhhhhhhh!

She then took a breath, and said, "Mel, what do you think I should do?"

I'm going to tell you the same thing I told my friend Molly, and I want you to remember this the next time you find yourself burning up with comparison or anger about what someone else is doing:

No one should feel sorry for you. If you are jealous right now about someone else's success, GOOD. I'm happy for you. Jealousy is an invitation from your future self. It is inviting you to look more closely at someone else—not to make you feel inferior, but to show you what is possible.

This woman was not stealing any success from Molly. She was not preventing Molly from changing her website or focusing on social media. This woman's wins online were not Molly's losses. Because other people are never going to stop you from achieving what's meant for you. They can't. Only you can stop yourself from achieving it.

This woman is a reminder to Molly that social media matters. She is a teacher who is leading the way. *Let Them* wake you up. *Let Them* be successful. *Let Them* dazzle you with their beautiful web design.

Let Them Show That It's Possible

Maybe you've been so caught up in your day-to-day that you've ignored what's right in front of you. Maybe you've been playing so small that you can't see how big and beautiful your life could be. Maybe you're so used to doing things the way you've always done them, you've been reluctant to try a new way.

Other people show you what's possible. When you see comparison as a teacher, you'll realize other people aren't taking anything from you; they are giving something to you. Other people have this beautiful capacity to show you pieces of your future that you cannot fully see for yourself yet. They show you possibilities that you didn't realize existed or told yourself you are incapable of achieving.

Whoever or whatever is making you jealous, GOOD. Their success and their wins don't shrink your chances of creating what you want. They expand it. *Let Them* lead the way. Flip your jealousy to inspiration. See what's possible through their example. The people you compare yourself to act as mirrors, reflecting back bigger possibilities—or in Molly's case, the formula and the work she was avoiding. And that's what I said to Molly. *Let Them* lead the way.

That brings me to a very important point: There's an important reason why this woman got under Molly's skin. The truth is, it had to be this irritating person. In life, if you're not motivated to do something, it's going to take something painful to force you to change.

In Molly's case, she had been watching famous interior designers for years. She had been talking about "doing social media" for years. She had every excuse in the book for why she didn't make it a priority.

Until now. . . all of a sudden, this irritating woman comes along, with no prior design experience, and Molly sees her doing all the things deep down she knew she needed to do years ago.

Molly knows that this woman from the neighborhood has no special advantage, talent, or resources. That's why she's so mad. This irritating woman is shoving a simple fact in Molly's face: *If I can do it, you can do it too.*

This is where comparison gets really interesting. These types of people in your life force you to look in the mirror and call yourself out.

So, *Let Them* make you mad. You need to be thanking this person that makes you mad, because you're not actually mad at them. That anger that is burning you up inside is you being mad at yourself, because you know that you could have gotten to work sooner, and you know you are capable of figuring this out. You just didn't. This was me in the speaking business. That's why I say this kind of comparison is your greatest teacher.

Not because it shows you what you need to be doing, but because it galvanizes your power and awakens your anger. And you need your anger as the fuel to get you going.

So whoever it is that's triggering you, *Let Them*. *Let Them* irritate you. *Let Them* burn you up. And *Let Them* show you EXACTLY what you want and what you need to be doing to get there.

Let's Talk About You

How do you turn these moments of jealousy and frustration into something good? How do you flip comparison into inspiration? Simple. Say *Let Me* and look at the data other people's successes provide.

Anytime you find yourself playing the game of comparison, there is something really important happening.

Comparison shows you the areas of your life that need more of your attention.

It means the time for thinking and excuses is over. *Let Me* get to work. Put in the reps. It's a phrase my buddy bestselling author Jeff Walker always says, "Success is about putting in the reps." What's that mean? Simple: To be successful, to lose weight, to write a book, or to become a YouTuber, you have to show up every day and do the boring, irritating, and uncomfortable work. You've got to put in the reps.

Think about any change you want in your life, like going to the gym. How do you build muscle? You show up every day and you put in the reps. The famous quarterback Tom Brady recently said about success, "The truth is you don't have to be special. You just have to be what most people aren't: consistent, determined, and willing to work for it."

All these people who stir up your jealousy are here to show you the simple fact that while you have been making excuses, they've been putting in the reps, slowly chipping away at the boring, hard stuff.

In the words of Tom Brady, they aren't special; they've just been what you aren't: consistent, determined, and willing to work for it. That is 1,000 percent the secret to my success.

That brings me back to my friend Molly. She knew in her heart that she needed to start prioritizing this several years ago. Part of the reason it's so painful right now is that she's seeing the fruits of someone else's efforts. This will keep happening if you don't start to move on the things that you want.

That beautiful website that Molly was so mad about—it didn't pop up overnight. That woman had been working on it for months. The social media strategy that was burning Molly up didn't magically happen. While Molly was making excuses, the other woman was researching, studying, learning, and creating all of the posts that Molly now sees.

The reason why these people make you so angry is because you know you could do it too. And you are just mad that you didn't start doing it a long time ago. The fact is, inspiration is not enough to get you motivated to do something.

This is why anger is important. This is why comparison can be one of your greatest teachers, and I am willing to bet when it happens, it will likely be someone you know who makes you mad. It will be Aron down the hall. All of a sudden he's quitting his job and he is working full-time on his custom boat business that he's been building in the dark on the weekends while you've been busy going out with your friends.

That's why it makes you jealous when you see him walk out the door. Because when the people that you know do it, it means that you can't make excuses for why you can't. If you've been sitting next to Aron at work for a year, you know there's no superpower, trust fund, or upper hand. They just started working on it. And now they're quitting. That makes you so jealous. That's why it had to be them.

It's perfectly normal to be upset as you see someone's beautiful website, or as you watch a colleague walk out the door to a new life, or as you step into your friend's beautiful new home. But if you're serious about being successful or healthy or achieving your goals, you have no time to be upset, and you cannot afford to waste your energy being jealous. You need that energy, because you have work to do.

These moments are really painful, and they are going to happen a lot in your life—so get ready for it. Using the Let Them Theory, you'll be able to recognize when comparison is trying to teach you something. Jealousy is a doorway to your future cracked open, and it's your job to recognize when it happens, kick the door open, and walk right through it.

When you let other people lead the way, you'll realize that beneath all the fear and excuses and time wasted is the life you've wanted all along. Right now the only things that are holding you back from taking control of your life are the excuses, fears, and emotions that we have been discussing throughout this entire book.

This is where you go from trying to control what everyone else thinks, feels, and does, and you take your time and your energy and use it to create the best chapter of your life. This is so important I'm going to give you one more example from my life.

The point of this story is that it's not always obvious what your jealousy is teaching you. In my 40s, back when we were struggling financially and before I had built any of the career I have today, I had a friend who was doing a huge house renovation.

Every time we went out to lunch or on a walk, I wanted to hear all about the renovations and see all of the progress photos. It was so fun to follow along. However, every time I left and went back to our house, I just felt. . . discouraged and sad.

I will never forget the day that Chris and I pulled up my friend's long, winding driveway when their renovations were complete and my mouth dropped to the floor. The house was beautiful.

As my friend led a bunch of us on a tour of the house, I found myself going down a comparison spiral. *HOW the heck do they have so much money*?! I remember thinking.

Of course, I was happy for her, but I was also so damn jealous. She absolutely deserved this, and she and her husband had both worked so hard for years. And they had earned every right to build it, to talk about it, to enjoy it, and to be proud of it.

I knew this deep down, but I did not know how to genuinely feel happy for my friend without feeling insanely jealous and insecure at the same time. When she swung open the doors to the playroom, I almost combusted.

"This is the upstairs play loft with the pool table and hangout area for the kids to enjoy now—and responsibly, when they are older, with friends," she told us.

With that, she gave us a wink, and we all laughed.

"And then here is the bunk room for all the kiddos and their friends to have sleepovers in. And my kids love it so much, they don't even want to sleep in their own rooms now."

My jaw dropped. No wonder my kids always wanted to go to my friend's house and didn't want to host friends at ours. Queen-size bunk beds? A playroom above the garage? Hello. . . this was a kid's dream, and it had always been my dream to have "the house" where all the kids hung out too.

At this point in the tour, I was ready to go downstairs, steal a bottle of wine, and crawl into one of these queen-size bunk beds—that's how sorry I felt for myself. I felt like such a horrible person for letting my jealousy sour my true happiness for her. Not only is she an incredible friend, loved by everyone, and gorgeous inside and out, she now has my dream home.

As the night went on, I tried to push the pit in my stomach down. I tried to act like I was completely unbothered by it all. But once I was in the car with Chris and on our way home, I didn't have to stifle the jealousy. . . so I threw it at him.

So like a typical eight-year-old, I had a full-blown tantrum in front of him.

"We'll never have a house like that," I snapped. "Why did you have to go into the restaurant business?"

Chris didn't know what to say, so we drove home in tense silence.

I can share this story with such detail because we have unpacked this moment in marriage counseling so many times. It would be easy to think this story was about a house. It wasn't. The truth that I needed to discover was so much deeper. Comparing myself to my friend and the anger that I felt was teaching me a life-changing lesson.

I wasn't mad at her. I wasn't even mad at my husband. I was mad at myself because I had given up on my own ambition. I had counted on my husband being successful and providing me with the financial support to have the things that I wanted in life. The truth is, your life is your responsibility. If you want financial success, it is your responsibility to create it. If you want a house that has queen bunk beds and a renovated kitchen, it is your responsibility to work for it.

I had been avoiding that responsibility for a decade. This experience forced me to look in the mirror and be honest with myself about what I wanted. Jealousy was in fact a message from my future self. Seeing my friend win allowed me to see bigger possibilities for me winning too.

And I kicked the door open, and I got to work. I am not special. I just did what I was unwilling to do before. I got consistent, determined, and willing to work for what I wanted. I started putting in the reps. It took 15 years of hard work to get my queen-size bunk beds. But I did it and so can you.

The Let Them Theory will help you dig deep and get to the truth of what jealousy is trying to teach you, and where you have let yourself down. If all you ever do is stay on the surface wasting your time and energy on other people and on things beyond your control, you will never discover the deeper meaning and possibilities in your life.

You have a beautiful and amazing life to live. You have potential beyond your imagination. You are not limited by where you live, or the circumstances you are facing, or the aspects of your life that you believe are limitations.

If you can be honest with yourself about what you truly want, and take responsibility for creating it, you will. You don't have to be special. You just have to get up every day, put one foot in front of the other, and work hard to do a little better, and be a little better, than you were yesterday. And one of these days, you are going to wake up and realize that you not only changed yourself, but you are in the middle of living the life you were once jealous of.

So let's summarize what you have learned about overcoming chronic comparison. Until now, you have allowed other people's success to paralyze you. The Let Them Theory teaches you to let others have their success while also using it as inspiration to build the life you want.

1. **Problem:** When you focus on how unfair life seems and compare yourself to others, you waste your precious time and energy on things beyond your control. You let others' success paralyze you, leaving you stuck, and feeling behind and frustrated. This mindset fuels procrastination and perfectionism, preventing you from taking action to create your own success.

2. **Truth:** There will always be someone who is luckier, has what you want, is further along, or achieves success more quickly than you. Comparing yourself to others is a natural instinct; but when it consumes your thoughts, it undermines your confidence and motivation. You can't control the success of others, but you can control how you respond to it.

3. **Solution:** Using the Let Them Theory, stop torturing yourself and use comparison to your advantage. Let others have their success and leverage it to fuel your own journey. Other people's success is evidence that you can do it too. By turning inspiration into action, you begin to build the extraordinary life you deserve.

When you say *Let Them*, you learn from other people's success and *Let Them* lead the way. When you say *Let Me*, you focus on playing the cards in your hand, turning inspiration into action, and winning by playing with others, not against them.

It's time to play your hand and win the game of life.

You've just finished the first half of this book, and by now, you've felt the power of the Let Them Theory starting to work in your life. You've learned how freeing it is to stop wasting energy on what you can't control—other people's behaviors, opinions, and expectations—and instead focus on yourself.

The more you say *Let Them* and *Let Me*, the more you'll free up mental space, emotional energy, and time you never knew you had. With that freedom, you can now show up differently for yourself and in your relationships—the areas where *Let Them* will have the deepest impact.

In the next section, we'll explore how to use the theory to navigate the delicate dynamics of adult relationships. Whether it's friendships, family, romantic relationships, or co-workers, you'll discover how to set clear boundaries, strengthen bonds, and finally release the exhausting need to manage everyone else.

Right now, you might feel frustrated, lonely, or unsure if the connections you want are possible.

But here's the truth: The best relationships of your life are still ahead of you. The most fulfilling friendships, the most beautiful love stories, and the most incredible bonds with family members are waiting for you if you learn to accept people for who they are and stop trying to force a relationship to be something it's not.

The more you release your expectations, control, and the need to fix others, the more your relationships will flourish. It's never too late to find amazing friends, make amends, strengthen family ties, or create the love you've always dreamed of.

How exciting is it that the most meaningful moments of your life and the deepest connections are just around the corner?

If you apply the Let Them Theory, they are. So let's get started.

Your Relationships and the Let Them Theory

Mastering Adult Friendship

Motivating Other People to Change

Helping Someone Who Is Struggling

Choosing the Love You Deserve

The more you let people
be who they are, the better
your relationships will be.

— Mel Robbins

Mastering Adult Friendship

CHAPTER 11

The Truth No One Told You about Adult Friendship

Let's be honest: Adult friendship is hard. Every person I know is struggling with adult friendships: creating them, losing them, or even just finding the time to keep friendships going.

If you've gotten to a point in your life where you're wondering, *Where did all my friends go?*, you're not alone. Perhaps you feel like you have no friends. Or, you're in different phases of life than the people you were once close with. Maybe you find yourself getting caught up in drama, waiting for someone else to reach out, or feeling unsure about where you stand. Or you feel like everybody else's life is a big party that you're missing out on. You want better friendships; you just don't know where to find them.

I've struggled with this too.

In this section, we are going to tackle adult friendship, which up until now, you've approached the same way you did as a kid: You just expected it to happen. Because of this, your friendships aren't what they could be.

The truth is, friendships change dramatically when you become an adult—and no one sees the change coming. That's why you need to use the Let Them Theory to take control of this area of your life.

Friendship is one of the best and most meaningful aspects of the human experience. You deserve to have amazing friendships in your life. Friends are awesome—they make your life more fun and fulfilling, and they can become the family you've chosen for yourself.

The Great Scattering

The reason why it is hard to navigate adult friendship is that when you reach your 20s, friendship changes from a group sport to an individual one—and no one understands this.

When you don't recognize that this change happened (and no one does), you don't change your approach to adult friendship, which is why you end up feeling lonely. You'll also find it challenging to stay connected to the people that you do love in an increasingly busy and distracted world.

As you grow and change and move jobs and cities and fall in and out of love, you'll constantly be confronted with the challenge of "finding your people" in new places and in new chapters of your life.

The Let Them Theory will help you understand adult friendship at a deeper level and it will empower you to strengthen existing friendships and set you up to meet your most favorite people in life, many of whom you haven't even met yet.

So what changes?

Let's talk about the difference between friendship when you were a kid and friendship after the massive change that happens when you're an adult.

When you were little, you and your friends and your classmates felt like a team, moving through life at the exact same pace, and in the exact same place. From kindergarten to high school, you and your friends had the same daily routine, you rode the same buses, you read the same books, and learned the same subjects in school.

You saw everyone your age all the time: in class, in the halls, on the sports fields, and in your neighborhood. You also had the same milestones. From birthdays, to graduations, to the exact same vacation schedule, you participated in the same clubs, activities, sports, and classes—which made you feel subconsciously like there was a big group of people moving through life with you, and you were a part of it.

This is why it felt like friendship was a group sport. Why? Because everyone traveled in groups, and that is simply what you did when you were younger.

For the first 20 years of your life, the structure of friendship was planned for you, by your parents, the school system, sports teams, college dormitories, fraternities and sororities, or extracurricular activities that made it easy for you to be around people your same age, going through very similar experiences at the exact same time.

Therefore it was not only easy to make friends but you were spending so much time together, and sharing so many experiences, that you also had everything in place to create really deep friendships.

And the reason why it was more of a group sport was that if you were part of a team, or a friend group, or a club, you expected to be invited whenever something was planned.

Your childhood trained you to believe you'd always be invited, friendship would be easy, that you'd see your friends all the time—and something fun would always be going on.

And then *BOOM*. You enter your 20s, and into a phase of friendship I call the *Great Scattering*.

The Great Scattering looks like this: High school or college ends, and all friends scatter in different directions. Suddenly, everyone is living in different places, and very soon, all your friends are on different timelines, working different jobs, hanging out with different people, and achieving milestones at different paces. And the structure that supported all your friendships is gone.

That's why you feel a tremendous loss of control about every aspect of your life. There is no longer a track, a template, a timeline, or milestones for what to do next or when you're supposed to achieve it. It's all up to you.

In other words, your adult life begins. For the first time in your life, you are officially on your own. It is entirely up to you to choose how you want to spend your time, where you want to work, what city you want to live in, and who you are going to hang out with.

And as time passes, those close friends of yours that moved to a different city start to feel further and further away. No one has any free time. Trying to coordinate everyone's calendars to get together feels impossible. And what is holding the friend group together is a text chain that gets quieter and quieter over time. Naturally, everyone is concentrating on living their lives and focused on the people right in front of them.

And this is when that loneliness really hits. This is when adult friendship gets hard. The structure that created the opportunity to see your friends 24/7, and the expectations that you would, is gone. Then you start to wonder, *Where did all my friends go?* You may feel out of control. And you cling. And feel insecure. And grip harder.

The reality is adult friendships come and go. Expecting friendship will destroy it. You need a more flexible and proactive approach. Which is why you're going to find yourself saying *Let Them* all the time.

Let Them move away. *Let Them* prioritize their new friends. *Let Them* not have time for me. *Let Them* not text me. *Let Them* not include me. *Let Them* go to brunch without me.

It happens to all of us, but it can still be incredibly confusing and disorienting. Now and forever onward, it's up to you to change the way you think about and approach friendship as an adult—because the Great Scattering has already happened, and versions of this will continue to happen over and over as you age.

When your single friends get married, they scatter. When your friends start having kids, they scatter. When people move out of the city and into the suburbs, they scatter. When people become empty nesters or get divorced, they scatter. When people get older, or downsize, or retire, or go through a loss, they scatter.

It's going to happen again and again in your life and with your friends. This is normal. This is why you need the Let Them Theory. It will teach you how to be more flexible in your approach to friendship, and show you how to use your time wisely to create some of the best friendships of your entire life.

The Three Pillars of Friendship

There are three factors that I believe make great friendships possible: proximity, timing, and energy. These pillars are the invisible foundation every friendship is built on.

When friends drift away, fall apart, or lose touch, it is because one or more of these three essential pillars is missing. Most of the time adult friendships fade not for personal reasons, but because of these three pillars: proximity, timing, and energy.

Understanding the role these three factors play will help you use the Let Them Theory to be more flexible, understanding, and proactive in your adult friendships.

The first pillar of friendship is proximity.

Proximity means how often you are physically near them. This matters because when you are physically near someone, you naturally spend a lot more time together. If you don't live near each other, you are not going to see each other as often. It will require more effort to stay connected.

You can absolutely do it, but it is harder. It is easier to grow closer to people you see all the time. And this isn't just common sense. It's a fact.

This concept of proximity has been researched and proven to impact who you become friends with, and who you don't. And the reason why this matters so much is that the more times you see someone in person, the more opportunities you have to get to know them, to spend time with them, to share experiences together, and to click and form a deeper friendship.

According to a University of Kansas study, to become a "casual" friend, you have to spend 74 hours with someone. And to become a "close" friend, you have to spend over 200 hours with someone. Let's put this research in the context of friendships when you are younger, and how they change when you become an adult.

In high school, you clocked 200 hours with friends every five to six weeks. In college, you spent even more time with your friends because you lived with them. You ate every meal with them. You spent every weekend with them. This proximity allowed you the time to fortify your connections and share infinite experiences and memories that allowed you to build trust in your relationships.

If you're physically next to someone, whether you're living across the street, or in the dorm, or across the hall, or sitting at the desk or the cubicle next to them, or seeing them every weekend at your kid's soccer game, you naturally spend time together because of proximity.

This matters. And it matters a lot. It also explains why it was much easier to create friends when you were younger. You were physically next to people your age all the time. This also explains why as an adult, when everyone scatters and is suddenly on a different schedule, it is hard to make new friends—because getting 200 hours with someone is a lot of time.

And get this: When you're an adult, you don't have as much free time as you did when you were younger to hang out, because you're working. According to the American Time Study, scientists found that from the age of 21 through 60, you will spend more time with your co-workers than your family and friends combined.

Which means your only chance to hang out with your friends is after work or on the weekends. Think of how many coffee dates, walks, and barbecues it takes to get 200 hours with a new adult friend! And it also makes you wonder, if proximity is so important, why are you not automatically best friends with all of your co-workers, since that is who you spend most of your time with?

The second pillar of friendship is timing.

Timing refers to the chapter of life you are in right now. If you're not in the same chapter of life with someone else, it's much harder to relate because you have less in common.

And nowhere is the impact of timing more evident than how it impacts friendships with co-workers. As you just learned, from the ages of 21 to 60, you will spend more time with your co-workers than your friends and family combined, but here's the catch: Everyone at work is in a different chapter of their life. That means for over four decades of your life, the majority of people at work who you spend the most physical time with are not in the same period of their life as you are.

For example, if everyone you work with is forty years older than you, it can be hard to relate. One of my daughters would always share that she would be on these team meetings at work and the "break the ice" question of the day would be something like "Where did you get married?" or "What is your retirement plan?"

She felt like she had to lie about her life every Monday morning when everyone was sharing what they did with their kids over the weekend, while she had gotten drunk with her girlfriends and thrown up in a garbage can.

This is why the timing of all life matters. Because despite spending so much time with her co-workers, and being really friendly with them, and liking a lot of them, they were in very different stages of life. It's why they never hung out on the weekends and they never went out to dinner after work—they had nothing in common other than work.

I can give you another example of how timing impacts friendship. Chris and I have family friends that we both love. I think they are so cool. I love hanging out with them. But we are fifteen years younger and they are grandparents. We have a lot less to talk about because we are in very different stages of our lives.

Are we still friends? Of course! I love them to death! But that friendship can only go so deep because we don't live near them, we don't see them a lot, and the timing is off—we are in very different stages of life. And what I love about understanding these three pillars of friendship is that it makes you realize that none of this is personal.

Friendships come and go. You can feel close and then you can feel distant. And none of this is personal. It's proximity and timing.

The Let Them Theory has really helped me loosen my grip on adult friendship. It will help you do the same, because the more you grow in your life, the more people will come in and out of your life. *Let Them.*

When you stop expecting to have everyone be your best friend, or to be invited to everything, or be included in everything, or that you will click with everyone, friendship gets a lot easier. There is an entirely different way to view adult friendship using the Let Them Theory; and it will make your life so much more fulfilling, healthy, and happy.

The third pillar of friendship is energy.

You either click with some people or you don't. You can't explain it, and neither can they, but you have to trust it. The energy is either on or it's off. There is no scientific reason to explain it. You just have to trust it.

And here is another hard truth: Energy shifts over time. Sometimes for the worse, and sometimes for the better. And that's a good thing, because it means that you and the people in your life are growing into new versions of yourselves.

For example, maybe you lived with five friends during college, and you loved them, and you clicked, and it was the best experience of your life. Then, two of you move in together after you graduate, and within four months, something just feels off. This is normal. It means you're both growing and changing, and it doesn't mean the friendship is over.

The mistake that we make is that we start to obsess over what is wrong, instead of just focusing on acceptance, kindness, and admiration for the other person. Just because you were best friends during one stage of your life doesn't mean you will be best friends during the next stage.

In fact, while we're on the topic, I hate the term *best friend*. It puts too much pressure and expectations on a relationship that will always need room to grow and evolve. As people come in and out of your life, *Let Them*. Trust the timing.

There are certain people who are meant to be in your life for a season. There are people that are meant to be in your life for a specific reason. And there will be people who will be with you for a lifetime.

This is normal. And when someone drifts away, or the energy feels off, do not make them your enemy. You can tell when a friendship is forced, and the energy is changing, because it starts to drain you. Conversations feel awkward. You'll start to feel like something is off or conversations are forced. Trust that feeling. I learned the hard way that gripping on to something, and trying to force it, just makes things worse.

We tend to hold on to things that we know deep down are not meant for us, because we know the second we stop forcing it, the relationship will fade. That is exactly what happened to me. All of a sudden, I found myself on the outside of what I thought was my closest friend group. I didn't know what to do, and I definitely did not handle it well.

CHAPTER 12

Why Some Friendships Naturally Fade

Here's what happened.

One of the most fun times in my life was when I was a young mom of three. We lived in a neighborhood with a huge group of friends, and were all raising our kids together, hanging out with each other, and building a really incredible community.

We all had kids the same age who went to the same public elementary school. It was one of the most social and fun periods of my life, because we were bumping into our friends all the time because of the kids, school, and their schedules overlapping. I honestly felt like I was back in high school again with constant plans, invitations, and groups of people to hang out with.

There were two couples in particular that we grew very close to, and we did tons of things together with our kids—going away for the weekend, Halloween trick-or-treating, coaching Saturday morning town soccer, Sunday brunches, football parties, barbecuing all the time, you name it.

Chris and I were genuinely happy. It felt like pure luck that we had moved into a suburban town not knowing anyone, and truly struck gold because we met so many amazing couples who we loved spending time with—and our kids loved their kids too! It was too good to be true.

At the same time, one of our closest friends was living in a different state and always remarked on how jealous they were of our community and our large, fun circle of friends. We thought that the only way things could get better was if they moved with their kids to our town too.

So Chris and I started encouraging them: "You've got to move here!"

And so they did. In fact, they bought a house right across the street from the two couples that we did everything with. At first, I was SO excited. Imagine this—one of your closest friends not only moves to your town, but lives on the same street, and is becoming neighbors, with your current two best family friends! We lived a five-minute drive away—it was perfect!

So naturally, I expected it was going to be one big block party: All four families together all the time. Now, in the beginning, it was just as I'd hoped. They'd call us and invite us to drive over and join in on the random weeknight dinners. But then over time, something really unexpected started to happen. The invitations became fewer and fewer. And what became apparent was that the three families were hanging out without us. . . all the time.

Looking back, I now understand that of course they would be. Proximity matters. They lived across the street from one another. They could wave to each other from their front doors. They all had kids the same age who took the bus together and carpooled to sports together every single day.

And looking back on this, I get it. It wasn't personal at all. When you're standing next to somebody waiting for your kids to get off the bus, you naturally turn and ask, "What are you guys doing tonight? Want to come over for dinner?"

It makes total sense that they would all become best friends! And they are allowed to! But for me, my experience was watching this Atlanta couple ultimately and unapologetically take what I thought was our place in the friend group. And I didn't handle it well.

I Was Horrible

I did what most people do when they feel threatened or excluded, because I didn't understand adult friendship. I found myself consumed with jealousy and anger. *That used to be us*, I thought. They *stole* our friend group. And as soon as my energy shifted toward them, everything changed.

At first, I wanted to be fun, friendly, and carefree around them, so the situation would change back to the way it was. But whenever I thought about the situation, or saw them, it was as if a demon took over my mind, body, and spirit.

I could not control my feelings. I was cold and bitter. My energy was off, and everyone could feel it. Chris could feel it. The three couples could feel it. And even friends in the wider group of families could feel it too. I was a complete bitch, even though I didn't want to be. I tried to not think about it, but any given weeknight, while we were at home eating spaghetti at the dining room table, our friends were all together grilling out in the backyard. It burned me up inside.

I'm embarrassed about how I felt and acted and how petty and insecure I was. But at this point in my life, I didn't understand my emotions or how to manage them. I didn't have the Let Them Theory. I became a walking friendship red flag.

If I saw any of the six of them at a Saturday morning soccer game, a school meeting, or a cocktail party, or the grocery store, I would feel so stressed. I wanted to be normal. I liked these people and wanted things to change. But I had no idea how to deal with my feelings.

I couldn't control myself. My tone of voice would shift. My arms would cross. And, while I didn't want to feel the way that I did, I had no idea how to change it. I don't think anyone purposefully excluded me or Chris.

And now, when I reflect back, I can see the situation for what it was. I can see how angry and jealous I was. I wouldn't want me at a barbecue either. I wouldn't want my negative energy there. It's a miracle we got invited anywhere at that point in my life!

My poor husband. It didn't bother him that the dynamic in the friend group had changed. He didn't take anything personally. But I just couldn't change how I felt. It's still deeply painful and personal to talk about even now, and I take full responsibility for my lack of maturity and toxic behavior. I was acting like a child. One minute I was pouting, the next minute I was pretending like I didn't care, and oftentimes in private, I was throwing a tantrum in front of poor Chris.

If I had had the Let Them Theory back then, I would have been able to *Let Them* be friends. I would have been able to rise above the situation. I would have taken responsibility for understanding and processing my emotions in a healthy way, like a mature adult. But at the time, I had no idea how to deal with my emotions or what I was feeling. It all felt like a personal attack. They became the villain in my story.

Why? I'll tell you: It's easier to blame someone else, and sit in your anger, than it is to take responsibility for yourself. I was making the single biggest mistake that you make in adult friendships: I was expecting to be friends forever, expecting to be included, and expecting it to be easy.

This story illustrates that proximity really does play a massive role in forming and maintaining adult friendships, and that is not always in your control. The story also illustrates how energy can destroy a friendship, and that is in your control. This situation happened when I was in my late 30s and early 40s, but it can happen in any stage of your life. At some point, you're going go from being on the inside of a friend group to feeling like you're on the outside. This is normal.

Because as people come and go, and scatter in different directions, and change their lives, and grow into who they are meant to become, every single one of the three pillars of friendship changes: proximity, timing, and energy. And that is why adult friendships require flexibility. That's why it's usually not personal when people come in and out of your life.

Let Them.

"I've Let Them. But Now I Have No Friends."

In researching this book, and analyzing the experiences of thousands of people around the world who have been using the theory, one of the most difficult experiences people have is concluding that the people you think are your friends are not your friends at all.

As you say *Let Them*, people will reveal exactly who they are, and they reveal where you stand in their life. You'll find yourself using the Let Them Theory a lot with your friends, and you will start to see many relationships where the effort you've been putting in is one-sided.

You're the one who calls, and when you stop calling, no call comes back. You're the one who always reaches out and makes all the plans, and when you stop making the plans, suddenly no one is reaching out and inviting you. It is painful to see the truth that you're the one putting in the effort. When that happens, and it will, I want you to come back to the three pillars of friendship: proximity, timing, and energy.

When a friendship fades, or someone reveals who they are, one of those three pillars is off. Maybe more. Before you feel sorry for yourself, and start isolating, or getting angry, look at the facts.

Have you or your friend changed or grown in new ways? Have the patterns and schedules of your lives changed? Are you physically bumping into them as much as you used to? Do you feel like the timing of your life is still the same, or are you in different chapters? Has some major change happened in one of your lives that has shifted the energy between you?

Asking yourself these questions is really important, because we tend to default to making ourselves wrong, or blame the other person and then decide the friendship is over.

Before you walk away from a friendship, assume good intent on the other person's part. Sometimes, you're just friends with someone who never makes plans, or is extremely introverted, or who has a lot of heavy or demanding things going on in their life. It's not that they are ghosting you; it's that they are exhausted by the chapter of life they are in. It's not personal that they've become distant. And the fact that you still reach out may be the lifeline that they need.

In doing the research for this book, I noticed a lot of comments from people specifically upset that their friends are not texting them back. I do not want you to use the theory to blow up your friendships because someone is not responding as often as you want them to.

Friendships are not a tit for tat. Do not keep score. Reach out to people because you want to. But don't expect a response. How quickly or how often someone responds is not a sign of how much they care about you. It's more likely an indication of how overwhelmed they may be. Everyone has a ton going on, and 99 percent of the time you have no clue what someone else is dealing with, so with friends especially, don't judge when you don't hear back, assume good intent.

Let Them Not Text Back

I can share personally that these last four years of my life have been the most overwhelming and demanding years ever, and it has had a huge impact on my friendships. After living right outside of Boston for 26 years, we moved to a small, rural town in a different state where I didn't know anyone my age.

At the same time, my company was going through a period of hyper growth, and I have never managed anything in business like this. My number one commitment has been spending time with my family and getting settled into our new community. So, any free time I have, I have poured into family and trying to make new friends in this small town.

I am sure there are many of my old friends who believe that I have ghosted them, or neglected the relationships, or thought that I'm a bad friend. And from their point of view, they are right.

It's not that I don't care. It's that I've been focusing my time and energy on different priorities these past three years, and have not made it a priority to proactively reach out to my old group of friends on a consistent basis. And that's okay.

When somebody "loses touch," it doesn't mean you've lost a friend. I hate the fact that a lot of people think that just because someone is distant, they are now your enemy. *Let Them* be distant. Just because they are not in front of your face doesn't mean you're against them. Make it a habit to just cheer for people and wish them the best.

I have found with some of my friendships that people will "disappear" for a few years and it turns out they were caring for an aging parent, or a child who was struggling, or were consumed by an unhealthy relationship, or a really demanding career. It had nothing to do with you. They are still your friend.

I say this, because I do not want you using the theory to make assumptions and to blow up perfectly amazing relationships because you haven't been flexible and allowed people to come in and out of your life, based on what is going on in your life and in theirs. All it takes is one text or phone call, and oftentimes, you're right back in it.

As I come out of these crazy busy four years, and I am now settled in our new house, and our Boston studios are up and running, and I've spent a lot more time with my aging parents, and we are now empty nesters, a new chapter has begun. And in this one, reprioritizing friendships is at the top of the list.

If you've ever received a call or text from someone you've lost touch with, it's one of the greatest surprises in the world. And there are people in my life that I haven't spoken to in several years, that if I had coffee with them, we would fall right back into a deep and loving connection. And I'm excited to create that for myself. *Let Me.*

The connection you have with another person never actually breaks. It's just the proximity and timing that makes you lose touch with them. So, it's never too late to reconnect with old friends and this is completely in your control.

Let Them will help you be flexible, be compassionate, and allow people to come and go. *Let Me* will remind you to stop sitting around expecting invitations, or assuming ill intent. It will motivate you to take the lead on reaching out to old friends, and put yourself out there to create new ones.

The Let Them Theory will help you find your people, even if you are starting from scratch. When you use it, you will create some of the most amazing friendships of your life. In fact, you'll soon see that you haven't even met some of your favorite people yet. Isn't that exciting, to live your life knowing that there are so many incredible people and connections and experiences, just waiting for you to be the one to go first and say hello?

So let's use the theory to go find them. I just did this at the age of 54 when we moved to a new community. I'm going to tell you the whole story and you and I are going to really focus on the *Let Me* part of friendship.

CHAPTER 13

How to Create the Best Friendships of Your Life

When we moved to our new town, I felt so lonely. I was brand-new to the area. I knew no one my age. And I was miserable.

At some point in your life you are going to experience this exact same thing. Every life change creates changes in your friendships. You'll experience it if you go through a breakup or divorce and people pick sides. You'll experience it if you or a loved one go through a major struggle and people either have no idea how to support you or are uncomfortable, so they distance themselves. You'll experience this when you have to move for your career or education.

And even if you're super excited about the change—you're going to your dream school or moving to your dream city—the reality is that, when you get there, you'll have no friends. The first time you may have experienced this in your life was when you went to college. You get to college and you expect to meet all your best friends right away, and that is not what happens. Everyone is nervous and latches onto the first person they meet and they try to form a group.

Within a week, it feels like everyone is already in a friend group. But, if you think about your college or even high school friend group, by the time you graduated your friend group changed a lot. That's because it takes time to find your people.

Give It A Year

When my daughter went to college, she called me crying all the time, saying, "I'm at the wrong school. My people are not here. I think I need to transfer." And I constantly told her to hang up the phone, go to the cafeteria, and ask to sit with someone who looked interesting. "You have to put yourself out there, and most importantly, you must give it a year."

She hated that advice. She called me all yearlong. She felt so lonely and desperate. And the two friends she had made early on felt the exact same way. (Hi Lexi and Micaela!) To their credit, they all kept putting themselves out there their entire first year.

I know my daughter, Sawyer, was asking to sit with people, DMing people online to get lunch, she joined a million clubs, tried out for the club lacrosse team (got cut), went to events on campus, but nothing clicked. It really took her a full year of trying. And then, in the last few weeks of school, she met one of her now closest friends, Mary Margaret, who then introduced her (and her two friends) to seven other girls who to this day are her people. She really had to give it a year.

And when I moved, somehow I forgot my own advice. I needed to be reminded it would take a year of trying. Within a week of moving, I was convinced that I had made a huge mistake. I felt bad for myself for an entire year. I cried all the time. And I was convinced I would never find a person that I would connect with or relate to. But what was I doing during that first year?

Nothing. Sitting in my house, feeling lonely.

I was not putting myself out there at all. I was not looking for opportunities to connect. I played sad music and felt bad for myself. I cried and complained to my husband. I was closed off. And I made the mistake of expecting friendship to fall out of the sky and land in my lap. It doesn't work like that.

I'm sure you've had an experience like this too. Maybe you moved, or changed jobs, or went through a breakup, or took care of a family member who was struggling, or became an empty nester and felt like you were starting over. In those moments, I'm sure you felt pretty lonely. This is normal.

And even if you have great friends who are far away, you feel alone if you don't have any friends near you. It got so bad for me that I was on a walk one day with my two adult daughters, sobbing about how I had no friends, and how I hated where we lived.

We passed by the house of a woman I had met once six months prior, and I mentioned to my daughters that I had met the woman who lived in the house and she seemed like she could be cool. And my daughters forced me to walk up her driveway, right then, and knock on her door and say hello.

I didn't feel like it. I was really scared to walk up the driveway. I felt like a loser. *Has it really come to this?!*

Yes, it had. When I really think about it, this was the exact same thing I told my daughter Sawyer to do when she called me crying freshman year of college.

It was embarrassing to knock on her door. I could feel my heart racing as I heard the dogs barking and footsteps coming. And when the door swung open, it wasn't the woman I had met; it was her husband.

I asked, "Is Mia here?" And then blurted out, "I met her a while ago, I'm brand-new, I'm really lonely, I thought I would stop and say hello. . ." My daughters chimed in, "Our mom needs friends. She thought your wife was cool, and so we made her come say hello."

He was so gracious, invited us in, gave us a tour of the house. We met the dogs, Mia was thrilled we stopped by, we exchanged numbers, and one week later, she and I were walking that very same loop together. And that was the beginning of turning this part of my life around and learning that adult friendship isn't something that happens. It's something you create.

I am happy to report, from that painful knock on Mia's door, and a hundred other awkward little moments—introducing myself to someone at a coffee shop, pulling into a field at a local flower farm to tell the owners that their flowers were incredible, saying hello to the person next to me at an exercise class—I was able to slowly but surely create my own new little community.

Over the course of the year, I started feeling like I not only knew the familiar faces in my small community, but by getting to know them, I found my people. This is why you need to focus on *Let Me*.

The Habit of "Going First"

Let Me be the first to introduce myself. *Let Me* be the first to say, "I'm new here. How long have you lived here?" *Let Me* be the first to say, "If you ever want to go for a walk, let me know. Here is my number."

Slowly but surely, one awkward conversation at a time, I not only met my people—I found some of my most favorite people I've ever met in my life in this small rural town. And if I can make amazing friends in my 50s, you can make amazing friends too, wherever you live, at whatever age you are.

It's never too late because everyone wants and needs friendship in their life. Even if people already have their "friend group," there is always room for someone you truly click with.

All you have to do is go first.

Be the one to say hi to whoever is around you. It makes all the difference. I didn't do that for a long time. For the year that I sat in my house crying, even when I went out, I was closed off. I would walk into a coffee shop, see the same people, and I knew no one's name. Because I didn't ask. That's why I didn't know anybody. I kept to myself. I didn't talk to anyone.

The second I started "going first," I walked into the same coffee shop that I had most days for an entire year, and as the cashier rang me up, I said, "I'm Mel. What's your name?"

"Kevin."

When he handed me the coffee, I said "Thanks, Kevin."

So when I sat down with my coffee, I immediately opened up my phone and created a new contact file for the coffee shop. In the notes section, I added "Kevin the tall barista with a beard." I did it right away because I was afraid I would forget his name if I waited until I got into the car.

Next I turned to the young couple who I had seen morning after morning at the coffee shop, but never spoken to before. "Hey guys, I see you here a lot; I just moved to the area. I wanted to introduce myself. I'm Mel, what's your name?"

Gregory and Jordan. Couldn't have been nicer. I immediately put their names in my coffee shop contact, under Kevin's name, in the notes section, with a short description: "Cute married couple. Moved from Los Angeles. Baby is adorable." Then I asked them how long they lived in the area. Turns out they had just moved here a year ago too.

Next I asked them what they did. You want to know something crazy? Gregory works in the podcast business. Jordan is a psychologist. What are the odds? And to think I spent a year sitting ten feet away from two people who I had so much in common with. What I was doing in the coffee shop goes way deeper than making small talk. I was starting to create a community for myself.

The warmth you offer others always finds its way back to you. Simply knowing all the names of the familiar faces around you will make you feel more connected to where you live. Plus, the more people you meet, the faster you will find the people you truly connect with.

And there are even more benefits to this. By going first, you create a connection that has a huge impact on your well being and happiness. And it is often overlooked. Researchers say the kinds of people you sit next to at the coffee shop, or stand next to in the elevator in your building, are not strangers—they are "weak ties."

These people are superpowerful and an important part of your life. They can become a foundation you build that lifts you up in your day-to-day routine. Learn their names. Say hello. Pet their dogs. Put descriptions in your contacts so that you can refresh your memory before you walk into the coffee shop tomorrow.

One conversation at a time, I started creating my social scaffolding, this network of people around me that I knew by first name: "Hi Kevin," "Hi Gregory," "Hi Jordan," which made me feel a little less lonely.

It's also how I met one of my now closest friends, David. We were living a mile away from each other for a year, and we never met because we were both sitting alone in our houses feeling sorry for ourselves. We started as a hello in a coffee shop, and now he is one of my most favorite people in the entire world, and he and his husband have become like family.

If I can do it, so can you. The Let Them Theory is going to help you take this on.

Will some people be a little awkward? Yes. *Let Them*. Will most people be warm and receptive? Yes. *Let Them*.

Creating friendship really is about the *Let Me* part. And here are some simple things I did to make myself go first:

1. Compliment people everywhere you go.

If you love their nail color, tell them. If you love their outfit, tell them. If you like their socks, say it! People love to be complimented because they feel seen and appreciated. And it's a foolproof way to break the ice with someone without feeling weird.

2. Be curious.

Ask them what they're reading. Ask them what they ordered. People love to talk about themselves. And even if it doesn't go any further than the other person saying thank you, you get points for being the one who goes first.

3. Smile and say hello to anyone and everyone you pass or meet.

Being a warm and approachable person is a skill. If you practice it, it becomes a way of life. When you move through life with a welcoming spirit, life opens up to you

4. Do this without expectation.

The reason to be warm to strangers is because simply creating connections with other people will improve your life. The warmth you give to others always finds its way back to you.

Trust that the more you do this without expecting someone to invite you out to dinner, or someone to immediately click, the faster the right people find their way to you. You can think about it in terms of energy. You are opening up your energy, knowing that the people that are truly meant to be in your life are going to match it naturally.

Loneliness is real. But you're not stuck there. It's hard to put yourself out there, but it's harder to stay in your house and feel lonely. I'd rather have an awkward moment than continue to feel lonely. And I know you would too.

And finally, give it a year.

Building a network of warm connections that make you feel like you are part of a community is a vital layer of friendship as an adult. It was shocking to me how simply starting to connect with all these people who were all around me made me realize that I was the one who was disconnected from the potential of friendship.

Creating Community Anywhere

I was the one who kept myself from connecting with the community that was right there around me. By isolating and separating myself, I had closed myself off to the community that was waiting for me. Your soulmate or favorite friend could very well be sitting two tables away from you at the coffee shop today.

Don't expect them to find you. Go first and you'll find them. And if you really want to accelerate your ability to meet people that you're going to click with, try these things that my husband and I did:

1. Look for events and group classes that interest you.

It could be anything: CrossFit, yoga, running, walking, cooking, painting, improv, or furniture refinishing. This will put you in proximity with people that have a similar interest in a particular topic. This will make it more likely for you to find people that you have things in common with.

2. When you click with someone, take it out of the class.

You go first, and ask them to grab a cup of coffee or take a walk. The more people you do this with, the more comfortable you will feel inviting someone you have just met to do things and the faster you will find your people.

3. As you meet more people, look for events that are interesting and reach out to the people you've been hanging out with to see if anyone wants to go as a group.

Maybe it's a concert, or a lecture, or a volunteer day. One way I did this was creating a walking group with one woman I met at a hair salon. Then she brought a friend one day. Slowly but surely I started inviting other people I had met. Every Wednesday, we meet at 6:30 A.M. to walk a particular loop in the neighborhood.

Three years later, it's still going strong. The text chain has so many people on it, we can't add any more. And new people keep showing up all the time. This is another example of why it takes an entire year.

But walking is just one example. I have invited groups of people to meet up and listen to jazz at a local inn, to go to a wreath-making class, to go to a drag queen bingo event, and to volunteer to help a local farmer dig up dahlia bulbs.

My husband, Chris, also used this approach. He joined a gym, signed up for a golf league, and took a bunch of paddle tennis clinics. He got involved at the local ski mountain. He became a hospice volunteer. All of these things led him to meet people with similar interests.

Chris then looked for fun things happening in town or nearby and invited a new friend to do it with him. He joined a team to compete in a men's ski race. He started a Tuesday-morning sunrise "climb the mountain and then ski down" group—they meet in a parking lot, the word has spread, and now on any given Tuesday you'll see 15–20 people of all ages, and from surrounding towns, hiking up the mountain together.

What does that tell you?

That slowly but surely you can make more friends—and that every single one of us is looking for opportunities to connect with other people and find new friends.

Instead of sitting around hoping that someone else starts a hiking group, or a walking club, or a book club, you go first.

Using the Let Them Theory, you'll not only make better friend-ships—you'll be a better friend too. This matters. Your relationships create a good life. Good friends make you happier, healthier, and bring your life meaning; and friendships are one of the things you'll cherish most as you go through your life.

The Let Them Theory will help you create the friendships you deserve, which are going to require you to be flexible. Remember, friends are going to come and go in your life. Stop expecting the invi-tation. Stop gripping so tightly when things start to shift. And start taking responsibility for how you show up. *Let Them* will help you be more flexible, not take things personally, and allow the right people to come in, and let the wrong people to leave.

It will also help you navigate this very awkward period where you are making new friends. If you say hello at a coffee shop and they aren't very friendly, *Let Them*. If their calendar is so busy they can't find time to go for a walk, *Let Them*. If they cancel plans this weekend because they've had a long week at work, *Let Them*. If they fall in love, or have a baby, and you are no longer a priority, *Let Them*. If they move away, and start a different chapter, *Let Them*. If they stop returning your calls, *Let Them*. If they are prioritizing other friendships or work, *Let Them*. If the timing, proximity, or energy is off, *Let Them*.

People are going to come and go in your life. And the more flexible you are, the more they do. It's such a beautiful thing to *Let Them*. Focus on *Let Me*, because that is what's in your control.

Let Me be understanding. *Let Me* make an effort. *Let Me* check in without an expectation, but just because I care. *Let Me* make the plans. *Let Me* trust when the energy feels off. *Let Me* call or text if someone crosses my mind. *Let Me* act with the belief that some of my most favorite friends I haven't met yet.

Let Me go first.

So let's summarize how to master adult friendship. You have been approaching adult friendship the same way you did as a kid—you just expected it to happen. The Let Them Theory empowers you to stop expecting friendship to happen and to take responsibility for creating it.

1. **Problem:** The Great Scattering happened and you didn't realize it. You have been approaching friendship the wrong way ever since. You have expected to be included. You have expected to be around your friends all the time. You have expected the text back. That expectation has led to feelings of disconnection, isolation, and uncertainty in approaching new or existing friendships.

2. **Truth:** There are three pillars to adult friendship: proximity, timing, and energy. It's your responsibility to understand these three pillars and adopt a flexible mentality and proactive approach to your friendships. You have so much power in your relationships and some of your most favorite people are just waiting for you to go first.

3. **Solution:** Using the Let Them Theory, start creating connections without any expectations. You go first. Start saying hello to people around you and building that feeling of community wherever you live today. Sign

up for that class. Create the book club. Send the text.
One awkward conversation at a time, you will find your
people. This approach empowers you to create the most
incredible community around you, filled with friendships
that are meaningful, supportive, and aligned with
who you are.

When you say *Let Them*, you release the need to cling to friendships that no longer serve you, making space for connections that truly matter. When you say *Let Me*, you take charge of your social life, reaching out, initiating, and cultivating the kind of friendships that reflect your values and bring you happiness.

It's time to stop waiting and start creating—building the best friendships of your life and surrounding yourself with a community that uplifts and supports you. You have so many laughs, memories to make, and incredible adventures in your future.

It's all there waiting for you to reach out and create it.

All you have to do is go first.

Motivating Other People to Change

CHAPTER 14

People Only Change When They Feel Like It

One of the most common questions that has been asked over the years is: "How do I motivate someone else to change?"

You can't.

The reality is, people only change when they feel like changing. It doesn't matter how much you want someone to change. It doesn't matter how valid your reasons are. Or that you are right in your opinion that they should change. Or how big the consequences are if they don't change. If someone doesn't feel like changing, they won't. And worse, when you pressure someone to change it just creates more tension, resentment, and distance in your relationships. I'll prove it to you.

I want you to think about someone in your life whom you care about and you wish would change. It could be anyone: your mom, your niece, your roommate, your brother, your husband, your ex, your kids, your sister-in-law, your best friend, your partner. Anyone.

You wish they would get a better job, lose weight, be more motivated, wake up earlier, stick to a budget, pick up after themselves, stop dating losers, be more proactive, drink less, help take care of the dog, stop being so negative, change their views on politics, be more appreciative, stop smoking, be more involved with their kids, or stop leaving their dishes in the sink.

You may worry about them. You may not understand why they don't see that this is an issue or why they aren't motivated. You've probably thought, *Why can't they just do this thing I am asking of them?!* I know exactly how you feel.

Here's the truth: When you push someone, it only makes the person push back. You're working against the fundamental law of human nature. People need to feel in control of their decisions. You want people in your life to change, but pressuring them creates resistance to it.

You may be acting with the best of intentions, but it is yielding the worst result. That's because every time you fight against human nature you will lose.

Using the Let Them Theory, you'll learn an entirely new approach to dealing with situations where you want someone else to change their behavior. It's true: You can't make someone else change. But I never said you couldn't influence them.

As I share examples from my life and walk you step-by-step through how to use the Let Them Theory to influence someone else to change, I want you to keep your relationships and the people who are frustrating you in mind.

Wishing Someone Would Change

"I wish you would take better care of yourself."

A good friend of mine is married to (and deeply in love with) a guy who needs to get healthier. Maybe you're in this situation with someone you love too. Over the years, she's tried everything to get her husband to take control of his health.

She's asked, pleaded, hinted, and even occasionally broken down in tears about it in front of him. It worries her... a LOT.

She's gotten angry with him and made passive-aggressive comments. She's signed him up for gym memberships. She's bought him new sneakers. She's cooked the healthy dinners. And she even got them a Peloton to work out on at home.

Nothing's worked. At this point, everything makes her mad. Whether it is his order off the menu, his resistance to working out, his post-dinner desserts, or the hours he spends watching television every night, it doesn't matter what the poor guy does—it frustrates the hell out of her.

Now, to his credit, he's tried. He's started diets, he's gone to the gym in spurts, and he's even taken some Peloton classes—but nothing lasts, and so he and his wife remain in this deadlock with each other about his health.

She's mad he won't change, and he's annoyed that she won't stop nagging him. Sound familiar? It does to me.

And I'm sure it does to you as well, as you think about the person in your life you wish would change for the better.

I know you want the best for them. That's why you want them to change. You love them. That's why you're stressed about this situation.

It's why you want them to get healthier. Get a better job. Study harder. Go to therapy. To move on after a divorce and start dating again. Or just get out of the house and spend more time with their friends.

Wanting someone you love to change for the better, and to be happier and healthier, is normal. It's a good thing to want someone to live a good life. It's a beautiful thing to see a bigger possibility for someone you love. It's an important thing to believe in someone's ability to improve their life, reach their potential, and achieve their goals.

The issue isn't wanting this for someone else. The issue is how you've been approaching this topic and how it's impacting the dynamic between you and the person you care about.

Or maybe as you're reading this, you're realizing that someone has been pressuring YOU to change. They don't even need to say something to you about your job, or your habits, or who you are dating, because their behavior makes it very clear that they don't accept you as you are right now.

They want you to be living your life in a different way. It's annoying. I know it is. And your natural inclination is to push back.

The Let Them Theory has challenged me to think a lot about this knee-jerk reaction to pressure people (and their innate reaction to resist), and why it's hard for anyone to change.

Why Is Change So Hard?

I mean, when you want someone else to change, don't you just kind of assume that it would be easy for them to... just do it?

I've definitely been there. All you have to do is just point out the obvious, right? Just tell the person how much better they will feel if they work out. Or constantly remind them of their ability to get a better job and how a better salary is going to solve all their current financial issues. Or the fact that they aren't going to meet someone amazing sitting on the couch all weekend playing video games.

I mean, clearly they've never considered these options for themselves. Right?

Now, flip that around. How many times has someone pointed out the obvious to you? As if you didn't already know that exercising would help you lose weight. Or crying alone in your bedroom won't win your ex back. Or that applying to nursing school is a requirement to actually get into nursing school.

It's almost offensive when someone else does this to you. You feel attacked. And it's also annoying when somebody sits on their high horse and acts like it would be easy to just snap your fingers and suddenly change or find a higher paying job. How dare they think they know what's best for you!

The fact is, change is hard for everyone, including you. No one wants to feel pressure from you, because they are already feeling it from themselves.

Just take my friend and her husband. Of course he wants to get in shape! He wants to lose weight. It's not easy to carry around an extra 50 pounds. He hates the fact that he's the biggest one in his friend group. It's not good for his heart. He knows this. He's not an idiot. And he also knows how hard it's going to be, and how much work it's going to take.

Waking up early, cutting down on the alcohol, feeling embarrassed at the gym, starting a new diet is going to be painful. It just is. Just like it's hard for a smoker to quit smoking. It's hard for someone who overspends to learn to stick to a budget. It's hard to be single, which is why people stay with someone longer than they should. It's hard to believe in yourself and land a great job if you've been fired.

Change is never a cakewalk. If it were fun and easy, the person you love would already be doing it.

The most loving thing you can do is to stop pressuring them and *Let Them* be. Right now, you have a completely unrealistic expectation and an approach that is backfiring. You have no other choice but to *Let Them*. Let adults be adults.

The Let Them Theory will force you to take a step back into reality, and approach your relationships with more compassion and humility and in a much more effective way. First, you need to understand the science of motivation and change so your approach is more effective.

Truth #1: Adults only change when they feel like it.

Stop trying to motivate people. It doesn't work. Based on the research, the motivation to change must come from within the other person.

Now, people love the word *motivation*—and maybe you do too. My friend complains about the fact that her spouse isn't "motivated" to take better care of himself. And maybe you feel a little frustrated that the person you want to change isn't motivated either.

However, it's just not that simple. Let's start with the definition of *motivation*: It means "you feel like doing something." And, as you're learning, adults only do what they feel like doing.

Your spouse doesn't *feel like* exercising. That's why they are not motivated! They don't want to do it. You can't motivate them, because the "feeling" of wanting to do it has to come from within them.

The problem with motivation is it's never there when you need it. If motivation were automatic, everyone would have six-pack abs, a million dollars in the bank, and the world's best side hustle. Plus, if you could magically make people "feel like doing" whatever you want them to do, you'd be practicing mind control. . . not motivation.

And look, even I mess this up.

For example, I spent years trying to "motivate" people to change the same way I got myself to change: by pushing them. I pushed my best friend to start dating again, I gifted my brother a personal trainer, I tried to force my mom to go to therapy. Giant. Fail.

Of course it failed because pushing someone just makes them push back.

Truth #2: Human beings are wired to move toward what feels good.

Another reason why pressure doesn't work? Humans are wired to move toward what feels good right now, and to move away from what feels hard in the moment.

This is neuroscience. In researching this book, I spoke to Harvard-trained psychiatrist Dr. Alok Kanojia, MD—also known as "Dr. K" to the millions of people who follow him online at the Healthy Gamer.

Dr. K is one of the leading voices on motivation and behavior change. He told me, point blank, that pressuring other people backfires because "you don't understand the way people are wired."

What you need to know, according to Dr. K, is simply that a human being will always feel like choosing what is pleasurable now, and avoiding what feels painful. In the moment, the work it takes to change is painful and hard. That's why no one is motivated to change—even when they know it's good for them in the long run.

My friend's husband knows it's going to take endless trips to the gym (and a whole other assortment of lifestyle changes) to improve his health. But the couch he's sitting on? It's comfy right NOW. The bag of chips he's eating? It's delicious right NOW. The game he's watching? It's entertaining him right NOW.

While he knows that the treadmill and the bench press will *eventually* create a good result, the gratification isn't there right NOW. In fact, the immediate thing he will feel when he pushes himself off the couch and hops on the treadmill is... pain.

The treadmill and the bench press are going to be tiring. They're going to make him sore. They're going to require a lot of work... and what if he can't stick to it? What if it's not worth it? What if the weight doesn't come off? What if he can't do it? Isn't it just a better and easier idea to finish the bag of chips and try again tomorrow?

Of course it is. And that is why he isn't motivated to change! He doesn't do it, because he doesn't feel like it.

Dr. K told me that when we pressure other people to change, "We are spending our whole lives swimming upstream. Instead of understanding our motivational circuitry, we are trying to conquer it. Instead of utilizing it, we're trying to fight against it and overcome it."

When you pressure someone, you're fighting against the wiring of the human brain. People are wired toward what feels pleasurable now. Dr. K says that in order to make a change, a person must be able to separate themselves from the pain they will feel in the moment and the action that they need to take.

That means while he is sitting on the couch, he is going to have to say to himself, "This is going to suck to exercise, but I'm going to do it anyway."

He has to do it. He has to separate himself from the pain. He has to decide to override his feelings and push himself to do it. You can't do that for someone else. So *Let Them* sit on the couch.

And that's not all. There are even more psychological reasons why pressuring is backfiring.

Truth #3: Every single person on the planet thinks they're the exception.

I also talked to Dr. Tali Sharot while researching this book. Dr. Sharot is a behavioral neuroscientist and the director of the Affective Brain Lab at University College London and MIT. Her research integrates neuroscience, behavioral economics, and psychology to study how emotion and behavior influence people's beliefs and decisions.

And one of her findings is groundbreaking: that people believe that warning labels, threats, and known risks do not apply to them.

That's why my friend's husband thinks he's the only person on the planet who can be overweight and sedentary and never have a heart attack. It's why he can convince himself that he can stay exactly the same, and nothing bad will happen.

That's why your friend thinks she's the only person on the planet who can vape several times a day and never see repercussions on her lungs. That's why you think "quietly quitting" your job by coming in late, leaving early, and phoning it in on effort will go completely unnoticed. That's why your significant other doesn't believe you when you say, "If this doesn't change, I am leaving."

Everyone thinks they are the exception to bad outcomes happening to them. Which explains why your tears, pleading, and ultimatums will also backfire.

Our brains quite literally tune out the worst case scenarios—which is why the contempt-filled sighs aren't doing anything.

They think they are the exception. (And by the way, so do you, when it comes to changes you are resisting in your own life.) By being passive-aggressive, constantly bringing it up, or using threats as a way of trying to pressure someone else to change, it will always backfire.

And, get this: Dr. Sharot explained that brain scans show that when someone is telling you something negative ("I'll leave if you don't stop drinking") or something you don't want to hear ("That dude you're dating is a narcissist"), your brain literally tunes it out.

You can see on scans that the part of the brain that is listening to negative information turns off! So what does that mean?

It means that all those threats, worst-case scenarios, passive-aggressive comments, eye rolls, and scare tactics aren't even registering in the other person's brain. You are wasting your time, your words, and your breath. No wonder you are so frustrated and stressed out by the situation!

That's why you need a different approach, and the Let Them Theory will help you put this science to work so you use your time and energy in a much more effective and compassionate manner.

And if you do it right, it may just inspire the person you love to want to change for themselves.

Let's go back to the example of my friend and her husband. I want you to picture yourself in their situation.

Say you walk in the house after a long day at work, and your spouse is there happily lying on the couch watching his basketball game and shoving chips into his mouth.

He's fine sitting there. In fact, he's really happy to be sitting there. He says, "Hey honey!" with a massive smile across his face.

You, though. . . you take one look at him, the stress hits, and the amygdala turns on. You're immediately annoyed. The anger starts to bubble up inside of you. You can't help yourself from audibly sighing, "Oh, hi."

You're not thinking about anything you just learned about the human brain or the science of motivation or any of the things we've talked about so far. You're just thinking about how easy it would be for him to get up and do something other than sit on his lazy ass.

Since you're coming from a place of judgment, not acceptance, you're not thinking about all those little moves he needs to make to go to the gym, and how painful it's going to be.

You're not thinking about him walking into the bedroom, changing into workout clothes, filling up a water bottle, finding his keys, driving to the gym, walking all the way inside the gym, finding a machine, and then actually having to do the work.

Instead, you jump over the reality, the science, and the truth about how hard change is for everyone—and you jump right into anger over the fact that they aren't doing what you want them to do right when you want them to do it.

In reality, what that situation requires is compassion, not contempt... and your audible sigh of disgust and bad mood isn't going to launch them off the couch. In fact, those sighs of contempt are going to keep your spouse lying on the couch until they've lost the remote in the cushions.

No matter how loving your intentions are behind the audible sighs, your spouse is feeling like you're trying to fix him—which feels more like pain, which means he's now going to move away from you. It makes him feel defensive, and that's just going to close him off from feeling like changing even more.

Enter: The Standoff

Pressure doesn't create change—it creates resistance to it. When you try to exert control over someone else's behavior, they instinctively resist your attempt to try to control them.

Instead of inspiring change, your pressure creates a battle over control.

When I spoke to Dr. Sharot, she reiterated that human beings have a hardwired need to be in control. It's a survival instinct. Feeling like you're in control of your life is what makes you feel safe. Feeling in control is what makes everyone else in your life feel safe too.

That means your spouse, your roommate, your mom, your boss, and your friends all have that same hardwired survival instinct to be in control, just like you do.

The people that you love only feel safe when they feel in control of their own life.

So when you start to push people around, pressure them, or tell them what to do, you are threatening their hardwired need for control over their own lives, decisions, and actions. You're getting in the way of their *agency,* the feeling that they are in control of themselves, their life, and their own thoughts and behaviors.

By hinting to someone that "it's a nice day for a run outside" when someone doesn't feel like going for a run, you just threatened them. Your suggestion—no matter how helpful you may mean for it to be— feels like you're trying to take away their right to be their own person who does what they want, when they want.

This is why you must let adults be adults. *Let Them.*

Acceptance of another person, as they are, is the foundation of a healthy and loving relationship. When someone feels that you accept them as they are, they feel safe with you.

The opposite happens when you pressure, change, criticize, push, or expect someone to behave differently than they are. This pressure puts you and your loved one in a battle for control, whether or not you realize it.

Remember Dr. K's research about how the brain is wired to move toward pleasure and away from pain? Feeling your pressure is painful, which is why they are moving away from you. Which only makes you push harder, and that makes them resist more.

This will be a never-ending standoff between the two of you. You have the power to end it.

Let Them sit on the couch, because if you want to end the standoff, you have to.

If you think about my friend and her husband, who has the control? The husband. As long as he ignores his wife, he's in control of his life, his decisions, and his behavior.

The second he does what she says, he loses his sense of agency and she "wins." At this point, the argument is not about exercising anymore, but who holds the power.

It also explains why she can't let it go. His health worries the hell out of her and makes her feel like she's lost control of an important part of her life... So she keeps trying to control him, to make herself feel more in control of this part of her life.

That just makes him feel threatened, and push back for the sake of his own survival. And, the more stubborn he becomes, the harder she pushes.

Can you see how this dynamic creates a gridlock that just keeps escalating?

And maybe you can see this same gridlock between you and one of your kids, or an aging parent, or you and your partner. Or maybe you feel this gridlock because somebody else is pressuring you.

Here's the truth: No one wants to feel pressured by their friends, family, or loved ones. What you want is unconditional love, acceptance, kindness, and compassion. You don't want to be controlled; you want to feel deeply accepted for who you are, and where you are in your life.

That's what allows you to truly be yourself and feel safe in your relationships.

You certainly don't want your best friend telling you she doesn't like your boyfriend, or your partner knocking you over the head with a gym membership, Peloton, and organic groceries.

That brings me to another truth.

Most of the time, the person probably does want to change, deep down. Dr. K talked a lot about this internal tension that people feel when they know their behavior isn't good for them in the long run.

That's exactly what my friend's husband feels. That's why he stops and starts. That's why he keeps trying. That's why he's struggling.

Change is hard for everyone. And it's even harder when you have someone breathing down your neck, and you not only have to deal with their pressure, but you'll also have to admit that they were right when you finally end up doing the work.

Dr. K couldn't emphasize enough that it needs to be THEIR idea to change, not yours. The husband needs to have a reason to push himself to do the hard work—other than just shutting his wife up. Otherwise, this change will never last, and the resentment between them will just grow.

People Do What They Feel Like Doing

People only change when they are ready to make that change for themselves. Stop punishing them for not changing on your timeline. Stop trying to "motivate" them into doing something they clearly don't want to do.

It is a waste of your time. It is stressing you out. It is ruining your relationship. It is not working. And most importantly, it is driving a wedge between the two of you.

Loving people means that you have to meet them where they are. You must learn how to let adults be adults. This is why the Let Them Theory is so effective.

When you *Let Them* be, you're accepting them for who they are right now. *Let Them* be on their own timeline. *Let Them* fail at their career. *Let Them* vape. *Let Them* give up. *Let Them* stay in that miserable relationship. *Let Them* make promises they don't keep. *Let Them* be messy. *Let Them* wear the sweatpants to the dinner party. *Let Them* play video games all weekend. *Let Them* feel the consequences of their inaction. *Let Them* sit on the couch and never go to the gym. *Let Them* live their life.

It's simple, but I didn't say it was easy. I know that you may read this, thinking, *Oh. So there's nothing I can do?* There's always something you can do.

Because there's always something within your control: it's YOU. The only behavior change that you can control is your own. And this is where your power is.

The first change in your behavior is to stop pressuring and start accepting. *Let Them* be. When you accept them as they are, the frustrating and ineffective battle for control ends and you set yourself up to win the war for positive change.

It's science.

But I'm sure you're wondering. . . if pressure doesn't work, what does? I said you couldn't change their behavior. . . but I never said you couldn't influence it. And this is where *Let Me* comes in and helps you unlock the power of your influence.

Decades of research from neuroscientists and psychologists say that you can't motivate someone to change, but you can "inspire" them to change and even make them believe it was all their idea to do so.

I'll show you in the next chapter how you can tap into someone's innate desire to change by choosing NOT to pressure them: *Let Them*. And instead, use your influence by saying and doing the right thing at the right time, based on the research.

CHAPTER 15

Unlock the Power of Your Influence

When you stop trying to pressure people to change and *Let Them* be, something magical happens. You now have time and energy to unlock the power of your positive influence.

People are social creatures that are highly influenced and inspired by the people around them. This has been proven over and over by decades of research on human behavior. This is why when you see someone online gushing about a protein powder, or a new style of jeans, or a pro golfer holding up a club that "improved their golf game," you suddenly feel yourself wanting to buy it.

If you see something working positively for someone else, it often makes you feel interested in it too. Whether you realize it's happening or not, when someone else is either having a lot of fun, or getting the results you want, or making something look easy and pleasurable, you are hardwired to move toward it. It's why when you hear a friend raving about a book, you naturally want to read it.

If someone starts eating a crisp, red apple on the train, research shows people around them start craving one too. If a co-worker starts taking a walk outside at lunch—you're more likely to suddenly feel like going for a walk at lunch too.

The reason why influence works is backed by decades of research on human behavior. We are social creatures and are highly influenced and inspired by the people around us. Dr. Sharot calls it "social contagion," which is a fancy way to say that people's behavior is contagious.

Using this with people in your life is very simple: Model the behavior change you want to see and walk the talk you've been asking for. If you have ANY shot at influencing them to move toward the behavior or change you want them to make, you need to show them how easy it is. You can't ask someone else to eat healthier while you're raving about the croissant you just ate. But you can influence them if you're always eating healthy meals yourself and raving about how good it tastes.

You can't ask someone to stop looking at their phone when you've got your phone in your hand. But you can influence them by keeping your phone in a different room and modeling better boundaries with your devices.

Model the behavior you want to see. What I love about this research is that it's a sneaky way to get someone else to change and believe it was *their* idea.

Let's just take the example of the co-worker who goes on a walk every day. If you see someone else do that every day for a few weeks, it starts to influence you subconsciously. You watch them leave every day at lunch, you watch them come back after their walk, and they are in a better mood, and have more energy, and they are smiling. And then you see it happen again the next day when, as they walk out the door, you're sitting at your desk, shoving a sandwich in your mouth, working through your lunch break.

A half an hour later, they walk back in, looking refreshed, energized, and happy. Their example influences you even though you're not consciously thinking about it. And guess what happens if you see this over and over, and they seem to enjoy it? All of a sudden one day, you look outside, you see it's a beautiful day, and you suddenly feel like going for a walk during your lunch break, instead of working through lunch like you usually do.

Here's what I love about the power of influence: As you head out the door for your walk, you think this was your idea. Nope. It was the influence of your co-worker working its magic on your brain. And they weren't even trying to do so! They were just going for a walk and enjoying it. Makes sense, doesn't it?

That's the power of your influence, and you can use this research to inspire anyone in your life to change. Here's how:

First, *Let Them* be.

Stop pressuring them to change. Accept that you can't control their behavior or actions. Adults only do what they feel like doing. Your job is to accept them for who they are and where they are.

Let Them be. Then, *Let Me*.

Use Your Influence

Remember, the power is in your influence. That means focus on what you can control: your behavior. Model change and make it look fun and easy.

Dr. Sharot's research shows that your influence is highly effective, but it requires a lot of patience because it will take time for your positive influence to take effect in someone else's brain.

So you're going to need to say *Let Them* a lot as you just focus on your own behavior and your attitude about it. It's important to do this without the expectation that they will change. The reason why you have to give up your expectations is that if you do this expecting them to change, you'll start to resent them when they don't.

Focus on yourself, model the behavior and the positive attitude because it works for you, and hold out the hope that the magic of your influence will work on them. Be prepared to give it six months or more. I know what you're thinking.

Six months?!

Yes. Six months. It could absolutely take six months or more of you going to the gym, making it look easy, and seeing incredible results with your influence to make the person in your life suddenly feel motivated to exercise for themselves. If you don't want to wait that long, or if you're already in a very frustrating standoff with someone that you care about, it's time for advanced techniques in the science of influence.

The ABC Loop

The ABC Loop is a tool that I've created, based on combining the best of what experts say will work, and I've put it into a simple formula that you can follow with anyone in your life.

In the ABC Loop, you have three steps:

A: APOLOGIZE, then ASK open-ended questions.

B: BACK OFF, and observe their BEHAVIOR.

C: CELEBRATE progress while you continue to model the CHANGE.

Let's take each of these three steps, one by one, and show you exactly what to do and explain with science and the Let Them Theory why this works.

1. The Ground Rules: Using the ABC Loop

If you want to use advanced techniques, you've got to be willing to do a little preparation.

The ABC Loop begins with a conversation that follows a proven, scientific technique. This conversation is very different from any of the conversations you have had about this issue in the past. You're going to follow a research-backed method that is used by medical professionals in clinical settings. To ensure that this conversation is successful, you need to take it seriously, and do the prep work before you have it.

If the issue has been around for a while, you probably have a lot of pent-up frustration and emotion about it. That's part of the problem, and it's why you're at a standoff. This preparation, and setting up the conversation correctly, will defuse your emotion and help you be way more effective.

The conversation needs to be in person, without any alcohol involved or time pressure to finish quickly. Do not have the conversation in a random place, or when you only have 20 minutes on the phone. It doesn't work like that. It's really about connecting at a deeper level with someone you care about on an issue that is bothering you.

This is also a time to show up and practice compassion and curiosity. It's not an invitation for you to vent or complain about how frustrated and worried you are. The point is not to be "right." The whole point is to communicate in a manner that neutralizes any tension and creates the space for positive change to happen.

The best way to do this is to come prepared to listen to the other person wholeheartedly without interrupting them.

If you follow the formula, you've got nothing to worry about, because you are coming from a place of love (and science). You got this.

2. The Prep Work: Using the "5 Whys" Method

Before you have the conversation, you need to get very clear about what exactly is making you so annoyed and why you want them to change. This is important because, before you can be honest with somebody else, you have to be brutally honest with YOURSELF.

Here's how you can get to the truth with yourself. Grab a blank piece of paper, crack open a journal, or get out your Notes app.

The idea here is to rise above your emotions and get to the truth of why this bothers you so much, using a proven technique called the 5 Whys method. The 5 Whys method was created by Sakichi Toyoda, an inventor and founder of the Toyota family companies, as a way to help engineers uncover the root cause of a particular problem, and it's now taught in business schools and engineering programs around the world.

The 5 Whys method is a formula that I've used in my life, business, and marriage to help me get unstuck and gain profound insights whenever I've faced a problem I can't seem to solve.

In this method, you'll ask "why?" five total times until you feel like you've gotten to a much deeper answer as to why this bothers you so much.

Here's how you use the 5 Whys method:

Ask yourself: *Why does this person's behavior (or this situation) bother me so much?* Think about it, and write or say your answer.

And then, ask it again:

Why does that bother you?

And then again: *Why does that bother you?* And then again: *Why does that bother you?* And then a final time: *Why does that bother you?*

Here's an example of how that could look with my friend who is upset about her husband's health. Let's ask her:

Why does this behavior/situation bother you? *It bothers me because he doesn't seem to care about his health.*

Why does that bother you? *He is modeling unhealthy habits for our kids.*

Why does that bother you? *It's like he's ignoring everything important for an extra beer, 15 minutes longer at the TV, and an ice cream... and it's making him unattractive.*

Why does that bother you? *He's the love of my life and I think he's being selfish. I don't want him to have a heart attack when he could just get off the couch and exercise.*

Why does that bother you? *I'm terrified that I'll lose him before I have to.*

See how that works? It's pretty obvious, 5 Whys later, that this issue is probably a lot deeper than her being mad at him. That's exactly why it stresses her out so much. And here's what else you need to know: Your answers will be deeply personal to you.

Give yourself permission to get to the root cause even if you discover something ugly about yourself. Having done this exercise with thousands of people, one theme that comes up a lot that is very hard to see in yourself is judgment of the other person, and how their behavior reflects badly on you (or so you think).

For example, you might answer the 5 Whys and conclude that the real reason you're upset about someone's drinking is because you're embarrassed to have a son with a drinking problem. Or you're ashamed to be married to someone who is not successful.

And whatever you learn by using the 5 Whys method is personal to you, and you do not have to share what you learn with the person. You can if you think it will help you apologize for pressuring them, but this is about you getting to the root cause of your frustration, and it will always have to do with their behavior making you feel a loss of control.

Allow yourself to be honest. When you see that it's been about YOU all along, and your need to control, it is easier to drop the pressure and *Let Them* be. And that puts you into a grounded place as you go into your conversation using the ABC Loop.

Which begins with:

THE ABC LOOP

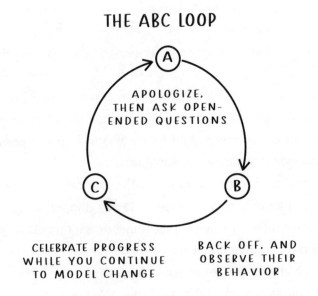

(A) APOLOGIZE, THEN ASK OPEN-ENDED QUESTIONS

(B) BACK OFF, AND OBSERVE THEIR BEHAVIOR

(C) CELEBRATE PROGRESS WHILE YOU CONTINUE TO MODEL CHANGE

Step A: APOLOGIZE, then ASK open-ended questions.

This first step utilizes an evidence-based technique to elicit change called *motivational interviewing*, which I learned about from Dr. K.

Dr. K says that this is one of the only ways that is effective in helping you influence someone else's motivation to change, and it's the technique that he uses with his patients, who are struggling to find the motivation to change.

My favorite part of this technique is that it focuses on asking open-ended questions. The thought behind this technique is that getting the person to talk about how THEY feel will encourage them to think about the disconnect between what they want and their current behavior.

This is the opposite of pressure. Instead of thinking you know what someone should do, you're asking open-ended questions because you're curious about where someone stands with their behavior.

The best way to start this conversation is to first apologize. You could say something like: "I want to apologize for judging and pressuring you, and I realized I've never asked you how you feel about your..."

Health.

Grades.

Job search.

Being single.

Living situation.

Marriage.

Drinking.

Finances.

Starting with an apology sets the tone for a compassionate and supportive conversation. Really listen, lean in, and try to learn about how this person feels about the issue.

Whatever they say, just keep asking them open-ended questions that reflect back the answers they just gave you.

For my friend, it could be something like: "How are you feeling about your health right now?"

According to Dr. K, the question invites someone to really experience the tension between how they truly feel about where they are, and the fact that they are not doing anything about it.

"Each action that you take in life is individual," he says. "And in motivational interviewing, we help people understand this principle. What we want to do is encourage people to think about their own situation."

Then, no matter what their answer to the first question is, you're not going to share your feelings about it. You're just going to repeat back their answer: "So it sounds like. . ."

So it sounds like you're feeling okay about your health?

If they answer in a one-word response—"Okay"—no problem. Just turn it into another open-ended question.

What makes you feel okay about it?

And then continue to just listen with curiosity and acceptance, and respond only with open-ended questions that repeat back what they just said.

It sounds like you're okay with your health because you've been this way for a long time.

Here are some follow-up questions that Dr. K recommended for just about any topic:

How do you feel about that?

So it sounds like you've gotten used to it.

I mean, you're saying you're comfortable. It almost feels a little bit more to me like resignation. Do you feel like it's going to take too much work to change?

What feels hard about it?

It must be incredibly frustrating to have me nagging you all the time, expecting more of you.

Can you tell me a little bit about how long you've felt that way?

So I hear you saying that you don't need me to do anything?

And I need to remind you again: You are just asking questions. Your opinions are irrelevant and they are not for this conversation.

The second you offer one, you'll be pressuring the person and it will kill the effectiveness of this technique.

This technique has been proven in research and clinical settings to be very effective in getting people to admit to themselves that there is a big disconnect between what they actually want and what their current behavior is.

And that is your goal: to make them feel the tension between these things.

I have to emphasize: Do not get discouraged if all you get is one word answers, or they keep trying to change the subject. The point of this technique is not to get them to tell you the truth. It's to create discomfort that they feel internally. They may not express it to you.

That tension is critical, because it ultimately becomes the source of their motivation to change. Seeing the disconnect between what they want and their current actions is what pushes them to eventually change for themselves.

That's why you can't insert yourself. You are just a vehicle for getting them to experience the disconnect, and you are doing it in a way that is loving, compassionate, and curious. You just want to know how they feel about this topic.

This conversation is a critical component for awakening their motivation to change. So *Let Them* talk. And *Let Me* listen.

Step B: BACK OFF, and observe their BEHAVIOR.

Now that you've *apologized* for your behavior and *asked* them the open-ended questions, you have to *back off* and stop pressuring them.

Don't expect them to launch into action. They are going to need to marinate on it. This is also why it's critical to model the change, and make it look easy and fun, while you give them the freedom to figure out for themselves why this issue matters to them.

Think of the example of the co-worker going for a walk. It might take watching someone do that for months before you feel inspired to go on a walk for yourself. And if you really think about it, every time you see your co-worker go on a walk while you work through lunch, you feel tension in your body as you sit there inside working through your lunch break. Eventually that tension transforms into the motivation that gets you out the door.

That's why you have to give this time. It takes time for tension to transform into motivation. *Let Them* be.

All you can do after you've asked the open-ended questions is observe the behavior and stop yourself from trying to change it. If you are seeing them change, amazing. If not, *Let Them* be.

This takes time, particularly with somebody that you love. So back off. They need enough space, time, and distance from the conversation with you to feel like they're not going to get an "I told you so." Space allows them to come to the idea for themselves. Time allows the tension to transform into motivation.

Step C: CELEBRATE progress while you continue to model CHANGE.

Once you've asked the open-ended questions and you've backed off while continuing to model the behavior change, you have to celebrate any progress you see. Whenever they make the smallest move forward, celebrate it.

Dr. Sharot's research says that immediate positive compliments are a key driver to influencing behavior change. For example, if your spouse one day heads down to the basement and hops on the Peloton, that's amazing. When they come back upstairs, give them a hug. Tell them you're proud of them.

Dr. Sharot says that one of the most effective things you can do is tell them how attractive they look, or give them a kiss on the cheek, as soon as they are done working out or doing what you want them to do.

It sounds cheesy, but it actually works.

It's Simple. People Want to Feel Good.

According to the research, immediate positive rewards after someone does something hard will boost their intrinsic motivation or desire to do it again. When you acknowledge their effort, it acts like fuel to keep them going.

The hard thing gets fused with something really pleasurable: the reward that you are providing. And remember what Dr. K taught you about the human brain: We are wired to move toward what feels pleasurable, easy, and fun.

The more my friend compliments, hugs, and admires her husband post-workout, the faster her husband will connect working out with compliments, desire, and the fact that his wife thinks he looks damn good. Her positive attention becomes the pleasure he moves toward, and what has been missing this entire time.

This isn't just common sense. It's neuroscience. You learned that humans are wired to move toward immediate positive benefits. The good things. The celebrations. So often, we approach change with negative reinforcements, threats, pressure, and fear, when the real success lies in being accepting, compassionate, and showing your support in a genuine and effective way.

It makes sense, doesn't it? *Of course it does.*

Adults only do what they feel like doing. Your power is in your positive influence. *Let Them* be. And *Let Me* use the science to inspire change. *Let Them* helps you rise above the emotions and broken dynamics to strengthen your connection, while *Let Me* influences positive behavior change in the people you love.

They may change immediately. They may change in a week. They may change in several months. It may take years. Maybe they might never change.

And that's okay too.

Later in the book, we'll discuss what happens when you've tried the ABC Loop, you've backed off for six months, and there's still no positive change. When this happens, you'll need to decide if this is a deal breaker or not. It's not fair to stay in a relationship where you are chronically complaining about someone else. You hold the power, always, to make something better or to learn how to accept things as they are.

The most important change in any relationship is the one that you can control: yours. You change how you showed up. You stop pressuring the person that you love and become more loving.

That's what makes you influential.

And in the process, if you do it right, you don't just reduce the friction between you and the person that you love. You also make the relationship much better along the way.

But what about when the stakes are really high, and it's not just a matter of someone getting in better shape, or being a little more motivated at work, or being more proactive and helpful around the house?

What if the person you love is spiraling? Do you just *Let Them* keep drinking? Do you just *Let Them* lie in bed with depression? Do you just *Let Them* fall apart?

I saw these questions over and over again while researching this book. In the next chapter, you'll learn an entirely new approach to supporting someone who is struggling, using the Let Them Theory and the latest expert research.

But first, let's summarize how to motivate other people to change. Yes, you want people in your life to change, but pressuring them only creates resistance to it.

The Let Them Theory encourages you to accept others, focus on your own growth, and inspire change through positive influence instead of pressure.

1. **Problem:** Pressure doesn't create change; it creates resistance to it. You are acting with the best of intentions, but it is yielding the worst result. Every time you pressure someone, it pushes them away. You are not only straining your relationships, you are fighting against the wiring inside someone's brain and body. You think the tension and frustration are due to the fact that the other person won't do as you wish. You are wrong. The tension and disconnection are being created by your pressure.

2. **Truth:** Adults only change when they feel like changing. Human beings have a hardwired survival instinct to be in control of every aspect of their life. Anytime someone feels like they are being forced to do something, they will fight back—and you will find yourself locked in a battle for control. What human beings want is to feel acceptance and love. They need to be in control of their own thoughts, actions, and decisions. Your power is in your influence.

3. **Solution:** Using the Let Them Theory, you will leverage the laws of influence to unlock someone else's intrinsic motivation to change for themselves. By using the ABC Loop to ask open-ended questions, model behavior change, and celebrate progress, you use your power to change other people. The key piece of this is creating the space for someone else to believe the change is their idea. Not yours.

When you say *Let Them*, you are accepting other people as they are, removing tension and pressure, and letting them have control over the way they live their life. When you say *Let Me*, you use neuroscience to your advantage and unlock your power of influence to motivate someone else to change.

Let adults be adults, and let your influence inspire them to change.

Helping Someone
Who Is Struggling

CHAPTER 16

The More You Rescue, The More They Sink

I know what you may be thinking: Let adults be adults? But what if the person I'm trying to change is in serious trouble? What am I supposed to do, just let them spiral? Let them drink and drive?

Of course not.

If someone is doing something dangerous or self-destructive, you don't just *Let Them*. You step in, take the keys, or do whatever is necessary to help because your response might just save their life—whether that's calling for help, or calling the police, or driving them to detox, or staying with them through a crisis until they are in a safe place.

The problem is that most people who are struggling hide it from you. They are not doing drugs in front of you; they are lying to you about it. They're putting on a brave face at work but secretly struggling with depression.

Part of the challenge with people who are struggling is not knowing the extent to which they have been, until it's really serious or it's too late. And, I guarantee you, there is at least one person in your life who is struggling immensely and you have no idea.

When people are struggling, they have a lot of shame and are often in denial about it. They already feel like a burden and often tell

225

themselves they are letting everyone down. Which is why people often don't ask for help or open up about what is going on.

Watching someone you love struggle with their mental health, crippling grief, or an addiction is one of the hardest experiences you will face in life. And an even harder truth is: Not everyone is ready to get better, be sober, do the work, use their tools, or face their issues. And not everybody can.

As much as you may love someone and believe in them and would do anything in the world to make their pain go away, you cannot want someone else's sobriety, healing, or health more than they do.

In this section of the book, we will unpack how, in your attempt to help, you may unknowingly be preventing other adults from finding their strength to face their struggles. The more you try to rescue someone from their problems, the more likely they will continue to drown in them. Allowing someone to face the natural consequences of their actions is a necessary part of healing. The fact is, adults only get better when they are ready to do the work, and you will be ready way before they are. It sounds harsh, but it's true.

You and I are going to take everything you've learned so far about relationships, friendships, and human nature, and build on it to show you how those truths apply even in the most difficult situations.

You will also learn a brand-new approach to supporting someone through their struggles, which is grounded in the belief that someone can do the work to get better.

But before we jump in, one BIG disclaimer: There is a difference between supporting an adult who is struggling and supporting a child who is struggling. When you are dealing with a child, you are responsible for their emotional, financial, and physical support.

When you are dealing with an adult, you are not.

The Hard Truth About Healing

As you learned, pressuring someone to change creates resistance to changing, and your frustration and judgment are only going to make the situation with someone struggling worse. The higher the stakes, the more shame and paralysis the other person feels.

People only heal when they are ready. And if they haven't, it's because they aren't ready. When someone you love is going through an internal struggle, they will not get better for you, their kids, or their family. They have to want to get better for themselves.

You may not understand it. You may think you would act differently if you were in the same situation. None of that matters. All of your opinions are judgment. And your judgment of the other person and what you think they should do is part of the problem, because it translates to pressure.

You need an outlet for your judgment—a therapist, a friend—because it won't help to aim it at the other person. In times of struggle, what the other person needs is acceptance. *Let Them* struggle.

People only heal when they are ready to do it for themselves. These are deeply personal, difficult battles. . . and they can only be fought by that person when they're ready to fight. You cannot make them fight. You cannot make them get sober. You cannot make someone financially responsible. You cannot make them heal.

Yes, they need your love and support. But here's the hard part: They do not need to be "rescued." I will say this again: The more you try to rescue someone from their problems, the more likely they will continue to drown in them. The more you judge someone for their behavior, the better they will get at lying to you about it.

It's imperative that you realize that rescuing someone isn't supporting them, and enabling someone's self-destructive behavior isn't loving them. There is a thin line between what constitutes support, and what is enabling people.

Enabling is when you justify or support someone's problematic behaviors because you think you're helping them. For example, it can include things like giving money to an adult child who is not using it responsibly and is not looking for a job. It can look like covering for people because they were out drinking last night, making excuses for your spouse's anger, or ignoring the problem to avoid conflict.

Often, loving someone will require you to let them learn the hard way. Sometimes, reclaiming your power means not fixing everyone else's problems or making excuses for their behavior.

When you enable others with your money, words, and actions, you don't foster independence—you hinder their healing. You prolong their suffering, their debt, their breakdown, and in turn, your own. You think you're making it easier, but you're actually making their recovery or their self-improvement harder.

Allowing other adults to face and feel the natural consequences of their actions is one of the most important steps of healing.

The Let Them Theory teaches you that helping others doesn't mean solving their problems for them—it means giving them the space, support, and tools to do it themselves.

Think of healing as a game that the person you love must choose to play. Offering support is like throwing someone the ball. You can toss the ball to them over and over, but they have to choose to catch it and run down the field. Enabling is when you grab the ball and try to run it down the field every time they won't.

Let Them drop the ball. *Let Me* stop throwing it. *Let Me* resist the urge to pick it up and run down the field. *Let Me* stop lying about what is happening. *Let Me* accept the fact that they are not ready to change.

I get it: One of the hardest things in the world is to watch some-body that you love struggle. I'm not a heartless person. I have lost too many people that I love to the diseases of hopelessness and addiction. I wish they would have caught the ball. But no amount of wishing can bring them back or make someone who's struggling do the work to get better.

All you can do is recognize the situation that you are in. If they are unwilling to catch the ball, you must stop throwing it. We both know that deep in your heart, the second they are ready to catch the ball, you will be waiting to toss it.

Adults Heal When They Are Ready to Do the Hard Work

You can't want somebody's sobriety or their healing or their finan-cial freedom or their ambition or their happiness more than they do. You will be ready for your loved one to get better, way before they are. Which is why you need to remain in control of your response to the situation. You are not dealing with someone who is capable of rational thought or healthy decision-making.

This is always true when you're dealing with a child, because their brains are not fully formed. Which is why you cannot allow a child to drive their own healing. According to the experts, a human brain from a developmental perspective doesn't mature fully until 25 years old. Legally you are an adult at 18, but from a neuroscience perspective, someone between the ages of 18 and 25 still needs a lot of guidance.

So you have to be the adult in the room getting professional help and steering what is happening. With adults over 25, it is different. Adults are responsible for their own healing. And they are also capa-ble of it.

But regardless of the age of the person who is struggling, they are likely in pure survival mode, from a neurological standpoint. Particularly if someone is spiraling from depression or addiction or facing a tragedy, they are in a chronic state of fight, flight, or freeze.

And this is why things get painful and tricky. You can't get them out of survival mode. You can soothe someone in the moment by giving them a hug, or sitting with them while they cry, or listening until they feel calm and present, but you can't get them out of a chronically stressed state. They are going to have to do the work to get there themselves.

Everything that you learned in the chapters about managing stress, influencing other people to change, and the wiring of the brain applies here. Dr. K taught you that human beings are hardwired to move toward what feels easier and pleasurable in the moment, and to avoid what is painful and hard.

When you are depressed, staying in bed feels easier. When you are grieving, it's easy to think you'll never get through this. When you are struggling, reaching for a drink eases the pain.

That is why the people you love can find themselves struggling with the same demons for years. They would love to get better. They probably doubt that they can.

In periods of my life where I've struggled with severe postpartum depression or crippling anxiety, that was one of my many fears: that I would never climb out of this. That's why the process of getting better will always feel worse in the beginning. That is why people avoid it and act out in ways that don't make sense.

I once heard an addiction specialist say that no one gets sober until being drunk is more painful than facing the thing you are running from. Hearing that made so much sense for me and it can help you move from a place of judgment into a place of understanding and compassion.

That person needs pain in order to galvanize the will to change.

It's true about any struggle. No one heals an eating disorder until restricting is more painful than facing the issues they are running from. No one faces sex addiction until hiding it is more painful than facing the truth.

What every expert I spoke to in researching this book said is that struggling is a critical part of the human experience, and it is one of the most necessary elements of someone choosing to get better.

Notice the word *choosing*.

Someone who is struggling is running away from their problems and numbing their pain. Healing is a choice. This fact creates a problem for you and me, because you will always feel this tension between letting someone struggle and, at the exact same time, desperately wanting to make someone's pain go away.

I've made this mistake. I thought, *If I can just make their life easier, I make change easier, right?* Wrong.

There is a huge difference between trying to make someone's pain go away and offering support that allows them to do the work themselves. What's difficult about this is that every situation is different, and you're going to have to figure out what support looks like for you.

These painful experiences are also part of the motivational circuitry that Dr. K talked about. In other words, if it's easier to avoid the problem, they will never face it.

"Let People Learn from Life."

Dr. Robert Waldinger is a practicing psychiatrist and psychoanalyst, as well as a clinical professor of psychiatry at Harvard Medical School. He also leads the Harvard Study of Adult Development, one of the most extensive and long-standing research projects on adult life. Dr. Waldinger addressed this specifically when I talked to him:

> Let people learn from life. Don't shield them from the consequences of what they choose. If somebody says, "I don't really want to get a job." "Okay, well, how are you going to pay your rent?" There are lots of things we can do to help people meet the challenges of life by not shielding them from the challenges of life. This often happens in the realm of addiction with loved ones. We have to let people deal with the pain of losing a job, or losing a partner because they're addicted to some substance. Don't try to run in and make it all better. When we let people face the real-world consequences of the choices they make, they hopefully learn from them.

Maybe they need to spend a night in jail.

Maybe they need to lose their job, or their family.

Maybe you need to take them out of college.

Maybe they need to live with you, because they need family around them.

Maybe they are so far gone, they are going to become homeless.

And it's not just in the most extreme cases like addiction and severe mental illness. This same principle applies when someone is struggling with homesickness, anxiety, or self-doubt.

Dr. Luana Marques, a clinical psychologist and lecturer at Harvard Medical School, told me that avoidance is a habit and coping mechanism that is very common when someone is confronted.

Your loved one is going to avoid situations, conversations, or behavior changes that feel hard. It's human nature to reach for what feels easy and move away from facing what is difficult. It's important to embrace the facts here, so that you can approach this from a rational and science-backed approach.

Stop Avoiding the Problem

I'll give you an example from my life when one of my kids was struggling. I didn't handle it the right way. In my attempts to lessen my daughter's anxiety, I actually ended up making everything worse.

While this book is really about adult relationships, the laws of human nature apply to parenting young adults as well. Just remember: When you're the parent, you are responsible for your child's physical, mental, and emotional needs.

When our daughter was in middle school, she had a very scary bout of anxiety. It would rev up all day long, and culminate in her waking up in the middle of the night and not wanting to be alone in her room. She would come to our bedroom, and I made the mistake of welcoming her into our bed for the first couple nights.

Every time I said it was okay for her to sleep in our room, I was helping her avoid the anxious feelings and I thought I was making things easier for her. But what I didn't realize is that I was actually making it harder for her to face whatever was underneath this anxiety.

Every single night, she would wake up just before midnight and wander down, and I tried to get up and reassure her, but she refused to go back upstairs alone. Eventually, she would wear me down, and after several nights of her climbing into my bed, I just started creating a little bed on the floor of my room for her.

This went on for six months, every single night.

This is what Dr. Marques meant when she explained that "avoidance is a coping mechanism when someone is struggling." Our daughter was scared to sleep in her room, so she was avoiding it. By allowing her to sleep on our floor, I made her anxiety worse. Every day, when I said, "You can sleep on the floor of our room," I was telling her with my actions, "I believe you're not strong enough to face this."

This may not seem like a big deal, but it's a really big deal. Over the next few years, her anxiety got way worse, because I had helped her learn how to avoid facing it. I had taught her that the solution to anxious feelings was to run away from them. That only made her anxiety worse and her impulse to run stronger.

Everything made her anxious: going to school, sitting in the car alone, sleeping at a friend's house, going to guitar practice. Any small, normal moment of nerves would escalate into an anxiety attack where she "needed me."

I flew home from a vacation with my husband because she was inconsolable, and our babysitter had no idea how to handle her—and neither did I. I blame myself. I'm the parent. And I allowed both of us to avoid facing this difficult situation head on. I was rescuing her, when the truth is, she had the strength, the ability, and the power to work through her anxiety and fears, and learn how to be okay whenever she was feeling anxious or uncomfortable.

It wasn't until Chris had finally had enough that we took her to see a therapist, and learned that the only way somebody gets stronger is by facing the things they feel too weak to face. And it's exactly what the Let Them Theory is going to help you do.

The fact is, it is normal to wake up in the middle of the night and feel anxious. It didn't have to spiral into a six-month ordeal. Anxiety didn't have to become the predominant issue in my daughter's life for the next decade.

You are way more capable than you give yourself credit for, and so is the person you love. You can't control whether or not someone else feels anxious. You can't control whether or not they get up in the middle of the night and come down to your bedroom. But you can always control what YOU think, do, and say in response.

When someone you love is struggling, I want you to picture your-self putting your arm around their shoulders and offering support, as you encourage them to face what they are avoiding.

You can't control their anxious reactions. Your power is in your response. Here's how you can use *Let Me* to offer that support:

Let Me validate what they are feeling: "Oh honey, I'm sorry you feel so scared."

Let Me separate my emotions from theirs: "This is hard for me, too, to see you so sad."

Let Me comfort the person I love who is struggling: A hug always does wonders.

And then *Let Me* support them by assuring them that they have within them the ability to do something that feels hard.

Then, stand by their side as they do the hard thing—which, for me, meant getting up every night, in the middle of the night, and walking my daughter back to her room, and putting her back in her bed.

And I'm not going to lie, for the first few nights, I felt like a monster as she would cry and plead. I wanted to fire the therapist and throw in the towel on this plan, and allow her to sleep back on the floor. *I mean eventually she will want her own bed, right?!*

But I didn't do that. It took about five days, and it was not easy for me to see her crying and pleading. It wasn't easy to tuck her into her bed and then go stand outside her door until I heard her drift back to sleep. Some nights she would wake up again and come down again, not once but a few more times, and I would take the time to comfort her, put my arm around her, and walk with her back up those stairs to help her face what she was avoiding.

Look at people's struggles as an opportunity to support them in discovering their strengths. If someone learns that they are too weak to face their struggles, they will never experience what is truly possible.

And if you always swoop in and rescue someone, they will start expecting you to do it when life gets hard. But if they see themselves moment by moment, day by day, facing the hard and scary things in life with you by their side, you teach them that they are capable of doing things that are way beyond what they see for themselves.

Stop rescuing people from their problems and start acting as if you believe in their ability to face them. Your actions are the loudest and truest form of communication. So when you act in a way that supports someone in facing what scares them, your behavior says, "I believe in you. You can do this. And I'll be here by your side as you face it."

Supporting people through struggle is very hard to do. It is draining. It takes a lot of time and patience. It is frustrating. That is why a lot of us resort to enabling or rescuing people. It is much easier to let them sleep on the floor, transfer schools, quit their job, ignore it and hope it goes away, or, the most common way people enable others: throw money at it.

So the question becomes: How do you support someone effectively?

CHAPTER 17

How to Provide Support the Right Way

Since there were so many questions about HOW to effectively balance supporting someone without rescuing them, I want to share a very specific suggestion almost every expert I spoke with raised.

When you are supporting an adult who is struggling, one of the biggest levers you have to pull is what you will spend money for and what you will not.

If you are giving financial support to someone in an attempt to help them through a hard time, you better be very clear about the conditions upon which you are giving that support.

If you give money without conditions, it will lead to massive resentment on your end. The money is not a gift. And unconditional love does not mean unconditional financial support.

Often unconditional love means withdrawing financial support. This is very hard, especially for parents of adult children who are struggling, and it's often the very last lever that is pulled.

There is this term in recovery called *rock bottom*. We tend to talk about rock bottom moments related to the person who is struggling.

But what we don't talk about enough, is that you, as the loved one, will have a rock bottom moment too.

It happens when you've "tried everything." Nothing is working. You are suffering. And then it hits you: There is one thing I haven't tried: I haven't stopped subsidizing their life. At some point, you'll realize that by paying someone's rent, bills, tuition, or giving them a place to live without any conditions, you are enabling their self-destructive behavior.

Remember what Dr. Waldinger said? "Don't shield them from the consequences of what they choose." At some point, you're going to decide to stop subsidizing someone's life, who refuses to do the work or get the professional help they need to get better.

Dr. Waldinger, and every other expert I spoke to, was adamant about this point: You owe people love, acceptance, and compassion. You do not owe them money. Because if you're funding any aspect of someone's life while they continue to refuse treatment, or won't get a job, or don't attend classes, or continue to lie or steal or be engaged in shady, avoidant behavior—you are part of the problem. Money without condition is enabling.

But providing money with specific conditions is support, and it can look like this: You can live here, if you're sober. I'll pay for therapy, as long as you and your therapist agree to a monthly check in with me. I'll pay for tuition as long as you get a 3.0. I'll pay your rent, phone bill, and car payments if you go to inpatient treatment for your eating disorder.

The hardest part is what happens when they don't agree to the conditions. Because if they refuse to go to inpatient facilities or refuse to get a job, you're going to have to take away all financial support, which means you stop paying their rent or kick them out of the house.

And I mean all financial support. They are not on your phone bill. You are not paying their rent. You're not giving them logins for your streaming accounts. You're not buying their groceries or paying for their Ubers. And yes, you may have provided a guarantee on the lease for their apartment. You are going to have to be willing to have that hit your credit.

They are going to hate you. They will likely spiral in the beginning. But when they refuse to honor the conditions upon which your support was given, you must be the adult. I am shocked at the number of parents who are asking about adult children who are struggling, whom they are financially supporting.

Let Them struggle. *Let Them* violate the terms of your support. And then, *Let Me* cut them off financially.

Very few people are willing to do this, because it feels cruel. That's why throwing money at a situation is so common. But removing your financial support is the only thing that will work. Because it's the only thing you have left when nothing else has worked. You do have power. And maybe this is the exact wake-up call that your loved one needs.

And if you're reading this, and your parents are paying for your therapy, or your rent, or your education, or your phone bill, or any aspect of your life, I have news for you: They get to vote on how you're living your life.

You don't get to have someone else fund your life, and then have an attitude when they have an opinion about how you're using their money. Having your parents pay for your therapy and then refusing to let them talk to your therapist is a form of gaslighting.

If you are sick of your parents' opinions about what you should be doing, then start paying your own bills. As long as you are financially tied to someone else, you can say *Let Them* all you want, but their money is buying access to your life, whether you like it or not. If you want independence, prove it and start being financially independent for real.

And let's be honest: The real reason why your parents' opinions frustrate you so much is because you need their money, and you know it. You're not mad at them; you're mad at yourself for not being financially independent.

Stop Bailing Out Other Adults

I can give you a personal example of why it's important to stop bailing people out without conditions. I mentioned earlier that when I was in my 40s, Chris and I were in crushing financial debt.

We had liens on the house and we were $800,000 in debt. Chris's restaurant business was profoundly struggling. The business was missing payroll. Chris hadn't been paid in months, I had just lost my job, and we were having trouble paying for things like groceries or even filling up the gas tank.

It was a really scary time. Chris and his business partner were desperately trying to raise money to keep the business afloat. I remember him asking his brother to loan him some money for the business.

His brother said no, and added, "I'm sorry if me not giving you this money is the reason why the business fails and you go bankrupt, but I won't bail you out. You have got to figure out how to do this yourself."

Was that harsh? No. It was honest. He wasn't responsible for Chris's business problems. Chris was. And he wasn't responsible for propping up a failing business or rescuing Chris from his financial problems. It was super painful for Chris to hear that, but it was the truth. A few weeks later, Chris hit rock bottom.

The business hadn't paid him in six months and it was running on fumes. He and his business partner had been working nonstop for years trying to make this business successful. It was this conversation with his brother that helped him realize that he had to get out.

The business couldn't support two owners. Plus, Chris had developed a major problem with alcohol. He was drinking away the stress and engaging in other self-destructive behaviors. He was depressed, anxious, and knew he could no longer live like this. That was his rock bottom.

If his brother had loaned him the money, it would have just prolonged this devastating situation. When his brother said no, he had no choice but to rescue himself. That's rock bottom and it changes your life for the better. Because, when you finally hit it, you connect with something solid inside yourself—the resolve to change.

It's important to point out that Chris's brother said no to money, but that doesn't mean he wasn't supportive. He listened to Chris, he validated his feelings, he felt a lot of compassion for him, and ultimately, by refusing to loan him money, he was saying, "I believe in your ability to figure this out."

And you know what? Chris did figure it out. The right answer wasn't propping up the restaurant. It wasn't running away from the situation. The right answer was saying, "I'm not doing this anymore. I quit."

The first step to changing your life is taking responsibility for the fact that your life isn't working. That's why you need to let the people that you love face reality, not help them run from it. It's your job to love them, and believe in their ability to do the work, and support them from a safe distance, which is what Chris's brother did. Because just like there are a million ways to solve a problem, there are also a million ways to provide support.

How to Create the Best Possible Environment for Healing

One of my favorite ways to provide support is thinking about how you can create an environment to help someone get better. What does that mean? There is a lot of research about the role that your physical environment plays in your mental, spiritual, and physical health. It's everything from the space you live in, the clutter around you, the food in your fridge, the people that you spend time with, and the plans in your calendar.

Ask yourself, *How can I create an environment that makes change and getting better easier?* There are a million ways you can do this, but I want to start with an example from my life.

When our first daughter was born, I had a very complicated delivery and lost a lot of blood. By the time I was finally discharged and sent home, I was not only physically destroyed, but mentally dealing with severe postpartum depression.

It was so bad that I couldn't be left alone with our baby for the first four months of her life. I couldn't breastfeed because of the medications I was on. And I was so depleted, I spent most of the day sleeping or sitting like a zombie on the couch.

What I remember most is that no one asked me how they could help. They just showed up and created an environment for my healing without asking.

My cousin came over to clean. My parents drove across the country and sat with me for weeks. A new friend, Joanie, who was pregnant at the time, would come and just sit and keep me company so Chris could go to work. And while I dozed off to sleep, she would do a load of laundry or make a simple lunch.

My in-laws came for a week and, every day, had something planned. Without even asking, they would say, "All right, come on, we are going to the Boston Flower Show." And they would load me and the baby into the car. And even though I was still a zombie, and still deeply depressed, they created an environment where I got out of the house and began to step back into life again.

No one asked me, "What help do you need?" No one asked me, "Do you want me to do the laundry?" No one asked me, "Do you want me to drop off dinner tonight?" They just did it. And that is an important note about people who are struggling.

Let Them doesn't mean leave them alone.

When you are struggling, you don't know what you want or what you need. Some days, you don't even know what day it is. Have you ever noticed that when you ask a friend who is grieving, going through a breakup, or just got out of the hospital how you can help, they often say, "It's okay, I'll be fine," "Nothing," or "I don't need anything."

When you're struggling, you don't want to burden anyone else, because you already feel like a burden. *Let Me* create the environment they need to get better.

Here are some examples of things you can do: show up at their doorstep, drop off dinner, help them clean up their apartment, fill their fridge with healthy food, walk into their bedroom and pull the shades open and lift up the windows to let the air in, do their laundry, make a playlist of great songs, send them podcast episodes that will help give them hope, send them care packages filled with thoughtful and nurturing things, or buy them a digital picture frame and load up photos so in their environment they are constantly reminded of happy memories and people around them.

One of my favorite things to do, especially for a new mom, comes from therapist K.C. Davis: Drop off a tower of paper plates and cups so they don't have to do the dishes while caring for a newborn.

And while we're on the topic, call or text a friend and say, "I'm coming over on Saturday, and I'm taking the kids or the dog to the park to give you a break."

Take your roommate to get manicures, or to a new exhibit at the museum, after her breakup. Text someone once a week and just say, "I'm thinking about you, you are not going to go through this alone, you do not need to text me back, I just want you to know I am always here." Invite your friend who just got out of a treatment program to do a yoga class with you every Wednesday morning, and better yet, pick them up.

You can create an environment for positive change by offering therapy, cooking healthy meals, or having conversations, and focusing on open-ended questions. Can you see how these examples are very different from throwing money at a situation, or enabling or rescuing someone from their problems? These are all examples where you are making it easier to step back into life.

You never know what someone else is going through. You get to choose what kind of friend, loved one, or family member you get to be. In this book, we've talked a lot about showing up in a way that makes you proud of yourself.

When you help someone else, do it without expectation. Do it because it makes you feel good to reach out to that friend that's in the hospital. Don't do it because you hope to get a long text back updating you on what's happening. Drop off dinner to someone who just had a baby, not because you are expecting a thank-you, but because it makes you feel good to know you show up for the people you love in life.

Remember that when someone is struggling they are often so overwhelmed they don't have the energy to keep you updated or to remember to thank you—but trust that your kind gesture is making all the difference, whether you receive a thank-you or not.

Your job is to stand by their side and hold the light high. Be a beacon of hope. Believe in their ability to get better.

People avoid healing because they do not believe they can face the pain they are running from. So *Let Them* borrow their belief from you. Because when someone feels accepted, loved, and supported, it's easier for them to believe in their ability to step back into life too.

So let's summarize how to help someone who is struggling. In this section, you may have learned how you are preventing other adults from facing their struggles. The Let Them Theory teaches you that helping others doesn't mean solving their problems for them—it means giving them the space and tools to do it themselves.

1. **Problem:** Rescuing people from their problems makes them drown in them. When you enable others with your money, words, and actions, you don't foster their independence—you hinder their healing. You prolong their suffering, their debt, their breakdown, and in turn, your own.

2. **Truth:** People only heal when they are ready to do the work. You will be ready for them to heal before they are. While your intentions may be good, constantly stepping in to solve their issues creates dependency and frustration, and hinders their ability to take responsibility for themselves. You cannot want someone's healing more than they do.

3. **Solution:** Using the Let Them Theory, you must step back and allow adults to face and feel the natural consequences of their actions. Instead of rescuing, offer support with conditions. This approach helps them take

responsibility for their own healing and growth, and demonstrates your belief in their innate ability to get better and do better.

When you say *Let Them*, you trust and empower others to handle their difficulties while understanding that facing hardship is a necessary part of growth. When you say *Let Me*, you focus on providing support without taking over while creating the environment and tools necessary for another person to get better for themselves.

Believe in their ability to heal, and create an environment where change is possible.

Choosing the
Love You Deserve

CHAPTER 18

Let Them Show You Who They Are

At the end of your life, what are the very last words you want someone to say to you?

"I love you."

Love is the most powerful force in the world. You deserve to feel loved, be loved, fall in love, express love, and experience one of the greatest joys in life: being in a loving relationship.

Whether you're single, divorced, dating, engaged, in a situationship, or you've been married for a very long time, I believe the greatest love of your life is ahead of you. Even the best relationships can become more meaningful and your connection to someone can always go deeper.

If you're single, your love story is far from over. The love of your life is not in your past. They are waiting for you in the future, and everything that has happened and every relationship you've been in has prepared you for what is about to happen next.

While I was doing the research for this book, I received so many questions about using the Let Them Theory when it comes to love. So, in the next three chapters, you and I will cover dating, commitment, how to know if a relationship is right for you, making love last, and surviving breakups.

Finally, we are going to talk about how you've been accepting less than the love you deserve.

The reality is, adults choose who and how they love, and sometimes they won't choose you. People's behavior tells the truth about how they feel about you. Too often, you chase love—or the potential for what you think it could be—and end up compromising on your values. By chasing love, you chase away the deep and meaningful relationship you're worthy of.

As extraordinary as love is, it's also the source of so much pain. You want to be loved so much that you can find yourself giving your power away to the other person.

For example, maybe some stranger you met online now dictates your mood. Maybe someone who ghosted you has now destroyed your self-esteem. Or your spouse is very dismissive and treats you like a roommate, which you have just learned to accept.

In your love life, you can fall into the trap of letting other people—and their own traumas and issues—make you compromise your standards and settle for far less than what you truly want and know you need.

When the heart is involved, logic goes out the window. You can find yourself explaining away bad behavior or creating a fantasy in your head instead of accepting reality. You can also convince yourself to stay in a relationship that isn't working because it feels better than breaking up and facing the unknown.

You deserve an amazing love story, and you should never settle for less than that kind of love.

Using the Let Them Theory, you will learn the difference between chasing love and choosing it. You'll learn who is worth a commitment and who isn't. You'll also learn how to use the theory to create the most loving, supportive, and committed partnership you have ever had.

The fact is, the best relationships grow and change over time—and changing how you show up will create connection and the loving partnership you truly deserve.

So, Let's Start at the Beginning ... How to Find Love

Dating today is really hard. I haven't talked to a single person who says they like dating and that it's easy and fun.

Absolutely everyone dreads the idea of "putting themselves out there," getting on the apps, and entering what feels like a very toxic, shallow hookup scene. So if you feel discouraged, bummed, or insecure about being single, you're not alone. This is normal, and it has a lot to do with the fact that dating apps and social media have turned love and relationships into a game, an industry, and a competition.

The other reason it's frustrating is that so much of the advice feels like tricks, tips, and rules to win someone over, or secure the next date, or attract as many likes as you can on the app. That's what I mean when I say that dating in today's world feels like a competition. That is the worst way to approach the topic of love and committed partnerships. It is not a game. You're not supposed to trick someone into liking you. You're not supposed to follow rules about when you can text or what you can say.

You are supposed to be yourself and trust that if you show up as your full self, the person that is looking to be with someone as awesome as you can actually find you. Anybody that is telling you the trick to "landing them" is leading you away from yourself and into shallow waters where you'll meet the wrong people. Instead of thinking you need to change yourself and start doing something different, I am going to teach you what you need to stop doing.

Finding love is more about saying no than it is about saying yes. When you have high standards for yourself and the kind of relationship you want, dating becomes a process of elimination. The Let Them Theory will keep you honest with yourself, and it will give you the courage to let other people reveal who they are while you stay true to yourself.

When you are brave enough to be yourself, you are in control—because you're the one who is choosing who gets your time and energy, and who doesn't.

It also takes bravery to see that someone's not interested in you. It takes confidence to remind yourself that texting you is easy—but if they truly wanted to see you, they would be making plans.

The second you start creating excuses and scenarios in your head, you are giving your power to the other person. Dating requires you to be very black and white when it comes to other people's behavior. And that is the hard part. Using the Let Them Theory, you're going to learn how to choose the right relationship instead of constantly chasing the wrong ones.

The Purpose of Dating Is Not Just to Find "The One"

A big reason why dating is hard is that you don't understand the true purpose of it. It's not just to find "the one." Dating helps you learn more about yourself and what you want and don't want. One person at a time, you are learning what you like and what you don't. That's why every single experience that you have—even the really crappy ones—teaches you something important.

One of the most important lessons is learning what kind of behavior you will not accept, and what kind of person you truly want to be in a relationship with. If you become obsessed with finding the one, you are going to miss all the lessons that dating is trying to teach you about the value of love in your life.

You weren't put on the earth to be somebody's wife or husband. You are here to fulfill your dreams; share your story; and create a big, beautiful, amazing life.

No one else is going to create that life for you. The person you choose to love gets to share that life with you. That's why I want you to be choosy.

When you're dating, have fun and meet a ton of people, but never forget the bigger picture: that you're looking for someone who is capable of helping you become your best self and co-creating a beautiful life together.

So, no. The purpose of dating is not just to find "the one."

That's why you need to think about dating as an opportunity to learn more about yourself by being open to lots of different experiences, that will ultimately lead to you choosing someone amazing who chooses you back.

The hard part is you can't control whether or not another person chooses you. You can't control whether or not the timing of your life lines up with the timing of someone else's.

People choose who and how they love, and sometimes it won't be you. But never forget: You get to choose who and how you love too. You get to choose who is worth your time and energy, and you get to choose how you want to be treated. Oftentimes with dating, the way you choose is by choosing to walk away when you aren't being treated the way you deserve.

And that brings me to a fact: People's behavior tells you exactly how they feel about you.

Your job isn't to interpret it or second-guess it. Your job is to let people reveal who they are and how they truly feel about you and accept it. And by the way, this is true at every stage of a relationship.

The Early Days

As you put yourself out there and start meeting people, you may find there are lots of people you "like" and are "interested in" because there are lots of attractive, cool, and fun people out there.

The early days can be energizing and exciting. . . which is why you'll probably end up saying yes to a lot of people who end up being wrong for you. It's so easy to say yes when someone is attractive, or when you feel that rush of emotion, or you've got nothing else to do this weekend, or you're tired of being single, or you're scared you'll never meet someone.

Dating is hard because everybody is so scared to be alone, and so desperate to find somebody and to have the fairy tale, that you're not as discerning as you need to be about the reality of the situation you may be in with someone.

How many times have you convinced yourself that something is more serious than it is, or that this is going somewhere, or that the repeated drunken hookups mean they like you just as much as you like them, or that you have a future together?

There's that famous saying, "If someone likes you, you'll know, and if they don't, you'll be confused." Feeling confused is a very dangerous place to be when you're dating because if you like them, your knee-jerk reaction will be to convince yourself that they like you. Do NOT do that. *Let Them* confuse you.

Haven't you noticed that the only people you feel confused by are the ones who don't like you back? See the confusion that you feel for what it is. It means they don't like you the way you want them to. When you convince yourself that something is happening when it's clearly not, you're chasing love. Chasing love only chases it away. Chasing the wrong person always leads you to the wrong places. Chasing the potential means you know something isn't right and you're ignoring the truth.

And here's how you know you're chasing it:

You're the one that is always texting, calling, and reaching out. You believe the drunk hookups are leading somewhere special. You try to be near them all the time, hoping they will fall for you.

You believe what they tell you, even if their behavior tells you otherwise. You think with time this will get better. You think you know what's best for them, and it's you. You only see them when you are out at the bars. You believe you can fix them. You believe there is a text that you could send that might get them to want you back.

These are all examples of chasing the potential and choosing not to see the reality. You can't get so attached to "making it work" that you keep chasing something that you know isn't the right fit. It's like taking a pair of shoes that you think are cute and trying to ram your foot into it even though it is two sizes too small. Your foot is not going to magically shrink, and just like the shoe isn't going to grow to fit you, neither will this person shape-shift into who you hope they will be. That's why you have to stop chasing.

The more time you waste chasing the wrong people, the longer it's going to take you to find the right one. *Let Them* ghost you. *Let Me* move on.

Stop chasing the potential of who someone might be. Stop pouring your time and energy into people who do not give it back to you. Stop explaining away their disrespectful behavior. Stop giving your love to people who do not love you back. Stop making excuses for people who are clearly not interested in you. Stop chasing people who are not choosing to love you back. Stop playing the game.

Yes, dating is hard. Yes, your emotions are all over the place. Yes, rejection is painful.

Yes, the sex is awesome. Yes, they are hilarious. Yes, it is nice to not be the single one in your friend group. Yes, it feels great to have someone who seems interested. Yes, it is nice to have plans this weekend or something to look forward to. Yes, there will be times when the person seems right, but the timing is wrong.

Remember: You will find the right relationship by saying no to the wrong ones. The faster you say no, the faster you will be saying yes to the love of your life. The Let Them Theory will be revolutionary when it comes to finding the love you deserve, because it forces you to be brutally honest about the situation that you're in, and who you're dealing with, and how they actually feel about you.

They Don't Like You. Wake Up.

The only way you learn who someone is and where you stand in their life is by watching their behavior. Forget what they say. Watch what they do. That can be hard to do, because in the beginning, your emotions and hormones are all over the place. They can cloud your ability to see the truth about how you're being treated.

One question that you can always ask yourself to snap out of the dating fog is: *If your best friend were being treated this way, what would you tell them?*

One of the fundamental principles of the Let Them Theory is that people's behavior tells you exactly where you stand in their life. You need to understand: This is very black and white. You are either a priority, or you are not. There is no middle ground.

Let Them show you who they are.

If you're busy chasing someone, you will never allow yourself to see the reality that someone else doesn't like you the way you want them to. If somebody is sending you mixed signals, it means they are NOT interested. Mixed signals aren't "mixed" at all. They send a very clear message that you are not a priority; you're a convenience.

For example, if they are texting you nonstop, but they never suggest a plan to get together, they are not interested in anything real. *Let Them* text nonstop. If they want to see you every time they are back in town, but never follow up whenever they leave, they are not interested in anything more than sex. *Let Them.* They aren't the problem. You are. You are not valuing your time enough to realize that this is going nowhere.

You need the *Let Me* part of the theory: *Let Me* wake up and be honest with myself. The more I chase this person, the more time I spend texting this person, and the more I live in my head creating a fantasy that they are eventually going to come around and see that we are meant for each other, the less likely I am going to meet a person who wants a real relationship.

Let Me respect myself enough to admit that this is going nowhere. When someone is stringing you along, *Let Them.* You always have the power to cut the cord. You are an active participant in the stringing along, because you're allowing them to do it. And if you were in a positive, loving relationship right now, you'd roll your eyes if they texted you for a hookup! So admit your part in your own demise right now, and take your power back.

Let Me remind myself that I don't want to be dating someone who is not choosing me back. One of the most important signs of a healthy relationship is that it is mutual.

Mutual effort. Mutual respect. Mutual feelings. Mutual attraction. Mutual interest.

If you're making excuses for someone else's behavior. . . stop. *Let Them* reveal who they truly are. *Let Them* reveal whether or not they make an effort. *Let Them* reveal whether or not they care.

The biggest thing that makes dating confusing is your refusal to see the fact that they don't care about you the way you wish they would. We've all been there. It's painful when you are interested in someone and those feelings are not returned. But you can't control who another person chooses to love.

Do not spend your time trying to shrink yourself into a tiny little box, or become someone new, or change who you are, just to be in a relationship with someone who doesn't love you back. Don't do it.

At the beginning of a relationship, it's so easy to fall into this trap. It's easy to jump straight to conclusions that this person is right for you (even if alarm bells are going off in your head that they're not). It's easy to blindly hope that people feel the same way you do. It's easy to think someone will love you if you change just a little bit more. It's easy to hold on tightly to the idea of being loved, even if it's not quite as magical as you'd hoped. It's easy to delude you into thinking they are not seeing anyone else even though they are not giving you a full commitment right now, or they "don't like labels." It's easy to fall into an unfulfilling relationship just so that you can stop being the "single friend." It's easy in the moment, but in the long run, it'll break your heart.

The emotional distress, the loss of self, the constant questioning of where you stand, the heartache over the fact that they will never quite commit. . . it's never worth it. I want to say it again: If they like you, you'll know. If they don't, you'll be confused.

Let Them not text you back. *Let Them* make promises when they are drunk. *Let Them* leave abruptly in the morning and never follow up on "I'd love to see you again." *Let Them* confuse you, infuriate you, and send mixed signals.

You must let their behavior be the clear message. Letting Them is the easy part. *Let Me* is the hard part, because you don't want to see the truth. *Let Me* see them for who they are. *Let Me* accept the truth in their behavior—I am not a priority. Stop choosing to chase people who clearly do not want to be with you.

If they are not making an effort, they are not worth yours.

CHAPTER 19

How to Take Your Relationship to the Next Level

"**B**ut, Mel. . . they are giving me the attention I deserve. I know they like me because they have told me. . . and they are acting in all the right ways. . . except for the most important one. They just don't want to commit to me."

This is really common, and it can show up in a number of ways: Maybe they don't want to put a "label" on it, be exclusive, officially be in a relationship, move in together, get engaged, or get married.

First, you have to ask yourself, *Is this a pattern of mine to chase people who won't commit?* Or is this just an issue with this one person? I am going to tackle these topics separately, because they are two different issues.

If You're Always Picking the Wrong People

If you are always finding yourself trying to date the person who is unavailable or can't commit, chances are it is not as coincidental as you think. You are probably attracted to people who you think you can change or win over, or who are unavailable because they are with someone else or just emotionally unavailable.

Ask yourself: Are you dating people who never commit? Are you the girlfriend before they meet their wife? Are you dating people you don't fully trust? Are you dating people who are jealous or controlling? Do you keep sleeping with people hoping it turns into something? Are you dating people who have serious struggles whom you want to rescue? Are you dating people who cheat on you or that you meet by cheating? When your relationships ultimately blow up, do you tell your friends they were the "crazy" one?

If any of these things ring true, it's time for honesty: You love the chase. This is your pattern and it's a problem. The relationship is largely happening as a fantasy in your own mind, because you live in the potential of what could be, not in the reality of what is.

This pattern in your life will repeat unless you break it. Research shows that people subconsciously pick the same type of person to chase time and time again based on previous relationships and childhood experiences.

A study from the University of Alberta shows that after the initial "honeymoon phase," a new relationship tends to follow the exact same dynamic patterns of old relationships. The eight-year study showed that people tend to repeat patterns, bring the same dynamics to new experiences, and avoid addressing their own issues... which, in turn, create the exact same broken relationship dynamics over and over.

If this is ringing true for you, you should really go talk to a therapist about your past, and get to the root of your issues—because they are not going to be solved by being in a relationship with someone else. In fact, if you chase another relationship, you will just keep chasing healthy love away.

Another relationship is not the answer. In fact another relationship right now is just going to make the problem worse.

You need to be single.

I am going to say that again. You need to be single.

If you truly want to fix this and create the healthy, loving relationship you've always dreamt about, you must be willing to be single for the next year and focus on figuring out how to be happy by yourself and to heal.

"But, Mel. . . I don't want to be single, and I don't think it's that much of a problem. I just have met the wrong people. It's not me. It's them. I just need to pick someone different."

Nope! The problem is you. I just realized, as I was saying this to you. . . that you're going to think you're the exception to this research.

Remember earlier in the book when you met Dr. Sharot from MIT, and she taught you why you can't get other people to change? Because everyone thinks they are the exception, and that is happening to you right now.

If you have this pattern of chasing love, but never getting to a healthy commitment, you are not the exception. You are the problem. The biggest challenge you're going to have is recognizing your own denial that this is in fact a pattern that you need to fix and that being in another relationship will keep you from fixing this problem.

You deserve an incredible love story, but you will not create it until you figure out the root cause of why you keep choosing people who are not healthy or won't commit to you.

And I say this to you with love.

Now, let's talk about using the Let Them Theory in situations where you are seeing someone or in a relationship, and you want to take it to the next level, but you are not sure where the other person stands or how to broach the topic of a bigger commitment without losing your power.

The Commitment Conversation

There comes a time in any relationship where you may wonder where this is going or if you are on the same page about what you want. The second you start to feel that way, it's time for a conversation.

Never feel bad about asking for what you deserve. Never hint about something as important as a commitment. Being able to have honest conversations is the foundation of a loving and healthy relationship.

So don't fear this, embrace it. If the relationship is meant to be, this conversation will make it stronger. A real conversation only destroys something that is fake.

The way you're going to frame the conversation comes from my friend Matthew Hussey, a *New York Times* bestselling author who has been helping people for more than 17 years to feel more confident and in control of their relationships. His YouTube channel is #1 in the world for love advice, with over half a billion views.

As I was researching this book, I spoke to Matthew about the mistakes that people make when they want to take a relationship to the next level.

And he told me a very poignant personal story. He said that when he met his wife, Audrey, he was dating a bunch of people; they were also living in different cities, and it was very casual. He admitted to me (while Audrey was sitting right next to us) that he was stringing her along. That is. . . until she sat him down and had a conversation that was structured in a very particular way, and it caught him completely off guard.

She didn't make him feel bad. She didn't go on and on about how much she liked him, or that she was falling for him. In fact, she didn't focus on him at all. She focused on the value of her time and what she was looking for.

As Matthew told me the story, he said that the #1 mistake that people make when they are trying to take something to the next level is focusing on the other person, rather than focusing on the value of their time and what they want in life. And it worked—because he stopped dating everybody else, and immediately committed to Audrey, and now they are married and partners in business together.

He walked me through what he learned from the experience, how he now teaches this technique, and the way you can frame this conversation too. So here's what you're going to do:

Similar to the ABC Loop, don't have this conversation at a bar, on the phone, or when you're short on time. Don't even consider having it over text. It's important to not walk into this with any expectation that the person is going to be wanting the same thing that you do. You're seeking clarification because you've gotten to a point where you know that if this isn't going anywhere, it's no longer worth your time.

This isn't about getting the answer that you want. It's about getting the truth about where you stand. This isn't a particularly emotional conversation. It's about the facts of what is worth your time, and what is not. This is what Matthew recommended, but make it your own:

> I have really loved spending time with you. And I know myself, and I'm really looking for a commitment. I wanted to talk to you because I want to see if we both have the same vision for where this is going. I value my time and energy, and I don't want to put time and energy into spending time with someone if it's not going to go to the next level. And I've

reached that point with you. It's been really fun. I love spending time with you. But I only want to invest more time and energy if we're going to go to the next level. And if you don't see the same thing, this has been great. But I just know myself and I need to choose to invest the time that I have with people who want the same things that I want.

Wow. I wish I had known this when I was dating. What strikes me about Matthew and Audrey's approach is how matter of fact it is.

As you read it, don't you respect the person who is saying it? That they "value" their time and energy? And did you also notice, they were super complimentary of the person they had been seeing?

No guilt trip. No accusations. No sob story. Just two adults having fun, and now one of them is being clear about what they want in life.

Don't you respect that? I sure do. Don't you want to value your time just as much? Of course you do! And don't you want to be with somebody who is so badass that they value their time this much, and actually mean it?

And, did you notice zero expectation? The door is wide open for the other person to say no.

This is the hard part: Sometimes the people you choose aren't going to choose you back. It will suck. You will feel demoralized. And you'll be okay.

And here's the thing, even if they say no, you still get to choose what you do after.

If they tell you—I don't want to move in with you; I don't want to be your boyfriend or girlfriend; I don't want to do long distance; I don't want to get married; I don't want to ever have kids; I am not moving back to your hometown—they have given you everything that they have to give you. And this is it.

Let Them.

As my friend and bestselling author Pastor Sarah Jakes Roberts likes to say, "Are these table scraps what you're willing to accept, or are you looking for a five star meal?"

If you choose to stay in this after they've told you they don't want the same things you want, that's on you. If you stay in something after they won't commit, the next phone call should be to your therapist, because there is something deeper going on.

As your friend, I'll ask you: Why do you want to be with somebody that won't commit to you? Why do you want to be with somebody that doesn't want the same things that you want?

Yes, it can be terrifying to be alone. Yes, it's deflating to know another six months just went by. Yes, it's tempting to be with the table scraps rather than back on the dating market again.

You may think you'll never find love. You may think you'll never find someone as smart, funny, attractive, complimentary, or as good in bed. But, you're wrong. It's not true.

Do not accept the table scraps.

Be brave. Saying no to the wrong situations is how you find the right person for you. *Let Them* reveal who they are, and where you stand. Then you must focus on the second part of the Let Them Theory, *Let Me*.

Let Me end a relationship with someone who won't commit.

Let Me trust this is another step in the direction of choosing the love I deserve.

Let Me stop chasing the potential of this and see the reality.

Let Me believe that I just took one step closer to the right person.

Let Me take my power back, because the love of my life is right around the corner.

CHAPTER 20

How Every Ending Is a Beautiful Beginning

One topic that kept coming up when I was researching this book was how to know when the issues you are facing in a relationship are something that you can resolve versus something that you need to accept.

When is overthinking, frustration, and bickering normal, and when is it a sign that something is broken? When should I just *Let Them* be versus admitting the painful truth that this relationship is no longer working for me?

Having been married for almost 30 years, I can tell you that mutual give and take and compromise are critical to a successful relationship. No one is perfect, no relationship is perfect, and every relationship changes with time.

In a long-term partnership, there will be periods in your relationship that are amazing, and there will be times that are extremely difficult. But every couple that has made a relationship work has had two important things present:

First, they both wanted the relationship to work. And they were both willing to do the work to make it better. Second, the issues that created problems did not require either person to give up their dreams or compromise their values.

So if you're sitting here wondering if you're in the right relationship, that's a good thing because it means you want to be with somebody that is going to bring out the best in you, and who will work with you to create a good life.

One of the hardest things that I've experienced is being with someone who is a really good person, and knowing deep down that they are not the right person for me.

Or, in a couple cases, being with a really good person and knowing that I was in the wrong place mentally and not the right person for them—in fact, I had no business being in a relationship at all. (I am thinking about the apologies I've made to my college and law school boyfriends. I was in a horrible place mentally in my 20s, and boy did I behave in ways I deeply regret.)

Admitting that a relationship is not working is one of the hardest things in the world to do, especially if you're in love with them. Often, it's not that obvious what the issue is. Deep down you just know that underneath the day-to-day, and the familiar routine together, something feels off.

Love the Person, Not Their Potential

Any time you find yourself questioning whether or not this is the right relationship for you, ask yourself: *Can you accept this person exactly as they are, and exactly where they are, and still love them?*

That means, do you truly love your boyfriend, girlfriend, wife, husband, or partner for who they are right now? Or do you love who they once were, or who you wish they would become?

Even if there are specific things that bother you, in the end they might not be deal breakers. They may be things you have to learn to accept, and that's just work you're going to have to do to make this relationship thrive.

Let Them.

For example, maybe you can't stand that they've started vaping, they don't take care of themselves, they are such a slob it is driving you crazy, they don't plan anything, the sex is boring when it happens, they never want to do anything, or they are not interested in moving to a new city or traveling to a new country on vacation.

Can you still love them despite all these things? Because, the reality of it is... they may never change. And here is the other thing, they probably won't.

Remember, one of the fundamental takeaways from this book: People only do what they feel like doing. Yes, you can influence them. But if you keep wanting them to change, and they don't, it not only weakens your love. It creates resentment.

What I have noticed with couples is that the longer you are together, the more you want your partner to be like you. That's not fair. So be honest with yourself. Do you just want them to be just like you, or is it that one of your fundamental needs in the relationship is not being met? This is very important because based on the laws of human nature you should assume the person is never going to change.

Let Them be. Instead of sitting there silently resenting them or criticizing them behind their back, be the loving and mature person in the relationship. Either stop trying to make them like you, and accept them as they are, or have the productive and loving conversation about what you need, and why this is bothering you.

Maybe they don't even know you're upset by it, or they don't know how you feel about the issue, or they don't know how important it is to you, or they do know, but you have just created a standoff.

So before you spend another year overthinking and wondering if this is your person, have the conversation, apply the science, and then sit back and wait. You know how to do this using the ABC Loop and the power of your influence:

A: APOLOGIZE, then ASK open-ended questions.

B: BACK OFF, and observe their BEHAVIOR.

C: CELEBRATE progress while you continue to model the CHANGE.

When you use *Let Me* to influence someone else, do it with the hope that they change, because you love them and want something better for them, and you want the relationship to work and this matters to you. But don't ever do it with the expectation that they must change.

Because even when you use science to influence someone else, they are still their own person and are in control of what they choose to think, say, and do. Give it at least three months without any negative energy, while you keep modeling the positive change and celebrating anything you see.

Let Them be.

Why three months? It's plenty of time for your energy to shift and for the other person to suddenly feel inspired to make the change and believe it was their idea.

Remember the example of my friend and her husband. This issue of his health had been bothering her for a while, and even though she loves her husband, it's made her wonder if he is the right person for her? Can she be married to someone who doesn't take care of themselves?

So she's been using the Let Them Theory to answer this question. She is letting him be, and meanwhile, she's been going for a walk every morning, she's been positive and happy, she's been complimenting him and hugging him, and she's been very affectionate whenever he exercises.

And now she has to wait. One of the hardest parts about waiting, and just letting them be, is that moment when your loved ones complain about the natural consequences of their behavior.

Like how much money they have spent on vaping. (But they are still vaping). Or how much they hate their job. (But they haven't looked for a new one). Or how depressed they feel. (But they refuse to go to therapy.)

My friend shared that her husband was complaining the other day that he was so winded during pickleball that he had to step out of the game with his friends.

When that happens, your tendency is to want to reassure someone. Don't do it. Let their complaint hang in the air. Don't respond.

Let Them sit with it. Say nothing. *Let Them* experience their feelings. Let the silence do the work for you. *Let Them* feel the consequences of their actions. *Let Them*.

And then, *Let Me* use science. Ask them an open-ended question. "It sounds like it bothers you?" "Is there anything you want to do about it?"

As you've already learned from Dr. K, these open-ended questions are what researchers call *motivational interviewing*. It makes your partner reflect on the conflict between what they truly want to change in their life and their current behavior, and what they don't.

The Deal Breaker Decision

But. . . what happens if you follow the ABC Loop, and you wait patiently for three months, and nothing changes?

It means that your partner doesn't feel like changing. Their behavior tells you that. So, you have a choice. Because you always have power if you focus on your response. You've followed ABC. Now it's time for you to move to the next two parts: D and E.

THE ABC (DE) LOOP

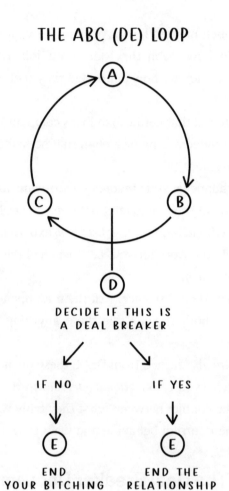

DECIDE IF THIS IS
A DEAL BREAKER

IF NO   IF YES

E   E

END   END THE
YOUR BITCHING   RELATIONSHIP

Step D: DECIDE if this is a DEAL BREAKER or not.

If after three months, the person hasn't changed or hasn't tried to change, assume they aren't going to. And, I'm sorry that I have to be the one to tell you this, but they're not ready. They don't want to do it. Doing it for you is not enough. It's not a priority of theirs, or maybe there is something deeper going on, and they are not capable of changing.

Or maybe they are just the way they are, and that's okay. Their behavior is their answer and they have made it clear.

Let Them. Not everyone wants to change. Sometimes in life, the most loving thing you can do is to stop fixing, start accepting, be more loving, and focus on what you can control.

And what you can control is choosing to love someone as they are.

I know it's not fair. I know it's disappointing. I know it's frustrating and sometimes even devastating that someone won't change for you. *Let Them* be.

Now it's time for the second part of the theory, *Let Me*. It's time to decide if this is a deal breaker for YOU. Because remember, you always get to choose who and how you love.

You can choose whether or not this is a deal breaker. A deal breaker is something you can't live with for the rest of your life. Here's how you figure that out.

Ask yourself: *Could you be with this person for the rest of your life if they never, ever change?*

Whether the answer is yes or no, move to Step E because something needs to end for this relationship to get better.

Step E: END your bitching or END the relationship.

You are at the point where they are not changing. You are in a standoff on the issue and you can either live with this or you can't. You have to choose to end your bitching or end the relationship.

Can you stop complaining about this issue, for real? Can you stop griping to yourself, holding it over their head, and acting in a passive-aggressive way and complaining to your friends?

If you're going to choose them, you owe it to them and to yourself to choose them exactly as they are. Take my marriage. My ADHD drives Chris crazy, and I understand why. I am a disaster a lot of the time.

I'll leave my dishes in the sink or stacked on my desk, I constantly misplace my keys, my stuff is all over my side of the bathroom sink, and anytime we are going somewhere I'm late.

Chris is usually sitting in the car patiently waiting for me while I run around the house like a lunatic looking for something I can't find. . . and this is just the tip of the disorganized iceberg that is Mel Robbins.

Over the years, Chris has sat me down. We've had countless conversations about it. How I leave dirty tissues on the counter and forget to throw them in the trash. ("It's disgusting, Mel.") Or how frustrated he gets when I am distracted and scrolling on Instagram. ("Are you even listening to me right now?")

And I know that my behavior makes him feel like I don't respect his time or care how my chaos impacts him.

I have tried to change. I want to change. I work on it. And it still hasn't happened. I am late. I lose everything. I make messes around the house and don't clean them up. I hate this about myself. I wish I could snap my fingers and change this aspect of who I am.

Chris is on time. Organized. Calm. Predictable. Always has been. Always will be. Chris would like me to be more like him. His life would be easier. He'd feel more supported and respected by me.

But relationships are about learning how to love someone for who they are, not for who you wish they could be. When you start using the Let Them Theory, you'll learn to see other people as they are, and then you'll see that it's up to you to figure out what you can accept and what you can't. That's how you hold on to your power. It's always in your response.

At the same time, as you let go of the surface-level stuff that is never going to change, you'll probably start to see the deeper things you have been taking for granted. For instance, while there is a lot about Chris that used to annoy me, one of the things I value most about my husband is how kindhearted, dependable, and peaceful he is. I never knew I "needed" that in a relationship. He, on the other hand, values my wild enthusiasm, fierce loyalty, and sense of humor.

It's why, as much as my behavior frustrates him, it is not a deal breaker. Chris has decided that everything else that I provide as his partner trounces the annoyances created by my ADHD.

Chris has accepted the fact that I will be like this for the rest of my life. And learned to both laugh, and live with it. Let Mel be... Mel.

That's why the Let Them Theory has made my marriage stronger. It's taught me how to accept Chris for who he is, and stop complaining about who he isn't... and vice versa.

You'll discover the exact same clarity in your own relationships. For my friend and her husband, this may mean that when she wakes up to hit the Peloton in the basement, she lets him sleep in. And that means being super quiet when she gets dressed, instead of slamming the bedroom door like she used to.

I share this example because loving someone as they are goes beyond ending your bitching. You demonstrate through your behavior that you do love them as they are. You lead with kindness and consideration.

Are You Actually Compatible with Your Partner?

Earlier, I asked you the question: Could you be with this person for the rest of your life if they never, ever change?

And what if your answer is: "I don't know" or "no?"

If you can't truly end your bitching, then you can't accept the other person and love them as they are.

That's not a very kind and loving thing to do. And if you can't stop slamming the door in the morning, or being passive-aggressive when they are running late yet again, that's not kind either.

Whether or not you end a relationship is a deeply personal decision that only you can make. In the case of my friend and her spouse, it's not a hard call. His unhealthy habits are not a deal breaker. Not even close. She loves him.

She knows that to make the relationship work, she has to work harder at accepting him and changing how she shows up in the relationship. She needs to bring more compassion and kindness to their dynamic. She can keep trying to influence him, but the expectations have to go, along with any complaining. This is about her, not about him.

And because he's not changing who he is, she needs to change who she has been in order for this relationship to be better.

But what most people are struggling with when they ask questions about using the Let Them Theory to determine whether they are with the right person are issues of compatibility. There's a difference between being committed to someone, and being compatible with them.

It is very common to fall in love with someone and experience what feels like the most incredible relationship of your entire life—and then over time the two of you start to grow in different directions, want different things, or realize that you've become different people.

This is incredibly hard when it happens, because you haven't fallen out of love. You just don't quite fit like you used to. I said that two things are required to make a relationship go the distance:

1. Both people want the relationship to work and are both willing to work on it to make it better.

2. The issues that create problems do not require either person to give up their dreams or compromise their values.

You may be in a situation where you both want the relationship to work, and you're both willing to do the work. When there's a problem with compatibility, no matter how hard you work at the relationship, there's a high chance it still might not work.

It's one of the saddest and hardest things to come to terms with when it happens, and it's a deeply personal choice.

For example, let's say you're in love with and committed to someone who is British and wants to move back home to London, but you've always envisioned staying close to your family in Atlanta.

Or another example that comes up a lot: One of you wants children, and the other doesn't.

You may talk about it. You may fight about it. You understand the reason why your partner wants to move back home to Europe and they understand why you don't. You've discussed the pros and cons of having children but never seem to come to agreement on your future. You've gone around and around on the topic. In the past, you have said, "We don't need to decide this now."

But now has come, and you're at an impasse.

They want to move. You don't.

You want children. They don't.

You're committed to each other, absolutely. . . but you might not be compatible right now.

How do you know this is truly a deal breaker?

Here's how you figure that out. Let's take the situation where you are in love with someone who has always wanted to move back home to London. And you have always envisioned being close to your family in the United States.

You ask yourself: *Will you regret breaking up with them more than moving to London with them? If you agree to move, will you resent your partner if you choose to leave your family and friends behind?*

Both choices come with heartbreak.

One requires you to give up on a dream you've had about living close to your family. The other requires you to leave the person who has been, until now, the love of your life.

And by the way, your partner is facing the exact same heartbreak because they won't compromise either. Your partner is not changing. They are moving to London. With or without you. *Let Them.*

And now, *Let Me* make a choice. Am I willing to compromise to be in this relationship?

The fact is, 69 percent of the problems in your relationship are not resolvable. This statistic comes from 40 years of scientific research conducted by Drs. John and Julie Gottman, the most famous relationship researchers on the planet (who also happen to be married).

They've found that the #1 issue that couples fight about is things that will never change: Like how someone runs late, or isn't as ambitious as you would like, or they spend every weekend in front of the TV, or their hobbies are different from yours, or they are messy, or they are a homebody, or they have different political opinions.

These are all examples of the 69 percent of the problems in your relationship that are not resolvable. That's why it is on you to figure out what you value at the deepest level. Is this something you can compromise on if your partner won't?

For some people, moving wouldn't be a big deal. They'd jump at the chance to move overseas with the love of their life.

Dr. John Gottman's research says that if you are constantly fighting about the same stuff and going around and around, it's probably because of a profound difference between your and your partner's personalities and your deepest hopes and dreams.

In other words, you value different things, and you have a different vision for how you want to live day-to-day and what you want to experience in your life. According to Dr. Gottman, almost all gridlock in your relationship comes from "unfulfilled dreams."

Take the couple fighting about moving to London, or the couple in disagreement over having kids. These are big issues. That's why you can't let it go. It's tied to a deeper vision that you have about your life. It's a very personal decision that you're going to need to make.

Moving to London seems like something that is worthy of compromising on. But if you've always wanted kids, you're going to regret wasting a decade with someone only to wake up in your mid-40s and realize this was something you truly wanted—and that now it's not going to happen.

Ask yourself, is this going to require me to give up on a dream? Because according to the Gottmans, if it does, that's a problem.

Is There Someone Better?

I've also noticed in my research that there are a lot of you in long-term committed relationships who wonder: *Is there someone better out there?*

The answer is, you'll never know.

I personally believe this worry is something that dating culture, social media, and romantic comedies have put into your head. There is no perfect person. Everyone has past issues. Everyone has baggage. And the older you get, the more baggage you have.

Most people haven't dealt with it. Only you know whether you don't appreciate what's right in front of you, or if you see everything in your life as half empty. You may think the grass is always greener somewhere else.

The fact is, the grass is greener where you water it.

That brings me back to the two things that are required to make a long-term relationship work:

1. Both people want the relationship to work and are both willing to work on it to make it better.

2. The issues that create problems do not require either person to give up their dreams or compromise their values.

At some point, you just have to choose. And that might mean choosing what is right in front of you.

As someone who has been married almost 30 years, I assure you every single couple has faced some really dark and scary times in their relationships. And for the couples who chose to lean in and work together through their issues, struggles, and challenges, not a single one of them regrets it.

But I know a lot of people who have gotten divorced and have a nagging regret that they wish they had worked a little harder to make it work and had the courage to face their issues sooner.

Maybe if they would have had the hard conversations and gone to therapy, things would have turned out differently. Because, even if it didn't end up keeping them together, it would have made the process of breaking up—and the aftermath of separating with kids involved—a hell of a lot better.

Ending a relationship is a very personal and difficult choice, especially when you wish it would work. It might mean choosing to believe in that deep intuition inside of you that something about this just doesn't quite fit.

You know it, you've just been terrified to admit it to yourself. Sometimes you have to end things before they end you. If you know what your dreams are in life, you deserve and need relationships that support you in achieving them. If you stay with someone who doesn't share the same hopes and dreams that you have. It will make you both miserable.

And look, it's easy for me to write that in a book. And it's easy for me to say, *Let Them* go. But there is nothing easy about breaking up with someone you still love.

That's when more than ever, you're going to be grateful that you have the Let Them Theory to help you get through it.

Surviving Heartbreak

I want to speak directly to you or someone you love who is going through heartbreak.

This will be one of the hardest things you ever experience. And you will get through this.

The worst thing someone can say to you when a relationship has just ended is that you should focus on "loving yourself." That is the world's worst advice, because when you're going through heartbreak, you often hate yourself.

You question everything. You wonder if you'll ever find love again. You want your old life and you wish you could go back to the way things were. You want what you used to have. It feels like your heart is shattering, because it is.

What you're feeling is grief. The life you thought you were going to live has died. Just like the experience of losing a loved one, when you go through heartbreak, you will experience all the same stages of grief. And it's going to consume you. For days, and weeks, even months, you'll think of the person nonstop.

You'll have to resist the urge all day, every day, to text, or call, or listen to their voice memos, or look at the photos, or check their location, or watch their stories online.

I was speaking to my therapist, Anne, about this, and she explained that:

It hurts so deeply because everything about them is intertwined in your nervous system. They have been a part of you and you have been a part of them for a long time. It is why you can still feel their presence and you can hear their voice. You are so used to talking to them every day, and so you naturally want to reach out. Yes, you miss them but your nervous system always misses them and the ways in which they've become intertwined with your experience of life. This is normal.

She was explaining the neurological, physiological, and neurochemical aspect of what it feels like to experience heartbreak. As you walk down the street, or you drive in your car, you'll imagine that they are there next to you. As you have a thought, you can almost hear what they would say back to you. If something good happens, you'll feel yourself wanting to share it with them. If something changes in your family, you'll wish you could tell them.

It's not just your heart that is breaking, it's all of these patterns in your life. It's the circuitry in your body. It's your nervous system. It's the thoughts in your mind. It's the images in your heart. It's the songs you used to listen to. When you get dressed for work, when you climb into bed at the end of the day and wake up alone in the morning, they will be on your mind.

You'll live in fear and in hope of bumping into them. You'll watch their life play out in pictures from far away. You'll be terrified of the day that you learn they've met someone else. The hardest part about a breakup is that you have to go through it.

There is no avoiding it. You experience it in every cell of your body because you must unlearn what it was like to be with them, and learn how to live your life again without them. This is why so many people hold on for so long.

Let Them will not make this easy. *Let Them* will not remove the pain.

My therapist Anne has a rule of thumb when it comes to heartbreak. No contact for 30 days. The reason is that any contact at all—seeing a photo, hearing their voice—will activate all the old patterns in your nervous system, and will really force you to take a step back in your process of unlearning life with this person.

This is the hard part. And you're going to be in the thick of it for at least three months. That is how long the research says it takes to grieve a breakup before you'll start to feel a little better.

By the 11-week mark, 71 percent of people feel better. I offer that as a benchmark to give you some comfort that, yes, it will get better. It may get better in 11 days. It may get better in 11 weeks. It may take a little longer. But it will get better.

The Let Them Theory will help you move through this, learn from it, and come through it stronger and more connected to yourself and what you want and deserve in your life. But, while you're in this first part, you just need to allow yourself to be in it. *Let Me.*

Let Me grieve. *Let Me* cry in my bed for days. *Let Me* tell the story over and over of how it ended. *Let Me* resist reaching out. *Let Me* be in a depressive state.

All this sadness is a mentally healthy response to heartbreak. And when you're ready, there are a couple of things that, based on the research, will help you accept that the relationship is over and that it's time for you to pick up the pieces of your life and move forward.

Here are a few recommendations for how you can get started on settling your nervous system and moving through this breakup in a healthier way—because it is not time that heals. It is what you do with that time that matters:

1. Remove all environmental triggers.

Take every visible reminder—trinkets, shirts, pictures—and get them out of sight. The patterns of this person are so hardwired in your body and mind that simply seeing things that remind you of them keeps you from moving forward. You don't need to burn things. You can just put them in a box and come back to them when you have time, space, and distance from all this emotion.

2. Give your bedroom a small makeover.

Chances are, you spent a lot of time together in your bedroom. Giving your bedroom a refresh really helps signal that a new chapter is beginning. Paint a wall or get that cool removable wallpaper. Get new sheets and a new comforter. Move your furniture around. It really helps.

3. Reach out to friends, siblings, cousins, and co-workers.

There is an empty space that this person left that needs to be filled. You need support, so ask for it. There is nothing to be embarrassed about. Everyone has gone through a breakup and understands how horrible it can be. Ask people to check in on you over the next few months and invite you to go for a walk or have dinner so you get out of your house.

4. Fill your calendar.

Look up events in your area and buy tickets so you're committed to go see an exhibit or go see a friend out of town. Reach out to friends and make plans so that you don't see an empty calendar, but you are experiencing a busy one. The distraction really helps. Nothing is worse for a breakup than an idle mind. If you don't have things to keep you busy, you will busy yourself by thinking about them.

5. Pick a challenge you have always wanted to do.

Whether it's a mountain you've wanted to climb, a triathlon you never had time to train for, a class you've always wanted to take, or even learning the guitar, this is the perfect time. Choose this challenge for yourself so that you are doing something for yourself that you are proud of. There is no better feeling.

6. Keep asking yourself this question.

If you knew the love of your life was around the corner and this breakup was bringing you one step closer to meeting them, how would you spend your nights and weekends while you are single?

One of the biggest fears when people go through a breakup is they will be alone forever and never find someone as good as the person that just walked out the door. That's not true, and being intentional about how you want to spend your time being single signals to your brain that you actually do believe that you won't be single forever— and that you better make the best out of this time right now.

One other thing: Don't do a revenge diet.

It's a huge mistake to use a heartbreak as an excuse to lose weight or get jacked at the gym or somehow make yourself more attractive with the hope of winning your ex back or rubbing it in their face as you get hot. Don't do that. It means you are still chasing your ex and they are still very much part of your day-to-day motivation.

If you want to go to the gym and get back into shape for yourself, fantastic. If you want to take care of yourself and prioritize healthier habits, amazing. But don't do it for them. Do it for you.

Most of all. . . give it time.

Time doesn't heal all wounds. What you do with your time does. No matter how busy you get, or how much better you start to feel, it will take time to process everything that happened. Let it take time. . . because it will take time. Often, it takes a LOT of time. But if you keep waking up every day and taking a step forward, one of these days you're going to wake up and realize that you're not only feeling better—you are better.

You Are the Love of Your Life

As you've navigated through the challenges of love, heartbreak, and everything in between, it's important to pause and recognize a fundamental truth: A relationship doesn't make you worthy of love. Your existence does. You will spend your entire life from the day you are born to the day you die with only one person: you. You are the only love of your life.

Throughout this book, we've focused on your relationships with other people. How to stop making other people a problem, and how to transform your relationships into the greatest sources of joy, meaning, and connection. But there's one relationship that underpins them all, and it's the one you have with yourself.

Whether you're single, dating, married, or healing from heartbreak, the power to create incredible relationships is already within you. The Let Them Theory has taught you how to navigate the complexities of human interactions, how to let others be who they are, and how to reclaim your power by choosing how you show up. But now, it's time to apply everything you've learned to the most important relationship you will ever have: the one with yourself.

Let Them be them, so you can finally *Let Me* be me.

You've learned that other people can be one of the greatest sources of happiness, better health, support, love, and connection. You deserve all that and more. You deserve relationships that elevate you, that nourish your soul, and that reflect the love and respect you have for yourself. But here's the key: The foundation of these incredible relationships lies in how you treat yourself.

Are you respecting your own boundaries? Are you showing yourself the compassion and kindness you offer to those you love? Are you allowing yourself to pursue your dreams without waiting for someone else's approval?

You are the only person you are guaranteed to spend the rest of your life with. This isn't a cliché; it's a reality. So, what kind of relationship do you want to have with yourself? I'm not going to tell you to go love yourself in some superficial way. But I am going to tell you that you have a choice—a choice to prioritize your needs, your desires, and your happiness.

This isn't about becoming self-centered or shutting others out. It's about recognizing that the love, respect, and care you give yourself set the standard for every other relationship in your life. When you stop chasing validation from others and start choosing to honor yourself, you send a powerful message to the world about how you deserve to be treated.

You don't need anyone else's permission to be happy, to pursue your passions, express yourself more, or to live the life you've always dreamed of. The only permission you need is your own. You've spent enough time waiting for others to give you what you crave—whether it's love, acceptance, or approval. But the truth is, everything you're looking for starts with you.

The Let Them Theory is more than just a tool for navigating relationships with others; it's a guide for how to treat yourself with the love, respect, and kindness you deserve. *Let them* be who they are. But more importantly, let yourself be who you truly are.

Let Me prioritize my own happiness.

Let Me pursue my dreams with passion.

Let Me set boundaries that protect my peace.

Let Me choose relationships that uplift and inspire me.

Let Me love myself enough to walk away when it no longer works.

This isn't about waiting for the right partner, the right friend, or the right opportunity to come along. It's about recognizing that you are the source of your own happiness, your own fulfillment, and your own joy. When you truly embrace that, everything else falls into place.

So, as you turn the page and move forward, remember this: You are the love of your life. And the life you create—full of meaningful relationships, joy, and fulfillment—begins with how you choose to love yourself. *Let Me.*

Now, let's wrap this up and remind ourselves of the incredible journey you've just taken. You've learned, you've grown, and you've discovered that the power to create the life and love you deserve has always been within you. And you learned throughout this section about how to best show up for yourself and choose the love you deserve.

Until today, you've been accepting less than the love you deserve. The Let Them Theory empowers you to recognize your worth, let go of those who don't treat you well, and focus on finding someone who truly deserves you.

1. **Problem:** You're accepting less than the love you deserve. You're chasing people who won't commit, or pouring time into people who don't love you back, or refusing to accept the person that you're with and learn how to love them as they are. Other people do not hold the power in your relationships, you do. It's time to show up differently.

2. **Truth:** Relationships are about learning how to love someone for who they are, not for who you wish they could be. In dating, this means letting people reveal who they are through their behavior. In relationships, this means accepting people as they are, and not punishing them because they are not who you want them to be. It also means having the hard conversations and making the hard decisions when someone can't be who you want them to be.

3. **Solution:** Using the Let Them Theory, you'll see that loving relationships are your responsibility to create, and your power is in accepting people's behavior at face value and changing how you show up. It is then that you open yourself up to attracting the love you truly deserve and showing up differently in your existing relationships, so that deeper love is possible. Welcome to your metamorphosis.

When you say *Let Them*, you accept people as they are, and you accept their behavior as the truth. When you say *Let Me*, you choose how love shows up in your life.

Stop chasing love and start choosing it.

CONCLUSION

Your Let Me Era Is Here

You and I have spent a lot of this book talking about others: their opinions, their emotions, and the ways their actions annoy, anger, frustrate, or disappoint you. But this book isn't really about other people. It's about you.

If you think it's about them, you've missed the point. If you still think other people are the problem, you need to go back and read this entire book again. The truth is simple: YOU hold the power. And YOU are the one who has been giving it away.

Imagine standing beneath a sky that's constantly shifting—sometimes clear and blue, other times filled with clouds, or rumbling with storms. You've spent so much time and energy trying to keep that sky clear, wishing away the clouds, hoping for endless sunshine. But the sky doesn't care what you want. It will do what it does, with or without your input.

The breakthrough moment comes when you realize this: The sky's beauty isn't diminished by the presence of clouds or storms. In fact, it's the variety, the unpredictability, that makes it truly magnificent. The storms highlight the calm; the clouds make the sun more precious. The same is true for your life.

You've been trying to control the uncontrollable, trying to force the world to conform to your expectations. But what if, instead, you focused on your own response to whatever the world throws your way? You can't change the weather. But you can change how it impacts you.

No matter what happens around you, you decide how it will affect you.

You decide if a comment from a loved one destroys your self-esteem or rolls off your back. You decide if all the bad dates you've been on cause you to lower your standards or become even more discerning. You decide if someone else's success makes you quit or inspires you to work even harder.

It's that simple. You have the power.

This realization is like finally understanding the true nature of the sky. The clouds that once frustrated you are now seen as part of a larger, ever-changing masterpiece. The storms that once frightened you are now moments of power and beauty, teaching you resilience and strength. You start to see that the sky's unpredictability is what makes it so magnificent, so endlessly fascinating.

Think about that for a moment. The sky will do what it does—clouds will gather, storms will come, and the sun will shine when it pleases. You can't control it, but you can control how you navigate beneath it. You can carry an umbrella; you can dance in the rain; you can chase the sun when you need to.

The people and situations around you are like the weather. The fact is, you can never control other people—how they think, how they act, whether or not they love you, or how fast they check you out at the grocery store.

So why on earth would you ever give them the level of control over you that you have been?

Why would you ever entrust something as precious as your confidence, your peace of mind, your happiness, and your dreams to the whims and moods of the people around you?

If you don't use *Let Them*, you are allowing yourself to be impacted by the worries, actions, insecurities, and opinions of others. If you don't use *Let Me*, you are leaving the things you want in life up to chance.

Ask yourself, and I mean really ask yourself: If all the energy and time you spent resisting reality—wanting lines to move faster, wanting people to text you back, wanting your boss to recognize your worth, wanting more friends, wanting people to like you, wanting your family to support your career change—if all those thoughts, feelings, and precious moments in your day were put toward something that truly mattered to you, where would you be? Who would you be? What would you have achieved?

THAT is the cost of not using *Let Them*.

Now think about all the missed opportunities—the people you wished you had introduced yourself to, the career you wanted to pursue, the music, the stand-up, the book you never wrote, the photo you never posted, the trip you didn't book, the thing you were afraid to say, the person you were afraid to love.

THAT is the cost of not using *Let Me*.

Can you really afford that price? I know I can't.

We all love to think of excuses for why people who have what we want are somehow different from us: They were born into money. They are more attractive. Their life has been easier. They've gotten lucky.

I'm sorry to break it to you, but that is a cop-out. There is no difference between you and the people you see achieving extraordinary things. They aren't special.

But there's one thing for sure they've figured out: They don't let the world around them derail their dreams. They've learned to navigate the sky, to accept the weather as it comes, and to keep moving toward their goals no matter what. At some point, they got sick and tired of worrying about what everybody else thought and just forced themselves to get to work.

They are laser focused on waking up every day and proving, over and over through their actions, that they are worthy and deserving of the vision they have for their life.

Every day that you allow your fear of somebody else's opinion, stress over friendships, or concern about how someone will react to prevent you from making the phone call, filling out the application, working on the business plan, starting the diet, or putting in the effort, you're holding yourself back. You're robbing yourself of your potential. You're standing still while life moves on around you.

Stop wasting your brain space on the million tiny things that don't matter. It's time to use every second of your day for all the amazing things you know you're capable of.

Stop letting the fear of what people might think paralyze you. It's time to go after your dreams boldly, relentlessly, and unapologetically.

Stop tiptoeing around everyone else's emotions. It's time to fiercely protect your own peace.

Stop letting other people's success devastate you. It's time to get to work.

Stop making your social life everyone else's responsibility. It's time to build the most incredible friendships you've ever had.

Stop trying to change people who don't want to change. It's time to let adults be adults.

Stop trying to rescue those who are struggling. It's time to let others heal how they need to heal.

Stop wasting your time trying to get people to love you. It's time to choose the love you deserve.

It's finally time to reclaim your power and reclaim your life.

The Let Them Theory is your key to taking back your power.

You can have the life you've always wanted. You can be a millionaire.

You can have the beautiful love story you've always dreamed of. You can build a career that challenges and fulfills you.

The question is, will YOU let yourself do it?

Because no one else can stop you. It's all on you.

The most important part of the Let Them Theory is understanding that you are responsible for your own happiness. You are responsible for the energy you bring and how you show up. You are responsible for waking up every day and doing the work to make progress on what matters. You are responsible for defining what matters to you. You are responsible for telling the truth even when it's really hard. You are responsible for paying for your life. Nobody owes you anything, but you owe yourself everything.

If you're not where you want to be, the great news is, it's all your fault. The even better news is, the second you decide to, you can change it.

You've wasted so many years being so consumed with other people, their feelings, their thoughts, and what they're doing. So let this book be your wake-up call: You are in charge.

This realization is not a condemnation, it's a liberation.

Isn't it incredible to know that others can't affect you? Isn't it liberating to know that they can say and do what they want—they can make fun, doubt, be the most successful person on this planet, and you remain unbothered?

How amazing is it that YOU get to be in control of what you think, what you say, and what you do?

How unbelievable is it that YOU get to choose where you pour your time and energy, and what you say yes to and what you say no to?

Taking back your power means reclaiming responsibility for your life. It means demanding more of yourself because time is ticking, and you've wasted enough of it worrying about things that don't matter. It means being laser focused on the things you can control, and not giving a single second to the things you can't.

Think of the sky once more. No matter what it brings, no matter how it changes, you are the one who gets to decide how to navigate beneath it. You are the one who gets to choose how to respond, how to act, how to live. The clouds, the storms, the sunshine—they all have their place, but they do not define you. You define yourself.

I won't lie to you: It won't be easy. It's not like the second you start saying *Let Them*, you get everything you've ever wanted. Anyone who promises you that is lying to you.

But the second you take your power back, you can take comfort in the knowledge that it's just a matter of time. The career, the partner, the friends, the body, the goals—they are now all in your control.

Now that we're here, I am so incredibly excited to personally welcome you to your *Let Me* era.

Let Me get started.

Let Me take a risk.

Let Me write the book.

Let Me be honest about what I want.

Let Me get in the best shape of my life.

Let Me apply for the dream job.

Let Me stop giving love to people who don't want me back.

Let Me create a better life. A life that makes me proud. A life that makes me happy. A life where I use my precious energy to enjoy every single moment I will have.

This book has shown you that you've always had control. You've always been in charge. You've always had the power. Now, it's time to take it back.

I want you to know that whatever that big dream you see for yourself is, however crazy, unlikely, or silly it may seem, I see it for you. If you don't believe in you, *Let Me* believe in you. If you don't know you can do it, *Let Me* know it for you.

And if you don't know where to start, *Let Me* help you take the first step. In case nobody else tells you, I want to be sure to tell you: I love you, I believe in you, and I believe in your ability to unlock all the magic and joy that your amazing life has to offer.

All it takes is two simple words:

Let Me.

APPENDIX

How to Apply Let Them to Parenting

One of the most common questions I get is how to use the Let Them Theory in parenting. Let's be honest—if you let your kids do whatever they want, they'd probably be eating ice cream at every meal, skipping homework, and avoiding chores. But as a mom of three, I've discovered that when you let your kids be themselves, your relationship improves and deepens in ways you never thought possible.

While this book primarily focuses on adults, the Let Them Theory is also a powerful tool for parenting kids of all ages. It's about connecting, supporting, and guiding—not controlling. Ultimately your job as a parent is to guide your children to become who they are meant to be, in other words—*Let Them*.

To help you strengthen your bond with your kids (and hopefully keep your sanity intact), I've put together a special bonus guide filled with practical tips on using the Let Them Theory in parenting. Because who doesn't want an incredible relationship with their kids?

Download it at **melrobbins.com/parenting** to get started.

How to Apply Let Them to Teams

Over the years, I've had the opportunity to work with some of the world's biggest companies, including Starbucks, JPMorganChase, Headspace, Audible, Ulta Beauty, and more.

One of the most common questions I've been asked is: *How do I motivate my team?*

The research is clear—having a good boss is what creates good teams. So what makes for a good boss? That's where the Let Them Theory comes in. You may be thinking, *You can't just let your team do whatever they want—they need to be managed*. True, but when you micromanage, you risk stifling creativity, damaging relationships, and creating a toxic work environment.

In other words, a controlling boss is a bad boss.

The Let Them Theory can help you find the right balance, empowering your team while providing the structure they need to thrive. After all, bad bosses kill good teams, and good bosses make great teams. In this special bonus guide, you'll learn how to use the Let Them Theory to be as good a boss as you can be.

Download it at **melrobbins.com/work** to get started.

Let Me Acknowledge You

To the millions of fans of *The Mel Robbins Podcast* and everyone of you on social media, who either follows me or has shared content from the "lady with the glasses"—thank you! Without you I wouldn't get to do what I love most. You are the reason this book exists. Your support, passion, love, and (of course) your tattoos inspired me to do something I swore I would never do again: write another book. Thank you for being a part of this incredible journey. Thank you for helping me create what I believe is the single most important piece of work I have ever done. One thing is certain, I wrote this book for you and it is yours as much as it is mine. I cannot wait to see how this book helps you improve your life and your relationships. You deserve more love, meaning, joy, and peace in your life, and the Let Them Theory will help you achieve it.

All the experts who have appeared on *The Mel Robbins Podcast* and in the pages of this book—thank you for hopping on planes and flying to Boston to sit down and spend time with me. I have learned so much from each and every one of you. Whether your research is cited directly in this book and bibliography, or not, know this; meeting, speaking, and learning from you has shaped every word and helped me improve my life. On behalf of everyone who will read this book, and every single listener of *The Mel Robbins Podcast* in 194 countries, thank you. Thank you for your work; thank you for sharing your wisdom with us.

Sawyer—my brilliant daughter, co-conspirator, co-researcher, co-writer, and co-pilot—you swore you would NEVER work for your mother, and here we are. I wake up every day grateful that you said yes when I asked "if you could help me with a 'small research project'. . . it's called the Let Them Theory." You dove in and never came back up for air. It has been one of the most fulfilling experiences of my life to not only be your mom but to now get to know you as a colleague. I love you deeply and I love every moment of working with you, even though I know you are having to say *Let Them, Let Them, Let Them* (about me) the entire time.

Tracey—my right-hand, right-brain, sentence-finisher, and executive producer extraordinaire—Where would I be without you? Lost at sea. You keep this ship afloat. Your single best quality: I have never once seen you with a frown on your face or a negative attitude; thank you for always bringing the sun. After eight years I am so grateful for your calm, steady hand guiding the way through this wild adventure.

Susie—thank you for bringing fun and storytelling into the writing process. You've made me a better writer. You've added so much depth and soul to this project, and your work is an undeniable part of the book's heart. You are an OG, and this book wouldn't be where it is without you. I am so happy it brought us together and thrilled to know that this partnership is just beginning.

Juna—you came in like a whirlwind, impressing me daily with your incredible writing skills. Your ability to nail down the language, the power, and the vibe of this book was remarkable. You were essential in shaping this story into something powerful. I absolutely love the way you think!

Lynne—you know that feeling when someone shows up in your life and you realize what has been missing. . . that is you Lynne. You filled a need in my life, and it is only in working with you that I now realize what true support and excellence feels and looks like. You set the bar impossibly high. I don't think I could do this job without you. Now, please put down your phone and turn off your laptop. . . stop working. . . and enjoy your weekend! I am not going anywhere, neither are you, so get some rest while you can. <3

Cindy—to our ROCKSTAR in pink Crocs and matching lipstick with the best Boston accent you have ever heard, I love you from the bottom of my heart. From the moment you walked into our lives, you brought so much joy and laughter. I never thought at the age of 56 I would find a "house mom" in real life—you know the amazing human who takes care of an entire sorority—that is you! You might as well be named Cindy Robbins and at this point Yolo and Homie get more excited when you walk in than when I do.

Amy & Jessie—to the OGs up here in Vermont. We first bonded over how much we HATED living in VT and had no idea what the heck we'd do in this tiny rural town. Moving here wasn't a coincidence; it was synchronicity. Over the past four years we have laughed, cried, and pushed our way through every obstacle—one cold plunge and card pull at a time (Amazing Amy!). And along the way, we managed to launch the single "fastest growing podcast" on the planet, from above our garage in the middle of nowhere. There's something magical about meeting some of your most favorite people later in life. And you are two of mine. I have a feeling this next chapter is going to be the most divine and epic one yet. The most surprising part is we absolutely love living here now.

Melody—our editor, copyediting champion, and fellow cool-eyeglass fashionista—thank you for gracefully managing my many, many late-night, last-minute delays. You always showed up with a smile and made sure this book was polished and perfect. I owe you a mountain of coffee and endless gratitude.

Marc—you already know how much I adore you. Not only did you make this book possible but you also ensured that its message would reach readers around the globe, with translations in languages far beyond the borders of the U.S. You are the best, a genius at making deals and helping me be the first author to do the "things" we do, the unique way we do them (top secret everyone)—I'm forever grateful. ;)

Christine—my sister-in-law, business partner, fellow Australian shepherd lover, and best friend—thank you for being my rock. I'm sorry I have had so many meltdowns over the writing of this book. I am embarrassed by all the emotional texts and late-night venting I did at you. No one on the planet needs the part of this book about managing emotions more than I do. Thank you for having so much grace. Thank you for guiding our company from an out-of-control start-up to a world-class business and global powerhouse in personal development. I am so proud of you. I am proud to be your partner. And I am so proud of what we've built together. I couldn't have done it without knowing you always have my back and our best interest at heart. I wake up every day and say to myself: *Can you believe we get to do this for a living?* I can always hear you say in the back of my mind: We are magical b*tches.

Chris—thank you for always going camping during the *Let Them* marathon writing weeks. A book can't be bound without a spine and you are that for me. You hold our family together. The thing I love most about my life is that I get to spend it with you.

Kendall and Oakley—based on what you have heard about how grueling this book process has been I can imagine you were grateful that you were at college and in LA as Sawyer and I duked it out. You have always supported me in pursuing my dreams, and know this:

Whatever it is that you choose to do with your lives, I'll be there every step of the way to cheer you on.

Mom and Dad—Mom: I think you get credit for instilling me with the *Let Me* spirit as a little girl. As I wrote this book, I kept thinking about that needlepoint pillow you stitched with the saying: *Pull Up Your Big Girl Panties And Deal With It*. LOL. Thank you for being my biggest supporters and for always being there when I needed you. I know you are proud of me, and I want you to know—I am proud of you, your marriage, and the life you've created too.

Anne—thank you for teaching me how to become a whole woman. Words cannot describe the impact you have made in my life, my marriage, and my ability to unlock my full potential. I love you.

David—whenever I need advice, perspective, coaching, a laugh, or a great gin and tonic—I got you on speed dial. Thank you for teaching me how to be a Good Boss and an even better friend. Christine and I couldn't do it without you, and we definitely wouldn't want to! Love you.

Pete—you absolutely nailed it with the book cover. The design is everything I dreamed of and more. I am sure I have been a giant pain in the rear end to work with, and I appreciate your patience with all the last-minute chaos. Thank you for your creativity—the cover is absolutely amazing, and I hope you are as proud of it as I am.

Julie—What can I say? The interior of this book feels clean, light, and exactly right. You made it all come together, and I'm thrilled with the result. Thank you for your hard work and dedication!

Lindsay—it is hard to put in words how much I appreciate your support even when I wasn't publishing a new book. You have been booking me on the *Today* show and sending me PR opportunities. You are smart, dedicated, and I am so excited to continue this rodeo with you.

To my entire team—thank you for giving me and Sawyer the space to write this book, all while you were producing two podcast episodes a week, a six-month online coaching program, keynote speeches, and productions for our partners at Audible, Ulta Beauty. . . and many more! You are THE BEST team on the planet. I couldn't have done it without your dedication and teamwork.

The tattoo artists and those who gave me your stories through your art—you are the true inspiration behind this book. Watching the *Let Them* concept take off has been humbling and exhilarating. It all began with you, and I'm forever grateful for the chance to share your meaningful, beautiful designs with the world.

Patty, Reid, Diane, Lizzi, Arya-Mehr, Marlene, Betsy, Kathleen, and the entire team at Hay House—I love being your partner. There is so much that you do that I don't even know what I should be listing, so to absolutely everyone who has supported this book, sold it, marketed it, and read it, it takes a village and it's an honor to be a part of yours.

Partners at Audible—WOW! We have been working together for seven YEARS. I cannot believe how much we have done together. Even as I write this acknowledgment, for partnering with me on *The Let Them Theory* audiobook, you and I are actively researching the topic for our seventh original Audible production together. I am so honored to be a part of your global and life-changing mission. Here's to the next seven Audible originals. I love you guys!

Align PR—You are the first PR agency I have ever hired and it is so worth it. I am amazed by the way you think, operate, and excel at your craft. I am proud to work with the best and that is YOU.

Bibliography

I've poured everything into this book—my heart, my soul, and years of learning from the best experts in the world. The Let Them Theory is built on research that's always evolving, just like you and me. What I'm sharing here is a powerful beginning, but there's always more to discover. Human behavior and relationships are endlessly fascinating, and as new insights emerge, our understanding will only deepen. The reason I've listed all the sources in alphabetical order is simple: I want you to focus on the bigger picture, not get lost in a sea of citations.

This theory isn't about isolating one study—it's about blending the most powerful ideas from psychology, neuroscience, and human behavior to create something transformative for you. As I said in the Introduction, this book is not a textbook or an academic paper, but rather a guide. The sources in the following pages are just a glimpse into the incredible work that has shaped the *Let Them Theory*. Your journey doesn't end here—it's just getting started.

Abbott, Alison. "New Theory of Dopamine's Role in Learning Could Help Explain Addiction." *Nature*, August 9, 2018. https://www.nature.com/articles/d41586-018-05902-7.

Alter, Adam. *Anatomy of a Breakthrough: How to Get Unstuck When It Matters Most.* New York: Simon & Schuster, 2023.

Amabile, Teresa, and Steven Kramer. *The Progress Principle: Using Small Wins to Ignite Joy, Engagement, and Creativity at Work.* Boston, MA: Harvard Business Review Press, 2011.

Amati, Valeria, et al. "Social Relations and Life Satisfaction: The Role of Friends." *Genus* 74, no. 1 (2018): 1–18.

Aron, Arthur, and Elaine N. Aron. "The Importance of Love and Commitment in Close Relationships." *Psychology of Relationships* 45 (2012): 150–172.

Aurelius, Marcus. *Meditations*. Translated by Gregory Hays. New York: Penguin Classics, 2006.

Bandura, Albert. "On the Functional Properties of Perceived Self-Efficacy Revisited." *Journal of Management* 38, no. 1 (2012): 9–44.

Barron, Helen C., et al. "Unmasking Latent Inhibitory Connections in Human Cortex to Reveal Dormant Cortical Memories." *Neuron* 107, no. 2 (2020): 338–348. https://www.sciencedirect.com/science/article/pii/S0896627320303470?dgcid=author.

Baumeister, Roy F., and Mark R. Leary. "The Need to Belong: Desire for Interpersonal Attachments as a Fundamental Human Motivation." *Psychological Bulletin* 117, no. 3 (1995): 497–529.

Ben-Shahar, Tal. *Happier: Learn the Secrets to Daily Joy and Lasting Fulfillment*. New York: McGraw-Hill, 2007.

Bilyeu, Lisa. *Radical Confidence: 11 Lessons on How to Get the Relationship, Career, and Life You Want*. New York: Simon and Schuster, 2024.

Bolte, Annette, Thomas Goschke, and Julius Kuhl. "Emotion and Intuition." *Psychological Science* 14, no. 5 (2003): 416–21. https://doi.org/10.1111/1467-9280.01456.

Bolte Taylor, Jill. *My Stroke of Insight: A Brain Scientist's Personal Journey*. New York: Viking, 2008.

Bolte Taylor, Jill. *Whole Brain Living: The Anatomy of Choice and the Four Characters That Drive Our Life*. New York: Hay House, 2021.

Brach, Tara. *Radical Acceptance: Embracing Your Life with the Heart of a Buddha*. New York: Bantam, 2004.

Brehm, Jack W., and Elizabeth A. Self. "The Intensity of Motivation." *Annual Review of Psychology* 40, no. 1 (2009): 109–131.

Brown, Brené. *Daring Greatly: How the Courage to Be Vulnerable Transforms the Way We Live, Love, Parent, and Lead*. New York: Gotham, 2012.

Brown, Brené. *I Thought It Was Just Me (but It Isn't): Telling the Truth About Perfectionism, Inadequacy, and Power*. New York: Gotham Books, 2008.

Bryant, Erin. "Dopamine Affects How Brain Decides Whether Goal Is Worth Effort." *NIH Research Matters*, April 17, 2017. https://www.nih.gov/news-events/nih-research-matters/dopamine-affects-how-brain-decides-whether-goal-worth-effort.

Buunk, Bram P., and Frederick X. Gibbons. "Social Comparison: The End of a Theory and the Emergence of a Field." *Organizational Behavior and Human Decision Processes* 102, no. 1 (2007): 3–21.

Buunk, Bram P., and Frederick X. Gibbons. "Social Comparison: The End of a Theory and the Emergence of a Field." *Perspectives on Psychological Science* 9, no. 3 (2014): 234–252.

Christakis, Nicholas A., and James H. Fowler. *Connected: The Surprising Power of Our Social Networks and How They Shape Our Lives*. New York, NY: Little, Brown, 2011.

Clark, C., and J. Greenberg. "Fear of Rejection and Sensitivity to Social Feedback: Implications for Mental Health." *Clinical Psychology Review* 84 (2021): 101945.

Clark, Margaret S., and Edward P. Lemay. "Close Relationships and Well-Being: The Role of Compassionate Goals." *Social and Personality Psychology Compass* 4, no. 5 (2010): 289–301.

Collins, R. L. "For Better or Worse: The Impact of Upward Social Comparison on Self-Evaluations." *Psychological Bulletin* 119, no. 1 (1996): 51–69.

Conti, Paul. *Trauma: The Invisible Epidemic: How Trauma Works and How We Can Heal from It*. New York: Sounds True, 2021.

Corcoran, Katja, and Thomas Mussweiler. "Social Comparison and Rumination: Insights into the Motivational Impact of Others' Success." *Journal of Personality and Social Psychology* 103, no. 4 (2012): 712–727.

Crum, Alia J., and Derek J. Phillips. "Self-Fulfilling Prophecies, Placebo Effects, and the Social-Psychological Creation of Reality." In *Handbook of Social Psychology*, 2nd ed. Springer, 2015.

Crum, Alia J., and Ellen J. Langer. "Mindset Matters: Exercise and the Placebo Effect." *Psychological Science* 18, no. 2 (2010): 165–171.

Csikszentmihalyi, Mihaly. *Flow: The Psychology of Optimal Experience*. New York: Harper & Row, 1990.

Damasio, Antonio R. *Descartes' Error: Emotion, Reason, and the Human Brain*. New York: Penguin Books, 1994.

Damour, Lisa. *The Emotional Lives of Teenagers: Raising Connected, Capable, and Compassionate Adolescents*. London: Atlantic Books, 2023.

Damour, Lisa. *Under Pressure: Confronting the Epidemic of Stress and Anxiety in Girls*. London: Atlantic Books, 2019.

Damour, Lisa. *Untangled: Guiding Teenage Girls Through the Seven Transitions into Adulthood*. London: Atlantic Books Ltd, 2016.

Davidson, Richard J., and Sharon Begley. *The Emotional Life of Your Brain*. New York: Plume, 2012.

Day, Kristen, Corinne Carreon, and Caitlin Stump. "The Influence of the Physical Environment on Health Behavior: Implications for Cancer Survivorship." *Public Health Reports* 126 (2011): 112–121.

Demir, Melikşah, et al. "Friendships, Psychological Well-Being, and Happiness: A Study on the Role of Socialization Goals in Emerging Adulthood." *Journal of Happiness Studies* 16, no. 6 (2015): 1559–1574.

Dijksterhuis, Ap, et al. "The Mechanisms of Social Comparison in Success and Failure Contexts." *Journal of Experimental Social Psychology* 46, no. 6 (2010): 923–929.

Duhigg, Charles. *The Power of Habit: Why We Do What We Do in Life and Business*. New York, NY: Random House, 2014.

Dunbar, Robin I. M. *How Many Friends Does One Person Need? Dunbar's Number and Other Evolutionary Quirks*. Cambridge: Harvard University Press, 2010.

Dunning, David. "The Dunning-Kruger Effect: On Being Ignorant of One's Own Ignorance." In *Advances in Experimental Social Psychology*, vol. 44, edited by Mark P. Zanna, 247–296. Elsevier, 2011.

Durvasula, Ramani. *It's Not You*. New York: Post Hill Press, 2024.

Durvasula, Ramani. *Should I Stay or Should I Go?: Surviving a Relationship with a Narcissist*. New York: Post Hill Press, 2015.

Dweck, Carol S. *Mindset: The New Psychology of Success*. New York: Random House, 2006.

Eagleman, David. *Livewired: The Inside Story of the Ever-Changing Brain*. New York: Pantheon Books, 2020.

Ekman, Paul. "What Scientists Who Study Emotion Agree About." *Perspectives on Psychological Science* 11, no. 1 (2016): 31–34.

Epstein, Mark. *Thoughts Without a Thinker: Psychotherapy from a Buddhist Perspective*. New York: Basic Books, 1995.

Evans, Gary W. "The Built Environment and Mental Health." *Annual Review of Public Health* 29, no. 1 (2011): 403–416.

"Exercising to Relax." *Harvard Health Publishing*, February 2011. https://www.health.harvard.edu/staying-healthy/exercising-to-relax.

Ferriss, Timothy. *Tools of Titans: The Tactics, Routines, and Habits of Billionaires, Icons, and World-Class Performers*. Boston: Houghton Mifflin Harcourt, 2017.

Festinger, Leon. "A Theory of Social Comparison Processes: Retrospective and Contemporary Perspectives." *Organizational Behavior and Human Decision Processes* 123, no. 2 (2012): 100–121.

Finkel, Eli J., and Roy F. Baumeister. "Attachment and Marriage: New Developments in the Science of Close Relationships." *Advances in Experimental Social Psychology* 42 (2010): 1–50.

Fiori, Katherine L., et al. "Friendship Quality in Late Adulthood: The Role of Positive and Negative Social Exchanges in Well-Being." *Journal of Aging and Health* 32, no. 3–4 (2020): 163–176.

Fishbach, Ayelet, and Stacey R. Finkelstein. "How Positive and Negative Feedback Motivate Goal Pursuit." *Social and Personality Psychology Compass* 6, no. 5 (2012): 359–366.

Fogg, B.J. *Tiny Habits: The Small Changes That Change Everything*. Boston: Mariner Books, Houghton Mifflin Harcourt, 2020.

Ford, Michael E., and Clyde W. Nichols. "A Framework for Explaining Social Cognitive Influences on Behavior." In *Advances in Experimental Social Psychology*, vol. 52, edited by Mark P. Zanna, 193–246. Elsevier, 2015.

Frankl, Viktor E. *Man's Search for Meaning*. New York: Washington Square Press, 1985.

Gallagher, Winifred. *Rapt: Attention and the Focused Life*. New York: Penguin Books, 2009.

Gallo, Amy, Shawn Achor, Michelle Gielan, and Monique Valcour. "How Your Morning Mood Affects Your Whole Workday." *Harvard Business Review*. Harvard Business School Publishing, October 5, 2016. https://hbr.org/2016/07/how-your-morning-mood-affects-your-whole-workday.

Garrett, Neil, and Tali Sharot. "Updating Beliefs Under Perceived Threat." *Affective Brain Lab*, August 2018. https://affectivebrain.com/wp-content/uploads/2018/08/Updating-Beliefs-Under-Perceived-Threat.pdf.

Garrett, Neil, et al. "Updating Beliefs Under Perceived Threat." *Nature Neuroscience* 22, no. 12 (2019): 2066–2074. https://affectivebrain.com/wp-content/uploads/2019/12/s41593-019-0549-2.pdf.

Grant, Heidi, and Carol S. Dweck. "Clarifying Achievement Goals and Their Impact." *Journal of Personality and Social Psychology* 85, no. 3 (2009): 541–553.

Greitemeyer, Tobias. "Effects of Exposure to Others' Opinions on Social Influence: Mechanisms of Conformity, Compliance, and Obedience." *Psychological Bulletin* 135, no. 6 (2009): 895–915.

Gilbert, Paul. *The Compassionate Mind: A New Approach to Facing Challenges*. London: Constable & Robinson, 2009.

Gilbert, Paul. *The Compassionate Mind Workbook*. London: Robinson, 2010.

Goldstein, Joseph. *One Dharma: The Emerging Western Buddhism*. New York: HarperCollins, 2003.

Gottman, John M. *The Relationship Cure: A 5 Step Guide to Strengthening Your Marriage, Family, and Friendships*. New York: Harmony Books, 2002.

Gottman, John, Julie Gottman, and Doug Abrams. *Eight Dates: Essential Conversations for a Lifetime of Love*. New York: Workman Publishing, 2019.

Gottman, John M., and Nan Silver. *The Seven Principles for Making Marriage Work: A Practical Guide from the Country's Foremost Relationship Expert*. New York: Harmony Books, 2015.

Greenfieldboyce, Nell. "The Human Brain Never Stops Growing Neurons, a New Study Claims." *PBS NewsHour*, March 25, 2019. https://www.pbs.org/newshour/science/the-human-brain-never-stops-growing-neurons-a-new-study-claims.

Grenny, Joseph. "4 Things to Do Before a Tough Conversation." *Harvard Business Review*, January 22, 2019. https://hbr.org/2019/01/4-things-to-do-before-a-tough-conversation.

Gross, James J., and Ross A. Thompson. "Emotion Regulation: Conceptual Foundations." In *Handbook of Emotion Regulation*, 2nd ed., edited by James J. Gross, 3–24. New York: Guilford Press, 2014.

Guell, Xavier, A. David G. Leslie, and Jeremy D. Schmahmann. "Functional Topography of the Human Cerebellum: A Meta-Analysis of Neuroimaging Studies." *NeuroImage* 124 (2016): 107–118. https://www.ncbi.nlm.nih.gov/pmc/articles/PMC5789790/.

Hall, Jeffrey A. "How Many Hours Does It Take to Make a Friend?" *Journal of Social and Personal Relationships* 36, no. 4 (2019): 1278–1296.

Hamm, Jill V., and Beverly S. Faircloth. "The Role of Friendship in Adolescents' Sense of School Belonging." *New Directions for Child and Adolescent Development* 2015, no. 148 (2015): 61–78.

Hartup, Willard W., and Nancy Stevens. "Friendships and Adaptation Across the Life Span." *Current Directions in Psychological Science* 8, no. 3 (2011): 76–79.

Hayes, Steven C., Kirk D. Strosahl, and Kelly G. Wilson. *Acceptance and Commitment Therapy: An Experiential Approach to Behavior Change*. New York: Guilford Press, 1999.

Heckhausen, Jutta. "Developmental Regulation in Adulthood: Age-Normative and Sociocultural Constraints as Adaptive Challenges." *Psychology and Aging* 27, no. 4 (2012): 937–950.

Heckhausen, Jutta, and Heinz Heckhausen, eds. *Motivation and Action*. Cambridge: Cambridge University Press, 2009.

Hill, Sarah E., and David M. Buss. "Envy and Status in Social Groups: An Evolutionary Perspective on Competition and Collaboration." *Evolutionary Psychology* 8, no. 3 (2010): 345–368.

"How to Strengthen Relationships Between Parents and Adult Children." *American Psychological Association*, May 18, 2023. https://www.apa.org/news/podcasts/speaking-of-psychology/parent-adult-children-relationships.

Hussey, Matthew. *Love Life: How to Raise Your Standards, Find Your Person, and Live Happily (No Matter What)*. London: HarperCollins UK, 2024.

Hyun, Jinshil, Martin J. Sliwinski, and Joshua M. Smyth. "Waking Up on the Wrong Side of the Bed: The Effects of Stress Anticipation on Working Memory in Daily Life." *The Journals of Gerontology: Series B*, 2018. https://doi.org/10.1093/geronb/gby042.

Insel, Thomas R. "The NIMH Research Domain Criteria (RDoC) Project: Precision Medicine for Psychiatry." *American Journal of Psychiatry* 171, no. 4 (2014): 395–97. https://www.ncbi.nlm.nih.gov/pmc/articles/PMC5854216/.

Kabat-Zinn, Jon. *Full Catastrophe Living: Using the Wisdom of Your Body and Mind to Face Stress, Pain, and Illness*. New York: Delacorte Press, 1990.

Johnson, M. D., and Franz J. Neyer. "(Eventual) Stability and Change Across Partnerships." *Journal of Family Psychology* 33, no. 6 (2019): 711–721. https://doi.org/10.1037/fam0000523.

Johnson, Colleen L., and Lillian E. Troll. "Friends and Aging: The Interplay of Intimacy and Distance." *Generations* 36, no. 1 (2012): 32–39.

Kabat-Zinn, Jon. *Wherever You Go, There You Are: Mindfulness Meditation in Everyday Life*. New York: Hachette Books, 2013.

Kahneman, Daniel. *Thinking, Fast and Slow*. New York: Farrar, Straus and Giroux, 2011.

Kanfer, Ruth, and Gilad Chen. "Motivation in Organizational Behavior: Insights and Directions." *Organizational Behavior and Human Decision Processes* 136 (2016): 121–133.

Kanojia, Alok. *How to Raise a Healthy Gamer: Break Bad Screen Habits, End Power Struggles, and Transform Your Relationship with Your Kids*. London: Pan Macmillan, 2024.

Kaplan, Rachel, and Stephen Kaplan. *The Experience of Nature: A Psychological Perspective*. Ann Arbor: University of Michigan Press, 2011.

Koob, George F., and Nora D. Volkow. "Neurobiology of Addiction: A Neurocircuitry Analysis." *The Lancet Psychiatry* 3, no. 8 (2016): 760–773.

Kross, Ethan, and Ozlem Ayduk. "Self-Distancing: Theory, Research, and Current Directions." *Advances in Experimental Social Psychology* 55 (2017): 81–136.

Kurth-Nelson, Zeb, et al. "Computational Approaches to Neuroscience: Modeling Belief Updating Under Threat." *PLoS Computational Biology* 15, no. 2 (2019). https://journals.plos.org/ploscompbiol/article?id=10.1371/journal.pcbi.1007089#ack.

La Guardia, Jennifer G., and Richard M. Ryan. *Self-Determination Theory: Basic Psychological Needs in Motivation, Development, and Wellness*. New York: Guilford Press, 2013.

Lavy, Shiri, and Hadassah Littman-Ovadia. "The Effect of Love on Personal Growth and Self-Perception in Relationships." *Journal of Positive Psychology* 6, no. 3 (2011): 209–216.

Leary, Mark R., and Roy F. Baumeister. "The Nature and Function of Self-Esteem: Sociometer Theory." In *Advances in Experimental Social Psychology*, vol. 32, edited by Mark P. Zanna, 1–62. Elsevier, 2012.

Leary, Mark R., and Roy F. Baumeister. "The Nature and Function of Self-Esteem: Sociometer Theory." In *Advances in Experimental Social Psychology*, Vol. 32, edited by Mark P. Zanna, 1–62. New York: Academic Press, 1995.

LeDoux, Joseph. *The Emotional Brain: The Mysterious Underpinnings of Emotional Life*. New York: Simon & Schuster, 1996.

Levine, Peter A., and Gabor Maté. *In an Unspoken Voice: How the Body Releases Trauma and Restores Goodness*. Berkeley, CA: North Atlantic Books, 2010.

Levitt, Mary J., et al. "Close Relationships Across the Life Span." *Wiley Interdisciplinary Reviews: Cognitive Science* 2, no. 1 (2011): 1–12.

LeWine, Howard E., M. D."Understanding the Stress Response." *Harvard Health*. Harvard Medical School, July 6, 2020. https://www.health.harvard.edu/staying-healthy/understanding-the-stress-response.

Luthar, Suniya S., and Natasha L. Kumar. "Friendship Quality, Social Skills, and Resilience in Adolescence." *Child Development* 89, no. 3 (2018): 876–890.

Lyons, Scott. *Addicted to Drama: Healing Dependency on Crisis and Chaos in Yourself and Others*. New York: Hachette Go, 2023.

Lyubomirsky, Sonja, et al. "Why Are Some People Happier Than Others? The Role of Cognitive and Motivational Processes in Well-Being." *American Psychologist* 56, no. 3 (2011): 239–249.

Maddux, James E. *Self-Efficacy, Adaptation, and Adjustment: Theory, Research, and Application.* Springer, 2013.

Margaret Mead, quoted in *The World Ahead: An Anthropologist Anticipates the Future,* edited by Ruth Nanda Anshen, 24. New York: Berghahn Books, 2000.

Marsh, Herbert W., and John W. Parker. "Determinants of Student Self-Concept: Is It Better to Be a Relatively Large Fish in a Small Pond Even If You Don't Learn to Swim as Well?" *Journal of Personality and Social Psychology* 47, no. 1 (1984): 213–231.

Marques, Luana. *Bold Move: A 3-Step Plan to Transform Anxiety into Power.* London: Hachette UK, 2023.

McGonigal, Kelly. *The Willpower Instinct.* New York: Avery, 2012.

McPherson, Miller, Lynn Smith-Lovin, and Matthew E. Brashears. "Social Isolation in America: Changes in Core Discussion Networks Over Two Decades." *American Sociological Review* 74, no. 3 (2009): 353–375.

Miller, William R., and Stephen Rollnick. *Motivational Interviewing: Helping People Change.* 3rd ed. New York: Guilford Press, 2012.

Mikulincer, Mario, and Phillip R. Shaver. *Attachment in Adulthood: Structure, Dynamics, and Change.* 2nd ed. New York: Guilford Press, 2016.

Mineo, Liz. "Over Nearly 80 Years, Harvard Study Has Been Showing How to Live a Healthy and Happy Life." *Harvard Gazette,* April 11, 2017. https://news.harvard.edu/gazette/story/2017/04/over-nearly-80-years-harvard-study-has-been-showing-how-to-live-a-healthy-and-happy-life/.

Mora, Florentina, Sergio Segovia, and José R. Del Arco. "Aging, Stress, and the Hippocampus." *Aging Research Reviews* 11, no. 2 (April 2012): 123–129. https://pubmed.ncbi.nlm.nih.gov/23403892/.

Morin, Alexandre J. S., and Christophe Maïano. "The Social Comparison Process and Its Implications for Goal Pursuit and Achievement Motivation." *Social and Personality Psychology Compass* 5, no. 6 (2011): 359–374.

Murray, Sandra L., and John G. Holmes. *Interdependent Minds: The Dynamics of Close Relationships.* New York: Guilford Press, 2013.

Murray, Sandra L., and Jennifer L. Derrick. "The Power of Reassurance: How Emotional Security Impacts Commitment in Relationships." *Journal of Personality and Social Psychology* 100, no. 4 (2011): 575–592.

Mussweiler, Thomas. "Comparison Processes in Social Judgment: Mechanisms and Consequences." *Psychological Review* 109, no. 3 (2012): 472–489.

Neff, Kristin D. *Self-Compassion: The Proven Power of Being Kind to Yourself.* New York: HarperCollins, 2011.

Nerurkar, Aditi. *The 5 Resets: Rewire Your Brain and Body for Less Stress and More Resilience.* London: HarperCollins UK, 2024.

Norbury, Agnes, and Raymond J. Dolan. "Anticipatory Neural Activity Predicts Attenuated Learning in Perceived Threat." *Nature Neuroscience* 22, no. 3 (2019): 437–448. https://affectivebrain.com/wp-content /uploads/2020/01/41562_2019_793_OnlinePDF_2.pdf.

Oettingen, Gabriele, Doris Mayer, A. Timur Sevincer, Elizabeth J. Stephens, Hyeon-ju Pak, and Meike Hagenah. "Mental Contrasting and Goal Commitment: The Mediating Role of Energization." *Personality and Social Psychology Bulletin* 35, no. 5 (2009): 608–22. https://doi.org/10.1177/0146167208330856.

Oettingen, Gabriele, Hyeon-ju Pak, and Karoline Schnetter. "Self-Regulation of Goal-Setting: Turning Free Fantasies about the Future into Binding Goals." *Journal of Personality and Social Psychology* 80, no. 5 (2001): 736–53. https://doi .org/10.1037/0022-3514.80.5.736.

Oliver, Mary. "The Summer Day." In *New and Selected Poems*, 94. Boston: Beacon Press, 1992.

Oswald, Debra L., and Elizabeth M. Clark. "Best Friends Forever? High School Best Friendships and Adult Friendship Development." *Journal of Adolescence* 84 (2020): 153–165.

Pilat, Dan, and Krastev, Sekoul M.D., "Why Do We Take Mental Shortcuts?" *The Decision Lab*. The Decision Lab, January 27, 2021. https://thedecisionlab.com /biases/heuristics/.

Platt, Michael L., et al. "Beyond Utility: Social and Biological Roots of Decision -Making in the Brain." *Nature Neuroscience* 19, no. 10 (2016): 1303–1310.

Porges, Stephen W. *The Polyvagal Theory: Neurophysiological Foundations of Emotions, Attachment, Communication, and Self-Regulation.* New York: W. W. Norton & Company, 2011.

Reeve, Johnmarshall. *Understanding Motivation and Emotion.* 7th ed. New York: John Wiley & Sons, 2018.

Reis, Harry T., and Susan L. Gable. "Social Support and the Regulation of Personal Relationships." *Advances in Experimental Social Psychology* 52 (2015): 201–245.

Roberts, Sarah Jakes. *Power Moves: Ignite Your Confidence and Become a Force.* Nashville: Thomas Nelson, 2024.

Robbins, Mel. Interview with Aditi Nerurkar. *The Mel Robbins Podcast*, podcast audio, May 23, 2024. https://podcasts.apple.com/us/podcast/1-stress-doctor-5-tools-to-protect-your-brain-from/id1646101002?i=1000656467802.

Robbins, Mel. Interview with Alok Kanojia. *The Mel Robbins Podcast*, podcast audio, June 5, 2024. https://podcasts.apple.com/us/podcast/the-mel-robbins-podcast/id1646101002?i=1000657879202.

Robbins, Mel. Interview with Alok Kanojia. *The Mel Robbins Podcast*, podcast audio, September 2, 2024. https://podcasts.apple.com/us/podcast/the-mel-robbins-podcast/id1646101002?i=1000668009088.

Robbins, Mel. Interview with Lisa Bilyeu. *The Mel Robbins Podcast*, podcast audio, March 28, 2024. https://podcasts.apple.com/us/podcast/the-mel-robbins-podcast/id1646101002?i=1000650685813.

Robbins, Mel. Interview with Lisa Damour. *The Mel Robbins Podcast*, podcast audio, May 18, 2023. https://podcasts.apple.com/us/podcast/the-mel-robbins-podcast/id1646101002?i=1000613472370.

Robbins, Mel. Interview with Luana Marques. *The Mel Robbins Podcast*, podcast audio, July 20, 2023. https://podcasts.apple.com/us/podcast/the-mel-robbins-podcast/id1646101002?i=1000621712441.

Robbins, Mel. Interview with Matthew Hussey. *The Mel Robbins Podcast*, podcast audio, May 27, 2024. https://podcasts.apple.com/us/podcast/the-mel-robbins-podcast/id1646101002?i=1000656851968.

Robbins, Mel. Interview with Robert Waldinger. *The Mel Robbins Podcast*, podcast audio, April 4, 2024. https://podcasts.apple.com/us/podcast/the-mel-robbins-podcast/id1646101002?i=1000651381441.

Robbins, Mel. Interview with Sarah Jakes Roberts. *The Mel Robbins Podcast*, podcast audio, July 25, 2024. https://podcasts.apple.com/us/podcast/the-mel-robbins-podcast/id1646101002?i=1000663279637.

Robbins, Mel. *The 5 Second Rule: Transform Your Life, Work, and Confidence with Everyday Courage.* Brentwood, TN: Savio Republic, 2017.

Robbins, Mel. *The High 5 Habit.* Carlsbad, CA: Hay House, 2021.

Rusbult, Caryl E., and Paul A. M. Van Lange. "Why Do Relationships Persist? The Role of Investment in Long-Term Commitment." *Psychological Science* 22, no. 7 (2010): 135–140.

Ryan, Richard M., and Edward L. Deci. "Promoting Self-Determined Relationships and Well-Being." *Educational Psychologist* 44, no. 2 (2009): 73–85.

Sangwan, Neha. *Powered by Me: From Burned Out to Fully Charged at Work and in Life*. New York: Simon & Schuster, 2023.

Sapolsky, Robert M. *Why Zebras Don't Get Ulcers*. New York: Henry Holt and Co., 2004.

Schore, Allan N. *Affect Regulation and the Repair of the Self*. New York: W. W. Norton & Company, 2003.

Schwartz, Barry. *The Paradox of Choice: Why More Is Less*. New York: Harper Perennial, 2004.

Seligman, Martin. *Authentic Happiness: Using the New Positive Psychology to Realize Your Potential for Lasting Fulfillment*. New York: Atria Paperback, 2013.

Siegel, Daniel J. *The Developing Mind: How Relationships and the Brain Interact to Shape Who We Are*. 2nd ed. New York: Guilford Press, 2012.

Seligman, Martin E. P. *Flourish: A Visionary New Understanding of Happiness and Well-Being*. New York: Free Press, 2011.

"Self-Acceptance Could Be the Key to a Happier Life, Yet It's the Happy Habit Many People Practice the Least." *ScienceDaily*. University of Hertfordshire, March 7, 2014. https://www.sciencedaily.com/releases/2014/03/140307111016.htm.

Seneca. *Letters from a Stoic*. Translated by Robin Campbell. New York: Penguin Classics, 2004.

Shapiro, Ron. "How to Have Difficult Conversations Without Burning Bridges." *Harvard Business Review*, May 15, 2023. https://hbr.org/2023/05/how-to-have-difficult-conversations-without-burning-bridges.

Sharot, Tali. *The Influential Mind: What the Brain Reveals About Our Power to Change Others*. London: Hachette UK, 2017.

Sharot, Tali. *The Optimism Bias: A Tour of the Irrationally Positive Brain*. New York: Vintage, 2011.

Sharot, Tali, and Cass R. Sunstein. *Look Again: The Power of Noticing What Was Always There*. New York: Simon and Schuster, 2024.

Smith, James M., and Nicholas A. Christakis. "Social Networks and Health." *Annual Review of Sociology* 36 (2010): 435–457.

Sprecher, Susan, and Pamela C. Regan. "The Importance of Friendship in Romantic Relationships." *Social and Personality Psychology Compass* 8, no. 8 (2014): 412–425.

Sprecher, Susan, and Pamela C. Regan. "The Importance of Reciprocity and Self-Respect in Romantic Relationships." *Personal Relationships* 8, no. 4 (2014): 419–435.

Swart, Tara B. "Impact of Cortisol on Social Stress and Health." *Journal of Neuroscience Research* 129, no. 2 (2023): 304–15.

Swart Bieber, Tara. *The Source: The Secrets of the Universe, the Science of the Brain.* London: Vermilion, 2019.

Tannen, Deborah. *You Just Don't Understand: Women and Men in Conversation.* New York: HarperCollins, 2011.

Tesser, Abraham, and Richard H. Smith. "The Meaning of Success: The Social Psychology of Competition and Achievement." *Annual Review of Psychology* 65 (2014): 519–546.

Tolle, Eckhart. *The Power of Now: A Guide to Spiritual Enlightenment.* Vancouver: New World Library, 2004.

Tsabary, Shefali. *The Conscious Parent: Transforming Ourselves, Empowering Our Children.* Vancouver: Namaste Publishing, 2010.

Ulrich, Roger S. "Evidence-Based Health-Care Architecture." *The Lancet* 370, no. 9597 (2011): 139–140.

Updegraff, John A., and Shelley E. Taylor. "From Vulnerability to Growth: The Influence of Successful Others on Personal Growth in the Face of Challenge." *Journal of Personality and Social Psychology* 102, no. 5 (2013): 936–948.

Vaillant, George E. "Involuntary Coping Mechanisms: A Psychodynamic Perspective." *Harvard Review of Psychiatry* 19, no. 3 (2011): 148–152.

Van Bavel, Jay J., and Dominic J. Packer. "The Power of Us: Intergroup Situations and Group-Based Persuasion." *Social and Personality Psychology Compass* 10, no. 8 (2016): 409–420.

van der Kolk, Bessel. *The Body Keeps the Score: Brain, Mind, and Body in the Healing of Trauma.* New York: Viking, 2014.

van der Kolk, Bessel, Alexander C. McFarlane, and Lars Weisæth, eds. *Traumatic Stress: The Effects of Overwhelming Experience on Mind, Body, and Society.* New York: Guilford Press, 2007.

Van Dijk, Wilco W., and Marcel Zeelenberg. "The Paradox of Envy: Comparing Ourselves with Better-Off Others May Cause Personal Growth." *Journal of Personality and Social Psychology* 86, no. 2 (2014): 192–203.

Vogel, E. A., J. P. Rose, L. R. Roberts, and K. Eckles. "Social Comparison, Social Media, and Self-Esteem." *Psychology of Popular Media Culture* 3, no. 4 (2014): 206–222. https://doi.org/10.1037/ppm0000047.

Vohs, Kathleen D., et al. "Decision Fatigue Exhausts Self-Regulatory Resources— But So Does Accommodating to Unrealistic Social Expectations." *Journal of Personality and Social Psychology* 104, no. 6 (2014): 940–950.

Vohs, Kathleen D., and Roy F. Baumeister, eds. *Handbook of Self-Regulation: Research, Theory, and Applications.* 2nd ed. New York: Guilford Publications, 2016.

Waldinger, Robert, and Marc Schulz. *The Good Life: Lessons from the World's Longest Study on Happiness.* New York: Random House, 2023.

White, Katherine, and Darrin R. Lehman. "Culture and Social Comparison Seeking: The Role of Self-Motives." *Personality and Social Psychology Bulletin* 31, no. 2 (2005): 232–242. https://doi.org/10.1177/0146167204271326.

Willis, Judy. "The Neuroscience behind Stress and Learning." *Nature Partner Journal Science of Learning.* Nature Publishing Group, October 16, 2016. https:// npjscilearncommunity.nature.com/posts/12735-the-neuroscience-behind-stress -and-learning.

Willis, Judy. "What You Should Know About Your Brain." *Educational Leadership* 67, no. 4 (January 2010).

Wiseman, Richard. *The Luck Factor.* New York: Miramax Books, 2003.

Wood, Alex M., et al. "The Role of Gratitude in the Development of Social Support, Stress, and Depression: Two Longitudinal Studies." *Journal of Research in Personality* 45, no. 4 (2011): 466–474.

Wood, Joanne V., and Abraham Tesser. "Ruminating on Unchangeable Success: Downward Social Comparison and Self-Improvement Strategies." *European Journal of Social Psychology* 41, no. 4 (2011): 387–396.

Wrzus, Cornelia, et al. "Social Network Changes and Life Events Across the Life Span: A Meta-Analysis." *Psychological Bulletin* 139, no. 1 (2013): 53–80.

Zaki, Jamil. "Empathy: A Motivated Account." *Psychological Bulletin* 140, no. 6 (2014): 1608–1647.

Zaki, Jamil. *The War for Kindness: Building Empathy in a Fractured World.* New York: Crown Publishing, 2019.

About Mel

Mel Robbins is a *New York Times* bestselling author and a world-renowned expert on mindset, motivation, and behavior change, whose work has been translated into 41 languages.

With millions of books sold, seven #1 Audible titles, and billions of video views, Mel's impact is truly global. As the host of *The Mel Robbins Podcast*, the Webby and Signal Award–winning #1 education podcast in the world, Mel empowers listeners in 194 countries every day.

Her media company, 143 Studios Inc., produces provocative, award-winning content, transformative events, and original training programs for clients like Starbucks, JPMorganChase, LinkedIn, Headspace, and Ulta Beauty. She was named one of Forbes' 50 Over 50 and serves on the board of directors of Amplify Publishing.

Known for her ability to simplify complex topics into practical daily actions, Mel Robbins delivers her most powerful and profound work yet with *The Let Them Theory*.

Learn more at **melrobbins.com**.

How to Stay in Touch with Me

If you loved this book—you'll really love:

1. **My Newsletter**

   One of the most popular newsletters in the world. Every week, the latest issue is sent to over 2,000,000 people. It's personal, inspiring, and packed with the best ideas and helpful advice.

   Sign up for free at **melrobbins.com/newsletter**.

2. ***The Mel Robbins Podcast***

   TIME magazine says "it gives listeners a reason to believe in themselves." *The Mel Robbins Podcast* is one of the top ranked podcasts in the world. New episodes release weekly and can be found wherever you listen to podcasts or on **youtube.com/melrobbins**.

3. **Connecting on Social**

   Connect with me daily on all your favorite social media platforms at **@melrobbins**.

Learn more at melrobbins.com

We hope you enjoyed this Hay House book. If you'd like to receive our online catalog featuring additional information on Hay House books and products, or if you'd like to find out more about the Hay Foundation, please contact:

Hay House LLC, P.O. Box 5100, Carlsbad, CA 92018-5100
(760) 431-7695 or (800) 654-5126
www.hayhouse.com® • www.hayfoundation.org

———

Published in Australia by:
Hay House Australia Publishing Pty Ltd
18/36 Ralph St., Alexandria NSW 2015
Phone: +61 (02) 9669 4299
www.hayhouse.com.au

Published in the United Kingdom by:
Hay House UK Ltd
1st Floor, Crawford Corner,
91–93 Baker Street, London W1U 6QQ
Phone: +44 (0)20 3927 7290
www.hayhouse.co.uk

Published in India by:
Hay House Publishers (India) Pvt Ltd
Muskaan Complex, Plot No. 3,
B-2, Vasant Kunj, New Delhi 110 070
Phone: +91 11 41761620
www.hayhouse.co.in

———

Let Your Soul Grow

Experience life-changing transformation—one video
at a time—with guidance from the world's leading experts.

www.healyourlifeplus.com